# My Health Is Better In November

# My Health Is Better in November

## THIRTY-FIVE STORIES OF
## HUNTING AND FISHING IN THE SOUTH

By Havilah Babcock

With drawings by Augusta Rembert Wittkowsky

*WITH A FOREWORD*
*BY IRENE LABORDE NEUFFER*
*AND AN ESSAY*
*BY CLAUDE HENRY NEUFFER*

SOUTH
CAROLINA

University of South Carolina Press

Published in Columbia, South Carolina, by the
University of South Carolina Press

00 99 98 97 96     8 7 6 5 4

Manufactured in the United States of America

ISBN 0-87249-440-3

Library of Congress Catalog Card Number 60-11238

*Affectionately dedicated to my Alice, without whose many suggestions it would have been finished in half the time.*

## ACKNOWLEDGMENT

Grateful acknowledgment is made to the editors of *Field and Stream, Outdoor Life, Sports Afield, Hunting and Fishing,* and *Outdoors* for permission to reprint stories which originally appeared in these magazines, as follows:

*Field and Stream* — How To Hunt Quail; Damn That Honeysuckle; Gun Shy; Billy And The Big Boss; Bass Are Dumber Than People; When It's Crappie You're After; I'm A Sucker That Way; Bees For Bream; Bob Is No Gentleman; Candy From A Baby; Puppies, Incorporated; Not Always The Smartest; The Other Fellow; Thank You, Sheriff; Sand Hill Quail; Old Muggins; Quail Guns And Loads.

*Outdoor Life* — Hell Hath No Fury; Bob White Is A Family Man; Sometimes You Can't Find Them; My Health Is Better In November; Irish; Are You Goofy Too?; When Dogs Fight; When Your Shooting Slumps; Birds Scare Me; Santee's Gentleman; How To Get Rid Of Chiggers; Indian Summer.

*Sports Afield* — Calling On My Neighbors; The Education Of The Wrecker; Fiddler; Just Cover It With Gravy.

*Hunting and Fishing* — Give Me A $40 Dog.

*Outdoors*—I'm a Top-Water Man, Myself.

# CONTENTS

# Foreword

IN 1947 the young University of South Carolina Press published its fifth volume, *My Health Is Better in November* by Havilah Babcock, then head of the University's Department of English. It was an unusual volume for any university press to publish in those days when such presses were generally expected to put the imprints of the universities on learned monographs that examined minutiae of history or literary criticism for the benefit of a few hundred impecunious scholars. But, then, Havilah Babcock was an unusual man with an unusual name who had found South Carolina to be an unusual state (incidentally, he had grown up in Virginia pronouncing himself huh-VIE-luh, rhyming with Samson and Delilah, but in South Carolina he answered without complaint to HAV-i-luh).

Much has changed in South Carolina since Babcock began to celebrate it. The first printing of the book sold out with unseemly haste and it was reprinted several times by Holt, Rinehart and Winston in New York. But the author had never heard the words "male" and "chauvinist" combined into one word, and his attitude to blacks, although it is clearly affectionate, was for a while embarrassing enough to keep the book out of print. To try to eliminate those aspects of Babcock's writings in a new edition would be less than honest, but they do not loom large in his work and can no longer overshadow the delights he offers.

Those delights were spelled out by Babcock's friend and colleague, my late husband Claude Henry Neuffer, in an essay in *The Georgia Review* (xxi, No. 3, Fall 1967). Claude was the founding editor of *Names in South Carolina*, an annual devoted to the study of South Carolina place names, to which Havilah was a contributing editor. That essay is reprinted hereinafter with the kind permission of Stanley Lindberg, editor of the *Review.*

Irene LaBorde Neuffer
*January 19, 1985*

# Calling On My Neighbors

SPORTSMEN are divided into two tribes: the *hithers* and the *thithers*. The former are content to cultivate their own neighborhoods, while the latter have an unshakable conviction that birds fly faster and bass hit harder in some other commonwealth.

The platform of the *thither* tribe is that hunting is good in inverse ratio to its accessibility. I know some rod-and-gun gypsies whose journals must read like the ramblings of some latter-day Ulysses. Each of us tries to penetrate the hinterlands a little farther than the other fellow, with the result that we oftentimes pass up prime sport.

I have made highly respectable catches in neighborhood ponds despised by my steeple-chasing friends. Only last week I found an enterprising family of bob-whites doing business within the city limits of my own town. Every other hunter had told himself: "That's a likely looking field, but it's so convenient everybody else has hunted it," and passed on. I once read the story of a man who wandered over the face of the earth looking for happiness and then returned to find it by his own fireside. Wayfaring sportsmen might ponder that parable.

Hunting, like charity, sometimes begins at home. In other days I have been something of an overnight gadabout, making an occasional passage into a "contagious" state for a bird hunt, but there is little of the Arab in me. I have found that the hunting under my own vine and fig tree is apt to be as good as it is anywhere else, and probably better.

For instance, the most enjoyable bird hunt I have had in many a day, and one I take regularly six or eight times every season, is right under my own nose. It is a made-to-order day's hunt, calling for scheduled stops at predetermined points. I have rambled over this territory so often that its landmarks, its familiar haunts and pleasant fields, together with the memories they conjure up, have for me a sentimental attachment.

Every covey of birds on the circuit has acquired for me a rather definite character. I know their habits of flight, their individualities and sometimes their genealogies. I can make the hunt leisurely in one day, leaving my visiting card at half a dozen way stations, and be back by nightfall. And the hunt derives an added pleasure from the fact that it is a round-trip ticket: when I have finished my swing around the circuit I am back at my own doorstep. My itinerary, in the order of visitation, is as follows:

> The honeysuckle covert.
> The chimney field.
> The half-moon pond.
> The sawdust pile.
> The railroad track.
> The old graveyard.

These six landmarks are associated with six coveys of birds that I can almost always count on. Like old friends, they seldom fail me, and then only with adequate cause. I am always careful to leave sufficient seed every year. In excessively rough weather I provide food for them. In their warfare with their natural enemies they find in me a puissant ally. Generally, I make things as hospitable for them as I can. And for their part, they follow the Biblical injunction: be fruitful and multiply. Each successive season they bring up for me a family of plump patricians, and in just about the same place. Bob-white is a creature of habit and a home-loving country squire. Barring undue molestation, he will establish and bring up his family in the same locality year after year. I suppose I have shot the great-great-grandchildren of the original coveys I found five or six years ago.

My first scheduled stop is at the honeysuckle covert, where Blue and I find our "crack-of-day" covey on the roost. I have to get out betimes to find them at home when I call, though. On fair days they are up and away by seven-thirty. On gray, lowering days they usually stay indoors until around nine, while in extremely raw weather they may not venture from their snug retreat at all.

The covert, a ragged rectangle of perhaps an acre, is interspersed with locusts. In addition to that, the vines are so heavily matted and the footing so insecure that getting through at all is a rather formidable job. Blue and I have to flounder through and fight for what we get here.

Of all the coveys on my day's schedule, these honeysuckle denizens are the most unsociable and most trying on my nerves. They never get up until I am fairly on top of them, then they simply explode on all sides. Usually it happens just as I step into a hole or trip over a fallen locust and revert to the quadruped state. In trying to get a shot I shilly-shally from one rocketing brown body to another, like the indecisive mule that starved to death between two stacks of hay. I normally miss with one or both barrels, for which I think Blue is thankful. Retrieving in that devilish mess is vexatious business at best.

But if this family is a bit inhospitable at home, they have a habit that equalizes matters and enables me to levy a reasonable tariff on their numbers every season. They invariably plummet down by an old rail fence in a near-by field. There the odds are about even. As the singles pop up from first one side of the crooked fence row and then the other, I manage to bag two or three, — all I want from this bevy this morning. Blue and I expect to call on this family again next week, and the week after that as well.

There is a cedar grove above the honeysuckle patch where these birds could put me at a sore disadvantage, but they seldom avail themselves of this sanctuary. Season after season they stick to the old fence row. Usually we dilly-dally with this first covey

until around eight-thirty or nine, then we hit a bee-line through
the squirrel woods for the old chimney field. The chimney field
is so designated because of its landmark, — a lonely brick chimney that stands as a tottering reminder of a once picturesque
old homestead. The wasted fields are now overgrown with a rank
growth of weeds and partridge peas. Between nine and ten, I
can nearly always count on finding a covey here around the
festive board. Not only do they feed here, but the birds like to
wallow and preen themselves in the ashes about the old chimney. It is fair shooting. If I am not dyspeptic and off-guard, I
get two on the rise.

But they regularly go down in a cane savannah two hundred
yards down in a bottom, where shooting is a sore tribulation.
It is a veritable jungle of cane where locating singles is next
to impossible. And if I am lucky enough to find one I have to
depend on snap shooting, a department in which the deponent
is unconscionably rotten. But Blue and I always follow them
into the canebreak for good measure. Occasionally we add a
prized savannah bird to our bag, which makes up for the dis-
comfort, and brings us back again.

It is now around ten-thirty or eleven, so we meander on toward the half-moon pond, where we hope to find a big covey
loitering in noonday dalliance about their favorite watering place.
Half an hour later I am looking down into a tiny crescent-
shaped lake. It nestles in a peculiar saucerlike depression, made
by the bleaching of limestone or organic matter, a geologist
tells me. There is neither inlet nor outlet. A 20-foot embank-
ment slopes gently down on all sides. A wide sweep of tan-
colored straw runs waist-high down to the water's edge. Around
the margin of the pond stretches a belt of soaring pines, through
which the breezes sigh plaintively. The water is as limpid as a
mirror, its surface serene and untroubled. If I were a poet —

But I am a bird hunter, so Blue and I saunter around the
margin to see whether the covey has come in yet. We are a
little early perhaps. We come back and sit against a big pine,
idly watching the doves standing like preachers in the treetops.
True, we might go out in the field and intercept the birds, but
that is a bit uncertain and requires walking. Blue and I have a
marked disinclination to unnecessary labor of any sort. Besides,

I am not in a hurry. I am never in a hurry when I am hunting. If I am in a hurry I don't go hunting.

Another circuit of the pond fifteen minutes later and we find our birds. Sometimes we hear them twittering companionably in the straw before Blue points them. I get two on the rise here. There's no excuse for my not doing so. They fly around the head of the pond and drop on the other side. We might follow them and get one or two more, but we don't. It is an idyllic spot to visit, and I want to make this covey last. I mean to eat my cake and have it too.

It is now one o'clock or thereabouts, a dead interregnum for hunting because birds are not moving about. They are apt to be dozing at water holes, or sunning themselves on lazy slopes. But Blue and I confidently amble over to our next objective, the sawdust pile.

What is there about a pile of rotting sawdust that attracts birds? You can find them there in even the most inhospitable weather. A windbreak and snug harbor, of course, but there must be something else. It sounds fantastic, but does the slow oxidation going on in a pile of sawdust generate any appreciable heat? A chemist whom I have just dialed tells me the idea is not fantastic.

Anyway, day after day a big covey convenes at the appointed rendezvous for a polite midday siesta. Some bask in the languorous sun and drowse; others coquettishly preen themselves, with many a flirt and flutter in the loose dust, while others still listlessly scratch for insects. This covey sometimes invites another to share its sunny retreat, both families contentedly disporting themselves in the freemasonry of the old sawdust pile. I have seen as many as forty birds scurry up from such a communistic covey at one time, an experience not especially soothing to the nerves.

I have got to "meet the train" to find my sawdust covey at home, however, and when I do find them they are as wild as hatters. I can count on bagging one or two birds on the rise, but then my tale is told. It is a swamp covey. As straight as a martin to its gourd, they hit for the darksome recesses of the swamp. I have tried following them, but it is too much sugar for a cent. Blue and I get disgusted with each other. Blue thinks these birds use bad judgment about getting up, and that I pick my shots with still worse judgment. She yields only the most perfunctory obedience to my cry of "Dead bird!" when we are after this bunch.

But just wait until high water hits that swamp! Then they will have to fly elsewhere, and I can whittle this covey down to my own ideas.

It is now time to pay our respects to the "snack" that has been bulging in my hunting coat all the morning. We sit by a cool, sequestered spring and share our lunch together. And while we are resting a spell, may I say a little about Blue, my unfailing companion on every hunt and the other half of "we" in this story.

I don't know what kind of dog Blue is. Several kinds, probably. I have never delved into her ancestry lest it prove a bit embarrassing. She is a gaunt blue-black pointer with a skinny frost-bitten sort of tail which she customarily keeps well hidden as if aware of the unsightliness of that member. She looks so much like a nondescript "nigger" hound that it has never occurred to anybody to steal her. She always prays when she points, with her blue rump pointing straight to the North Star and her long head snake-like on the ground, — a comical spectacle but a terribly tense one. Regardless of her lack of pulchritude and family tree, Blue is a matchless hunting companion. I hunt birds rather than ancestors anyway. If "pretty is as pretty does" she stands ace high.

Saying *auf wiedersehen* to the sawdust pile, Blue and I mosey over to socialize a bit with our Atlantic Coastline covey. Why are birds so fond of feeding and loitering near a railroad track? I have often conjectured about it, but like Omar the tent-maker I have always "come out by the same door as in I went." Here is a friendly little mystery I wish some bobwhite biographer would unfold for me. Are they pecking up cinders for their grist mill?

The fields adjacent to the track stand waist-high with tawny broomstraw, with here and there a pea patch or cornfield sandwiched in between. Along the right-of-way runs a low thicket of briers and honeysuckle. If our covey is not on one side of the track, we are certain to find them on the other. Sometimes we raise them in the briery undergrowth on the right-of-way itself. In fact, I have known the redoubtable Blue to point, or "stand" as we unreconstructed Southerners still say, with her gaunt body athwart the crossties.

It is around four o'clock, and the mellowest part of the day, when we call on this bevy. It is beautiful shooting, with all the accompaniments even an artist could ask. Autumn, the flaming courtesan, is abroad. In the background lordly pines stand silhouetted against the sky. The sun is a firebrand in the west. Nearby a clump of blackjack oaks are ablaze with the burnished gold of late fall. The straw is a frozen flame sweeping across the fields.

This covey almost invariably plummets back into the broomstraw from which we have raised them. I have to summon such Christian forbearance as I have to keep from overshooting them year after year. If I levy too high a tariff one week, I force myself to skip them the next. But bird hunting is serious business with Blue. She has more of the sport than the sportsman in her makeup. She has never gotten it through her thick head why I sometimes raise this covey, drop my gun on a scuttling brown body, and take it down without shooting.

Two years ago my railroad family was ravaged by prowling house cats, a nuisance to which I put an expeditious and permanent ending. Last year hawks began to prey on it, but steel traps planted on tall poles netted me six hawks and $2.50 in bounty from the county clerk.

It is now half an hour "be-sun." We have just completed our circuit and are nearing home. Perhaps we should go straight on, but there's the old graveyard a hundred yards off the path. It is a lonely and unfrequented spot on the brow of a red knoll. A mouldering rail fence runs around the dark rectangle. A ragged locust grove overgrown with honeysuckle and a bristling fringe of blackberry vines make it a welcome caravansary for the homing covey. It is the unfailing rendezvous of our twilight birds. The graveyard is also a sanctuary for harrassed cottontails, but they are graveyard rabbits and hence inviolable. Not even the most venturesome darkey in the neighborhood will invade the forbidding precincts.

We get a brace of fat graveyard birds. I might manage to bag one or two more by picking them out against the skyline, but we already have a round dozen to show for the day's hunt. So Blue and I pass on, like Pippa, and agreeing with her that "all's right with the world."

We are now within a few hundred yards of home. An autumnal chill is stealing into the air. We pass a gnarled old persimmon tree laden with its frost-bitten delicacies. I must make another barrel of persimmon beer this year, I reflect. Thence homeward, to crackling bread, cold buttermilk, and by your leave, chitterlings! And our dame is not "nursing her wrath to keep it warm," but is waiting to pick the birds, — mainly, I suspect, because she wants the feathers.

One day next week Blue and I will call on our neighbors again.

# Bob White Is A Family Man

"THAT WAS luck. Both cocks," my companion remarked as he pocketed a double.

"Got a grudge against 'em?" I inquired.

"The more cocks you kill, the more coveys you'll have next year. They fight among themselves and break up the nests. Didn't you know that?"

"No, I didn't — and don't know it yet."

My companion's sentiments are shared by about 99 percent of quail hunters. And that's a pretty respectable majority. They all congratulate themselves on eliminating the cocks, as if they were a bad rubbish and a good riddance. And not a few keen-visioned and self-possessed gunners deliberately single out the white-collared gentry on the covey rise, though I confess I'm never sex-conscious at such a time!

As the most misunderstood game bird in America, I nominate the one which is most shot at — the bob-white quail. The male of the species in particular. Bob is a much maligned fellow, more sinned against than sinning, and I should like to appear in court as a sort of character witness.

Not that you need waste any sympathy on him, or have any compunction about connecting with him whenever you can. He is fair game, neither expecting any quarter nor giving you any. But as an observing hunter said to me: "A reasonable amount of shootin' won't hurt the old rooster. May be good for 'im in fact — a *reasonable amount* — but you can shoot 'im without misrepresentin' him. I'd as lief shoot a cock as a hen, *but no liefer.* And that's the p'int!"

The notion that Bob may be shot almost unrestrictedly without detriment to the covey is based on the assumption that he is a polygamous fellow who will serve any number of mistresses. This supposition, so deeply rooted in common belief that to challenge it is to invite a one-way argument, is doubtless based on a comparison with domestic fowl.

Everybody knows that a guinea, for instance, is about as moral as a coat hanger, and that an old Dominique hen wouldn't know an ethic if she met one in the middle of the road. Just about the most promiscuous wench agoing.

But Bob is a gentleman, and under ordinary circumstances, a strict monogamist. He believes in "one wife, thank God!" And his marital fidelity is equaled only by that of his mate. What I say about his family affairs is, of course, applicable to his behavior in the wild state only. *Birds unnaturally confined may be expected to behave unnaturally.*

During his courting days, Bob *is* quite a playboy and philanderer. When the balmy days of spring come, with the cry of the huntsman and the clatter of guns a waning memory, he dons his Sunday-go-to-meeting clothes and puts on the dog for the coy damsels who covertly admire his gallantry. Then is Bob a robustious and swaggering fellow. With a flower in his coat and a chip on his shoulder, he is ready for fight or frolic, and he will throw down the gauntlet to any other swain who comes a-philandering around his true love.

But these set-tos that the touchy swains engage in are of brief duration, seldom lasting over a few seconds, and are almost never fatal. Indeed, the cocks seldom inflict any appreciable damage on each other. Likely as not the vanquished gallant will be back in a minute making amorous passes at the same female.

I have never known a single case where these swashbuckling encounters proved fatal to either contestant, except when the birds were confined in too small an area.

If Bob is something of a lady-killer and cut-up during his wild-oats days, he is never a love pilferer and home wrecker thereafter, as he is commonly represented to be. Once the apple of his eye requites his affection, which is done on the spot and without benefit of clergy, Bob is a changed man. The erstwhile playboy becomes a home body and a devoted family man.

Once he has committed himself, Bob usually follows the strait and narrow, devoting himself exclusively to his mate and she to him. Through thick and thin, fair weather and foul, the pair stick together. He almost never has what divorce courts call extramarital relations with another hen, nor does he show any dubious biological urges in that direction. Premarital rivalries there are aplenty, but few corespondents and postmarital triangles. And that's saying right much, brother!

Not even the repeated destruction of their nests will bring any rift between a couple, or lessen their determination to raise a family. When their efforts are frustrated by one of the countless dangers that beset them, when their eggs or young are devoured by some sneak thief of the hedgerows, the same pair go right back and start housekeeping again. I have known a pair to make as many as three attempts before bringing off a hatch. That is why the hunter often encounters immature birds when the hunting season opens. "Squealers" do not mean a second brood, but a delayed one.

Another count against the cock is that he struts contentiously about and breaks up the nests of other pairs. This is accepted as almost axiomatic even among bird hunters themselves. Yet not a *single case* of such home-wrecking has ever come under my observation, *although for twenty years I have been looking for just that.* Nor have I ever known a creditable witness who has seen such a case. Cocks do not interfere with the family affairs of other birds once housekeeping is under way.

On the contrary, I have seen as many as four nests in a weed-overgrown graveyard, each family apparently living on amicable terms with its next-door neighbors, and each pair successfully bringing off its hatch without molestation from the others. Indeed, I often observed the four head men basking together in a near-by sawdust pile in the friendliest fashion, chatting amiably together and doubtless bragging about the virtues of their respective wenches. Say what you will against him, Bob is a tolerant fellow and a first-class neighbor.

And a better-than-average husband. Now and then you might hear some lucky stiff bragging to the countryside about having a

"Nice good wife, that never goes out,
Keeping house while I frolic about."

But they often divide the domestic responsibilities with their mates. Cocks sometimes do the nest building, while their pampered spouses stand idly by and boss the job. And they sometimes relieve their mates at the tedious business of sitting on the eggs. Occasionally they appear to follow well-ordered shifts in this respect, alternately relieving each other.

And I knew one luckless old codger — in the corner of our garden — whose wife, discovering that she had hooked a sucker, turned the sitting completely over to him while she went traipsing off to bridge parties and whatnot, like the irresponsible hussy she was. Old Bob took off his vest, put on his apron, and took over the housework. Did a good job of it too, hatching them all out by himself.

Often some skulking mischance of the fields removes the nesting hen entirely, and the whole duty of hatching the eggs and rearing the young devolves upon the cock. When this happens, Bob rises to the occasion right gallantly.

When I was a boy, and curious about everything under the sun except a book satchel, I discovered a nest in the corner of an old rail fence. On one of my daily visits, I was horrified to find the nest ravaged. The gory remnants strewn about were mute evidence of the stalking tragedy that had overwhelmed the patient little mother. I was grief stricken that I had one less bird, and when I reached home I soon had one less cat. I'd seen her skulking in the vicinity too often to be beguiled by her plea of innocence. A few hours later, having certain visitations of conscience over the swift vengeance I had meted out, I performed a postmortem on the cat and verified the findings of the jury.

That afternoon, when I went to retrieve the eggs and place them under a bantam hen, I was immeasurably surprised to find the cock sitting dauntlessly on the nest. This in spite of the gruesome reminders about him, and the danger of a revisitation from the same marauder. And all along I had regarded him as a trifling fellow! Unaided, he hatched out every egg, and looked after his troublesome brood like a much harassed but determined old bachelor who has inherited a houseful of youngsters.

This happens often under normal conditions. Just how often there is no way of determining, but offhand, I venture the estimate that one third of the nests are incubated entirely or in part by cocks.

Whenever the role is thrust upon him, Bob makes a first-class mother. When the job of running the incubator falls to him, he devotes himself patiently to the tedious task and guards his nest with courage and cunning. He will fight furiously to repel an invader, and if such heroics prove ineffectual, he will resort to melodrama. Fluttering excitedly away, he will limp and piteously drag his wings as if *in extremis,* until he has lured the intruder from his precious cache, whereupon he will effect an instant recovery and blithely sail away.

His dramatic talents, however, are hardly equal to those of the mother bird who, when occasion demands, is the greatest little tragedienne in the world. How often as a boy have I been tricked in this fashion, pursuing a seemingly disabled bird across the field in high hopes of effecting a capture, only to have the base malingerer suddenly regain her health and sail maddeningly away.

Even when his mate is doing the housekeeping alone, Bob is seldom far away. Often you may hear him in subdued communication with her, or flush him from his listening post near by. At big recess, when the brooding hen may leave the nest for hours, he habitually joins her for an intimate stroll, takes her out to lunch on luscious insects he pridefully captures for her, and no doubt acquaints her with the latest neighborhood gossip.

One day a neighbor's lad came to our house with his upturned cap in his hands.

"Want what's in this cap?" he questioned tantalizingly.

"My-name's-Jimmy-and-I'll-take-all-you-gimme," I answered.

Whereupon he presented me with a dozen young quail chicks he had hatched in his mother's incubator. If I remember rightly, he had found the eggs in the wake of his father's mowing machine. I was delighted with the gift until it occurred to me that I had no bantams ready to take them. But for my grandmother, I should have been in a quandary indeed.

"Put them in the cage with the old bob-white rooster you have. Since his mate died, he might be lonesome enough to adopt them," she suggested.

My grandmother was right — as she too often was! The lonely old gentleman adopted the orphans at once and made a great fuss over them. When I released them a month or so later, he marshalled them all off to the wheat field as proud as you please.

When a pet covey I had mated and paired off, one rooster was left out in the cold. Either because there were not enough debutantes to go around, or because he just didn't have a way with the women, the old fellow was doomed to a wifeless existence.

When the other couples brought off their hatches and were surrounded with chirping progeny, the bachelor was most unhappy. But a few weeks later he had acquired a foster son, a spry little fellow he'd found somewhere and adopted. Possibly the lone chick had become separated from its mother in a heavy downpour, and the grandfatherly cock had been touched by its plaintive piping. I used to lie in the garden and watch him fussing over his heir apparent and spoiling him to death, as a father does an only child.

Unattached cocks — there are normally one or two in every large covey — often adopt foundlings and homeless waifs in just such fashion. The adoptive instincts are strong in quail, particularly in the males. Which is fortunate, since the birds remaining unattached during the rearing season are apt to be males, according to the normal ratio between the sexes. There is generally a slight preponderance of cocks.

This adoptive impulse makes the cocks a valuable ally in propagation. Many a tender bevy, violently bereft of its rightful parents, is taken over and brought to maturity by some family-loving old rooster. Many a covey, orphaned by harsh chance, would otherwise be lost.

Indeed, this adoptive instinct is often taken advantage of by quail raisers. Instead of using bantams and brooders, the quail farms take the chicks from the incubators and turn them over to unencumbered cocks for adoption. Rarely do they fail to do a good part by the "parcel o' chullen" thus inherited.

Bob has a great horror of becoming an old bachelor. If there are no eligible females in his neighborhood, he will extend his courting range for miles around. Wherever he goes he notifies all and sundry that he is frankly in the market for a wife, making the welkin ring with his unabashed declaration:

"I needa WIFE! I needa WIFE! I needa WIFE!" And he keeps it up until midsummer, when the best he can hope for is some pensive little widow whose erstwhile spouse met an untimely end.

This persistency of his not only brings belated comfort to many a lovelorn damsel, but it is a powerful factor in the restocking of overshot and relatively birdless areas. Many an extra covey is due to his perseverance and the amount of geography he covers in his wife hunting, since the female of the species, with a modesty conventionally feminine, is rather inclined to trust to luck and wait for some gallant to come a-whistling at her door.

I well remember one instance when Bob's amorous persistency was rewarded in the face of circumstances that might have daunted a less determined swain. Several years ago most of the birds around my home in Virginia perished in a memorable blizzard.

We thought all had perished, but one spring morning a gallant old gent appeared from somewhere, stationed himself on a half-rotten post in our yard, and began to tune up his whistle — for the benefit of the pet birds in the yard which we kept from year to year for restocking purposes.

Having scoured the countryside in vain for a wife, he had somehow detected, perhaps through some lovers' sixth sense, the presence of our stock birds. His desperation to renounce the ranks of celibacy brought him again and again to our yard, where he would sit by the hour, with one leg rakishly tucked under him, and broadcast to the sleek damsels in the convent.

His impassioned courtship kept up from morn till night, his throaty notes running the whole gamut of invitation.

"Listen to him, will you?" said my wife. "He's promising her the whole world and a big fat grasshopper. Just like a man. And likely as not some dizzy sub-deb in the pen is falling for his line."

"Shouldn't be surprised," I laughed. "One little idiot spends most of her time traipsing up and down the fence."

A few days later the troubadour failed to show up, and a hurried census revealed one of the hens missing. She had contrived to get through a broken mesh and had presumably eloped. Which shows that love will find a way.

"O well," I sympathized, "what is life without a wife! I wish him luck — and a large family!"

## Bees For Bream

"COME FULL moon in May, I'm headin' for the Edisto." Or maybe it's the Peedee, or the Cumbahee, or the Cooper, for each of these cypress-crowded low-country streams has its devotees. But it's always full moon in May. That's about the only common denominator among us.

During the full moon in May, we South Carolinians have a seasonal sickness. It is the bream fever. We go around with rapt expressions on our faces. We talk a language of our own. We are subject to strange goings-and-comings, to sudden exits and unpredictable absences. Our tolerant women-folk have the benefit of their spouses only now and then. Bream-widows, they call themselves. For it is during the aforesaid full moon that bream fishing is at its traditional best.

The methods of taking bream are, to use an old-fashioned phrase, divers and sundry. There are those who insist that a fly rod is the only weapon a gentleman will use. There are others who hold in disdain everything except a "jigger" — a fly skittered adroitly over cypress pockets and under overhanging banks and mossladen trees where no fly rod could operate. It is perhaps the simplest and deadliest fish-getter ever contrived — if you just want fish.

There are others still who verily dote on catalpa worms, horrendous green customers of so unpleasant an aspect that even the sight of them will induce nausea if you are the least squeamish. In June and July, whole groves of catalpa trees are riddled by them, to the delight of our citizenry. It is the immemorial bream bait.

Nearly every confirmed breamer is apt to have a "catawba" in his back yard, pridefully planted and nurtured as a private bait-factory. A former governor planted an entire grove on his plantation for the benefit of himself and his constituents. Provident indeed is the father who leaves his sons such a legacy! And a host of others smile indulgently at the foibles and conceits of the city slicker, asking nothing more of this mundane sphere than a can of good, honest earthworms — and the requisite full moon.

I belong to none of these schools, but to the brotherhood of the drone bee. Of all imaginable baits, the larvae of the drone are, in my judgment, the best. I should like to enlarge on their virtues a bit, but may I bring in the bream now and go back to my drones later?

The copperhead bream is almost legendary with South Carolinians. In a manner of speaking, he is our state fish, the piscatorial laureate of the commonwealth. Bound up with memories of the ante-bellum, with States' Rights and pistols-for-two and coffee-for-one, the bream is held in unique esteem. From time out of memory, anglers have acclaimed his mettle, epicures his meat.

We have other fish, to be sure. Bass that grow up to fourteen pounds, pickerel, (ignobly dubbed "jack" hereabouts) up to six or seven, and crappie in profusion. But it is none of these that brings that rapt expression to our faces. Indeed, every true South Carolinian is a little wacky on the subject of bream. And not without precedent aplenty! Does not his fame go back to the Revolution? Did not the doughty Lord Cornwallis assure the dubious war masters of Britain that South Carolina was worth fighting for "for the bream in the Santee River, if for nothing else?" And did not Yates Snowden, more than half a century ago, write:

And here was mooted many a day
The question on which each gourmet
Throughout the parish had his say:
Which is the best:
Santee or Cooper River bream?

"Any of various fresh-water sunfishes," the dictionary safely generalizes. Surely Webster never had one on a fly rod. Another dictionary dismisses him as merely a perch, a definition which any bream fisherman will hotly repudiate. And most of them insist that he is pronounced "breem," whereas any Southern boy big enough to button his "britches" knows it is "brim." Ichthyologists, who blithely Latinize everything from a spring-lizard to a whale, throw up their hands in despair when they come to the bream. He has more aliases than a jailbird.

Shaped like a perch, he is bigger and gamier. In color he is olive or greenish, with a purplish luster, the coloration varying somewhat with his habitat. And if he is big enough to brag about, he is apt to have copper bars across his head. Hence the sobriquet, "copperhead." The finest tribute to him I ever heard came from an old bream fisherman with a week's beard on his face and poetry in his heart. "The bream," he fervently announced, "is one fish Goda'mighty made for a fly rod and a gentleman!"

How big is a bream? It is always disillusioning to weigh your fish and measure your golf drives. Smart men estimate them. But a 12-ouncer is a good average. A 16-ounce bream you will swear to be twice as heavy. And although a pound and a half is supposed to be the maximum, not far away is an ancient and overgrown pond where they are occasionally caught up to $2\frac{1}{4}$ pounds. A bream that big is as wide as an unabridged dictionary; and when you see one, you'll say: "Whoever caught that fish is a liar!" What the virtues of unpicturesque Bull Swamp are nobody knows, but there these heavyweights grow.

As to the palatability of the bream, the fish books say he is "unsurpassed as a table delicacy." It is one of the few things they all agree on. "Unsurpassed" is right! I will risk my reputation as an epicure — such as I have — on this statement: the best-eating fish that swims in the wide, wide world is the Edisto River redbreast, and next to him comes the copperhead bream. I will challenge anyone who differs with me to a duel, at such a time as may be convenient to me and with such weapons as I shall choose, in spite of the fact that South Carolina still makes its state officials swear not to engage in duels during terms of office.

We look wistfully toward the full moon in May because it is then that bream traditionally bed. Unlike most fish, bream bed collectively. Often as many as five hundred circular beds may be found in a single acre. Unlike most fish, too, they feed avidly while bedding.

Most sportsmen concede fish a sort of inalienable right to spawn without molestation, to do their romancing in privacy. But I have yet to find a Southerner who evinced any scruples against fishing in a bream bed. Perhaps immemorial usage has made our consciences a little obtuse. It is sometimes the only way bream may be taken and, truth to tell, the practice does not seem to make any serious inroads on the stock.

State laws? Although the game warden may occasionally close a stream or a pond on account of low water or for some other extraordinary reason, the fishing season never closes in South Carolina. We have no laws whatever protecting fish during the spawning season. Our state has the dubious distinction of being unique in this respect! When an expert bream fisherman gets in a large bed, about the only bag limit is his conscience and his bait supply.

An experienced hand locates a bream bed in a novel way: he smells it out! Whether such smelling is really possible is a moot question, and we argue interminably about it. There are old-timers who accept it as an unquestioned fact, who methodically smell out their bream beds year after year, and hold in contempt anybody who cannot. It is just taken for granted. Such a bed, they say, secretes a sweet, musky odor that can be detected fifty yards away by a person who has a trained nose.

One of the best-known doctors in the state regularly pays an expert smeller five dollars a day for his nose. I am something of a fence-straddler on the issue. I have a suspicion that some beds are found first and smelled afterward, but never would I dare to communicate such a suspicion to certain friends of mine. Foolhardy indeed is he who questions a South Carolinian's ability to smell a bream bed!

I do little bed-fishing myself. Not that I have any more scruples than the other fellow. It just happens that I catch as many bream as I'm entitled to in another way — with drone bees. And my fishing is not dependent upon mutations of the moon. Time and again I have pitted my drones against artificial flies, catalpa worms, earthworms and other lures. Time and again they have justified my confidence in them.

Bream are omnivorous feeders. When they are really biting, they will bite almost anything, and anybody can catch them. But when all the signs are wrong, a smart bee-fisherman can still count on a fair catch. However apathetic a big copperhead may be, he can seldom resist the enticement of a fat, juicy drone that has been wafted downstream into his hangout.

The technique of bee-fishing is simple. Your equipment will consist of a light fly rod or slender cane, a fine silk line, and a small long-shanked hook. The shank will facilitate removal of the hook from the fish. If you have designs on a bed, anchor the boat a safe distance away. Remove all weight from your line, put two immature drones on the hook, and let it drift gently down of its own accord.

If you are fishing in running water, attach a single buckshot about eight inches from the hook. Stand upstream and let the current waft your lure under an overhanging bank or likely log jam. Mr. Bream is facing upstream, you may be sure, and is on the *qui vive* for any edible morsel which fortune brings his way. If a strike does not materialize, gently withdraw the hook and drop it upstream again. Don't let it remain in one place too long. Tantalize your customer by moving it slowly back and forth. When an overgrown copperhead unsuspectingly pounces upon that luscious tidbit and makes the belated discovery that he caught a Tartar, your line will sing across the pool. And you will be very, very happy.

Be careful not to disconcert your quarry by hitting the bottom of the boat or by trampling up and down the bank. They are sensitive to any such vibration. You can be as garrulous as you please, since fish can't hear, but how they can feel!

What are the best places to fish for bream? In the exact spots where you are most likely to get your hook hung! Especially in creek fishing. A little study will disclose their favorite hangouts. You will find them lurking under overhanging banks and root-hammocks, in shadowy pockets and foaming eddies.

In my favorite bream stream, a black log-jammed creek that winds snakishly through a swamp, there is a certain spot that I call my bread-basket. It is a small pocket at the base of an uprooted tree where I never fail to take half a dozen bream during the first ten minutes. It never goes back on me. Yet a bait which is not placed in the exact spot is ignored. We sometimes dislodge trees and make hammocks of our own, or nail scrap boards together and anchor them in the current.

In March and April, I fish below spillways. Bream run upstream, especially during high water, as far as they can negotiate with safety. After a heavy rain you will find them waiting for you below the dam. I know one pond owner who, whenever he wants bream, opens his flood-gates for a few hours and pulls fish from miles of trackless swamps. That's bream fishing de luxe.

Be careful not to mash your drone comb. To do so will squash the larvae and make their removal difficult. Don't break it in two with your hands. Use a heated knife, letting it sink through the wax. Then with a penknife shave away the sides of the cell and extract the larvae, one at a time. I confess I always take along a little pickaninny who performs this duty expertly for me.

The larvae of ordinary worker-bees are good bait, but, as anybody who has used them will testify, they have certain disadvantages. They are much smaller than drone larvae, and so tender that it is almost impossible to keep them on the hook, especially in running water. They simply melt and drop off. Again, the worker-bees are the sustaining force of the hive. When you mutilate the combs by cutting them out, you correspondingly weaken the hive. I have too much compassion for the tireless little workers to harm them. They never have any fun, anyway; they are born sexless so that they can keep their minds on their jobs.

But the drone never does a lick of work anyway. He is the playboy of the hive, an abdominous and square-butted loafer who sits around all day, bossing the womenfolks and browbeating everybody he meets. When you remove some of the drones, you do not necessarily impair the hive. They will get it in the neck anyway before very long.

As cold weather approaches, the workers inventory their winter stores and decide to liquidate their free boarders. On an appointed day an execution squad will methodically single out the drones, dispatch them on the spot, and drag their erstwhile handsome carcasses outside. Being stingless, the drones quickly succumb to the tiny amazons.

The workers know they can raise more when the mating season comes again. A queen bee lays at will two kinds of eggs: fertile and infertile. The infertile eggs hatch into males, or drones. The fertile eggs produce either queens or worker-bees, according to the diet they are raised on, which in turn is dictated by the exigencies of the tiny commonwealth.

Drone larvae are easily recognized on a movable frame by the protruding caps over their cells. Those of immature worker-bees are smaller and flat-topped. The larvae are in the best fishing stage after the head has been formed, but while they are still milk-streaked in color. The undeveloped white worms are too small and soft for bait.

With the right handling, a hive may be made to produce an abnormal quantity of drones. If you insert full-width foundation in the frames, you will have few drones, since the small cell bases were manufactured for the rearing of worker-bees. If you insert only half sheets, letting the bees construct the lower half, you will have patches of drones near the bottom corners, since the bees will build some cells specifically for drones. And if you buy and insert one full sheet of drone foundation, you will have almost all drones on that frame. In this locality the principal season for drone-rearing is March, April and May.

"But I haven't any bees," bemoans the prospective bee-fisherman.

Well, cultivate the acquaintance of an obliging bee-keeper, or get yourself some bees. Several years ago a neighbor gave me a section of drone larvae. After one fishing trip, I bought a hive. Now I have twenty.

In spite of the fact that I live in the center of a city of nearly one hundred thousand, my bees do a thriving business. My roof, porches and yard are full of them. My home is easily identified: "It's that old house on the corner, with the bird dogs and boats and fishing poles in the back, and bees all over the house. And a spindlin' fellow in the front yard casting or practicing chip-shots."

Not only am I assured of a plentiful supply of bait for myself and my friends, but I make half a ton of honey a year as a by-product. And in this age of shortages, well, as the Bible says, what is sweeter than honey in the honeycomb? Sugar-ration *me* with twenty hives of bees?

"But," sayeth the average fisherman, "I'd rather do without bream than get stung to death. I'll dig or buy my bait."

The danger of getting stung is greatly exaggerated, especially if your bees are docile Italians rather than black daughters-of-war. We rarely come into "unpleasant proximity" with our little householders. They respond to good treatment. Bees seldom sting, anyway, unless they are provoked or maltreated.

Or unless you smell bad! Yes, sir. If there is an obnoxious odor about your body or your clothing, look out! Or if you are afraid of them. Bees can smell a coward ten feet away. When you are scared, your body secretes an odor that bees can instantly detect. "Ah, here's a poltroon trembling in his boots. How sweetly he stinketh! Let's sock it to him."

But if you are a real bream fisherman, nothing will stop you. Bee stings are supposed to be good for rheumatism, anyway.

# Gun Shy

CAN A gun-shy dog be cured? All of us have heard of devious devices, some more noted for ingenuity than practicality, some as innocuous as recipes for curing the hiccoughs. And a few that are more "scientific" than humane, suggesting the remark attributed to a famous surgeon: "The operation was a success, but the patient died."

Many cases of gun-shyness might ultimately yield to patience and understanding, if the cause of the disease rather than its symptoms be treated. This is not only good sense, but good psychiatry. With most hunters it is a matter of academic interest anyway, since it is usually cheaper to "buy another dog."

In all of my experience, I have known but one really gun-shy dog to be cured — permanently cured — and in that case it was not effected through human agency. The dog was mine, but I was mostly a bystander, or at best a minor actor. Since the cure was brought about under circumstances that might suggest a possible procedure to others, I should like to "get it into the minutes" of the meeting.

"So I'm sending her down to you," my friend wrote. "She's incurably gun-shy. Even the experts have given her up; so you needn't entertain any illusions on the subject. She has been that way for two years — ever since I recovered her from those thieving blacklegs. Before that she was a magnificent little hunter. Since your dogs are getting old, you might want to raise some puppies. She's already in a 'family way' — by Tennessee Jake. You might save me one if they look good.

"P. S. I'm shipping her prepaid."

"I'm always in favor of prepaid people," I said, as I lifted the latch on her crate. "Come on out, honey, and let's get acquainted."

I walked over and sat down on the porch steps. Stepping daintily from her crate, she gave her tail a trial-and-error wag and gravely appraised me. A high-headed and lithe-limbed little dame she was.

"Come on over for a visit," I invited. "I've never been known to repel a lady's advances — not if she has brown shaggy ears, nice eyes and the right amount of blue-tick in her make-up."

She walked over and rested a tentative muzzle against my knee.

"I ain't so bad." I fondled a shaggy ear. "I'm a Cleveland Democrat, a circuit-ridin' Methodist and a middlin'-good shot. And I set a good table. Them's my papers, and I hope you like 'em. So they call you Ole Mistiss, do they? Well, we'll make it Missy, if you don't mind."

Nuzzling closer, she contentedly shut her eyes and surrendered herself to my caresses. A confiding and affectionate little miss she was, and we got along famously together.

"So you're not overly fond of guns," I said. "Well, I've got a few faults too. Not exactly a candidate for celestial translation myself. We'll just make allowances for each other. In the meanwhile, there's a friendly covey over there in the old orchard, and if you say . . . "

Half an hour later, she had pinned down the covey and most of the singles, and with a neatness and dispatch that made me fall in love with her all over again. A precious little hunter she was. What wouldn't a dog like that be worth but for her affliction, that strange psychoneurosis which makes a dog useless to his owner and a source of humiliation to himself — that terrible taint which sets a dog apart like a thing condemned.

By the way, I wondered, just how gun-shy is she? Slipping back to the house, I buttoned a gun beneath my overcoat and re-entered the orchard. Joyously she took the field again. Then she spied the gun, and looked like one betrayed. In her eyes shone a sudden and overmastering fear. Her tail sagged in self-debasement. The gun barrel wavered in my hands, and Missy fled madly and shamelessly for her life.

Under the house she scudded. There she stayed, in spite of my tenderest overtures, for the rest of the day. When she did come fearfully out, I took her in my arms and said: "Missy, I love you as much as ever, and I'll never embarrass you again. Not as long as I live." And I never did.

Behind a gun-shy dog there is apt to be either a conscienceless scamp or a blundering ignoramus. How little it takes, I reflected, to make or mar. The woebegone face of Missy haunted me.

"How I would like to get these two hands on the fellow who implanted in you so unnatural a fear, who took such a sensitive soul and stamped it with a bar sinister. Such a waste," I said, stroking her delicate head. "Such an awful waste."

My friend had sent Missy to me toward the end of March. A few weeks later he wrote:

"The old maid will soon become a mama. Let me know how the youngsters look."

As early as that? I shook my head dubiously.

"Great events are supposed to cast their shadows before, Missy. Maybe there's a mistake somewhere in our friend's chronology."

A week later I understood. Returning from a two-day absence, I was met by Missy, who obviously had a great announcment to make. Leading me to the back porch, she pridefully exhibited her family: one solitary pup!

"Well, I'm damned, Missy!" I said. "The mountain went into labor and brought forth a mouse. Is that the best you can do?"

Beside herself with pride, she panted excitedly and lolled her red tongue. Over she switched to lick my hand, back to nudge her precious pup in an excess of affection.

"One dog is enough for a man," she said, "if he's good enough. And this son of mine — well, take a look at him yourself."

Whereupon she pranced over, daintily picked him up, and brought him to me for inspection. A sturdy, well-boned youngster he was, who enthusiastically mistook my finger for something better and went after it lustily.

"I'll admit he looks O. K.," I conceded. "Mighty O. K., in fact. And with a whole cafeteria to himself, he ought to outgrow the world in no time at all!"

By September, Buck — for that was his name — was following me all over the place, perpetually getting himself into hot water with my wife, and pointing everything that would stand still long enough. Big of bone and sturdy of build, he was already as large as his mother. And the very image of her. I liked his looks, decidedly, and had high hopes for him.

"Missy, that's a strapping son of yours. We may make a dog of him yet, you and I, if we bring him up right."

Little did I realize then the part Missy was to play in his upbringing. For instance, it was really she who taught him retrieving. When I brought him into the house at night for his lessons, she invariably followed. A smart retriever herself, she watched the proceedings alertly. Following him about, she would poke her nose into dark corners, sniff excitedly, and fussily pretend to be looking for the ball herself. When he failed, she would make a spirited recovery, giving the pup the benefit of both precept and example.

Wherever Buck went, Missy went. Wherever he was, her eyes dotingly followed. Never was a mother so devoted. He had wrapped himself around her heart-strings, as she had wrapped herself around mine. But in spite of her affection, she was a firm disciplinarian. A lady herself, she was determined to make that son of hers a gentleman.

In sheer animal spirits, Buck would jump up on me and almost bowl me over. When he continued to disregard my peremptory "Down! Down!" she would growl an admonition, which he likewise disregarded. Deciding one day on summary measures, she seized him by the ear and sent him a sprawling belly-whopper. After a few such discouragements, the blithesome Buck learned to wait for an invitation.

Buck early developed a passion for chasing chickens, which brought him into many a sharp skirmish with my wife. Missy looked on tolerantly for a while, hoping he would put away such childish things of his own accord. Finally, her patience frazzled, she turned wrathfully on him. Thereafter, whenever he sprinted for a chicken, she repeated the dosage. After a few weeks, Buck conceived a profound respect for chickens in general and those of my wife in particular. With a comical, sidelong glance at his mother, he would make a stiff-legged detour around the lowliest Dominique on the place.

"I declare," remarked my wife, "I never saw anything to beat Missy and that scoundrelly son of hers. She watches him like a hawk. And does she make him mind his p's and q's!"

But it took many a cuff to teach Buck that Missy and I were law and order. As soon as she got him out of one trouble he was into another. Poor Missy went about with a perpetually harried look on her face.

"Don't take it so seriously," I laughed at her. "If it's any comfort to you, I was a bigger fool than he is, at his age."

"This thing of bringing a son into the world," she sighed.

Around the first of November, Missy and I started Buck to work in the old orchard. Without a gun, in deference to her. As for Buck, that rough-and-ready dearly loved a gun — the sight, sound and smell of it. I had seen to that earlier, without the old lady's assistance, of course.

Our season was to open in late November. If Missy and I could teach the young dandy his abc's during the intervening three weeks, I could put the finishing touches on him later. There was a bumper crop of quail that year — two oversized coveys in the orchard alone — so we had plenty of drill work right at home.

Buck's first lesson I shall never forget. Missy was down on a point. Buck, construing her sudden pause as an invitation to frolic, barged up and began tugging at her ear. Missy frowned, averted her head, and chided softly. Switching around, Buck went to work on the other ear. Again she turned her head, her lips writhing in menace. Cautiously she backed away, approached from another angle, and resumed her point. Emboldened by her non-resistance, Buck went up and yanked again.

"In just about two-thirds of a second," I said to myself, "that fool Buck is going to find himself in the middle of next week."

The next instant he was somersaulting through the air, landing "ka-thump!" in the middle of the skulking bevy. And there lay the masterful Buck, with eyes tightly shut and a chastened look on his face, as twenty birds exploded around him.

I laughed. Missy just lolled her tongue appreciatively.

"Now let that be a lesson to you," she growled.

But one lesson was not enough. The next time Missy pointed, Buck stood irresolutely for a moment, and then threw himself headlong into the covey. Again she gave him a thorough overhauling, softly throttling the prone Buck and snarling: "Nobody can flush birds around here and get away with it. The sooner you learn that the better off we'll all be."

Thus Buck learned afresh that a doting and indulgent mother can become an avenging nemesis when occasion demands.

Two days before the opening, the puppy got his final pre-season instruction. Missy was on point. Buck came up to her shoulder and manfully backed. It was as far, I think, as he intended going, and his conduct was thus far unimpeachable. But old Missy growled on general principles. Whereupon Buck, allowing a margin for error, discreetly edged back a step and planted himself on his inalienable rights and instincts. The muttering in her throat died softly away.

"That's putting it on a bit thick, honey," I chuckled. "Sort of gilding the lily, don't you think?"

By Thanksgiving, Missy and I had the puppy doing good work, allowing for the exuberance of youth. She had worked harder, much harder, than I had.

"Missy," I told her, "tomorrw is the day. Buck and I are going out alone. If I don't miss my guess, we'll have a lot of fun, find a lot of birds, one way and another, and maybe bring back a few for you to smell."

I lay awake for hours, waiting for the dawn. After a hasty breakfast I pulled on my hunting coat, picked up my gun, and called to Buck. Into the car he jumped. While I was putting the gun in I chanced to see Missy standing indecisively between the porch and the car. Well, that was understandable. She knew what the puppy would do with her. She didn't know what he would do without her. She knew what it meant to me, and had just come to see us off. That was it.

But then she came a few steps nearer, wagging her tail irresolutely, looking now toward the car, now toward the house.

"I wonder just how close she will come to that gun. Maybe. . . . "

Leaving the back door open, I ignored her altogether. Walking around the car, I got in and fussed around the dashboard while I watched her over my shoulder. More out of curiosity than hope, I admit.

A step nearer she came, with eyes intent on the pup. A step nearer still. Then to my amazement, she slipped quietly into the back seat with him. I closed the door without looking back, grinning to myself.

"Well," I tried to sound casual, "glad to have you along. Handn't counted on it exactly, but glad to have you anyway. You can just sit in the car and watch us."

When I stopped the car, Buck sailed out and hit a ragweed lot at a smart clip. There were birds in that ragweed. I knew it. The puppy knew it. And Missy knew it. I took my gun and followed, leaving the car door cracked just in case.

Two hundred feet away, Buck sniffed eagerly and began to stalk forward. Here was the just-abandoned and reeking roost. The birds were running ahead of us, presenting the puppy with a new problem in deportment. He wanted to point in all directions at once. Creeping forward a few paces, he dropped. Reconsidering he advanced and dropped again. Once more he crept forward, quivering. Then, baffled, he turned and looked at Missy for help.

Over my shoulder I saw her, standing by the car, watching the puppy with her heart in her mouth. She didn't see me. She didn't see the gun. Only that son who was in trouble. Behind me I heard her padding softly. Moving up beside Buck, she daintily lifted her muzzle to test the air, turned to the right, and dropped conclusively. With returning courage the puppy strode up and stretched out beside her.

"Lord," I breathed. "Whoever would have thought of it!"

Suddenly I realized the quandary I was in. The puppy was entitled to present his case. If I shot with Missy there . . . I was more scared, I think, than either she or the puppy. But there was no escape. Lifting my gun, I walked in, dropped a bird on the rise, and swiftly turned away to shut out the expected sight of a panic-stricken and woebegone Missy fleeing homeward.

When I dared to look again, there was Buck, fetching me the bird, with Missy tripping confidently by his side. I thought it best to ignore her, but the puppy I complimented and hugged hugely. The light in Missy's eyes told me that was thanks enough, a mother's recompense.

The rest of the day we hunted together, with Missy always in the shadow of the pup, zealously guarding him against many a grievous mistake. When the trail grew devious, there she was to set him straight, to steady him against impulsiveness, to nab the wounded bird that eluded him. I don't believe she heard the gun the entire day, so wrapped up in him she was.

Thereafter we hunted regularly together. There was never any more evidence of gun-shyness on her part. The pup made a good dog, but it was Missy, his mother, that no man's money could buy. She was the dog who had come back, the dog who has a special niche in my memory after these twenty years.

Thus was a gun-shy dog cured, and perhaps not so strangely after all, if one considers a simple fact: her love was greater than her fear. She loved me, and she loved that pup, more than she feared death itself. After all, love is a great psychiatrist. The greatest, I expect, in the whole wide world.

## Sandhill Quail

A FRIEND of mine was bemoaning the decadence of old-time quail hunting in the South. Bob-white, he complained, has lost his open-field cockiness, the saucy indifference that made him the field target par excellence.

"Why, he used to be an upstandin' field bird, and huntin' him was a pleasure. Now he's degenerated into a skulkin' bushwhacker and a pain in the neck. He's lost his nerve, I tell you. Now when I was growin' up — "

I had to admit the force of the indictment. Year by year the Southern partridge is becoming warier and more elusive. He has abandoned the mellow fields about the old homestead, the orchard back of the barn, the friendly hedgerow. He is becoming a refugee, a lover of the darksome covers and impenetrable haunts he once scorned, and shooting him is a snare and a delusion.

To be sure, even nowadays we find an occasional covey sunning on a pleasant hillside, or meadow lush with ragweed, but most of the birds we raise are liable to be loitering in the edge of a swamp or woods, ready for instant flight. Bob is becoming as jittery as an escaped jailbird. He is like an old darky I knew down in Mississippi, a foxy old fellow who had ignominiously skipped out on a free-for-all fight.

[ 37 ]

"Why did you run, Uncle Tobe?" I asked.

"Cap'n," he answered owlishly, "I'd ruther hear 'em say, 'Cyan't dat nigger run!' dan have 'em march down de church aisle and say, 'Don't he look natchal!'"

"What would have happened if Bob had not become a bushwhacker?" I asked Henry. "What with fast automobiles and good roads, restricted ranges, automatics and what-nots, and ten of us bombardin' him to every one in the old days?"

Henry stretched his long legs before the fireplace, jammed a handful of ready-cut into the cavernous bowl of his pipe, and contemplated the ceiling through the swirling fragrance.

"Guess it would have been curtains, all right. Guess the little scutter figured that a good run is a sight better than a bad stand. Yes, sir, his name would have been Dennis if he hadn't gone into retirement. Can't say that I blame him much. Rather be a live woodpecker than a dead bird of paradise myself. Matter of fact, I don't like 'em too easy. All a fellow can rightfully ask is half a chance."

"If all you ask is half a chance, what about tryin' a few sand-hill quail this afternoon?" I suggested.

"Are sand-hill birds any different from others?" he asked.

"Not after you get 'em."

"Well, I've shot quail in the James River bottoms where Johnson grass was waist-high. I've shot 'em in Florida where you had to wear tin leggings to keep rattlesnakes from osculatin' you, and I've shot 'em in the Blue Ridge Mountains where they fly straight up, like autogyros; so if you've got anything new in birdshootin' it's Barkis with me. Let's go."

An hour later we were standing on a flat sand-ridge overlooking an endless succession of other sand-ridges, all studded with a bristling growth of pygmy oaks from five to eight feet high. Their naked gray branches interlocked to form a dreary and unbroken landscape extending for miles around us. Here and there a towering pine etched a lonely silhouette against a burnished sky. A buzzard wheeled listlessly overhead. In the barren sand beneath the thicket of black-jack only the scantiest of vegetation found sustenance.

The sand-hills extend in a ragged belt for perhaps two hundred miles through South Carolina, stretching from Cheraw to

Augusta. A great part of the forlorn waste is covered with dwarf oaks in splotches of from fifty to a thousand acres. The work of erosion, some geologists say; sand dunes marking the original shore-lines, others say. The last place on earth to pick for a bird hunt, anybody would say.

"Whoever saw so much sameness!" muttered Henry. "The only game in that stuff is chiggers and doodle-bugs. Why, even a crow would have to pack provisions to cross it. What would a partridge find to eat in such a God-forgotten place?"

"If you're half as good a shot as you think you are, maybe we can find out," I hedged.

My companion glanced appraisingly at the scraggly oak growth. Mathematical fellow that he is, he was figuring the probable line of flight in case we raised birds. His look of complacency told me he had doped it out that they would level off just above the interlacing tops, in comparatively open shooting. But when he turned, I was smiling contentedly.

"Looks fair-to-middling to a man up a tree," he commented.

Sally Anne, like the irrepressible coquette she was, went streaking through the black-jacks. Before she had hardly entered a thicket she was flashing through the other side, bestowing her capricious and frisking favor on whatever came her way. You had to have eyes in the back of your head to keep up with Henry's racy little Llewellin.

Not so with my heavy-bodied old pointer. Judge jogged along in front of us like a sedate Victorian gentleman, regarding the effervescence of the young setter with genteel tolerance. Judge is getting old and a trifle phlegmatic now, like Shakespeare's country squire "in fair round belly, with good capon lined." Not that there are any flies on the old fellow. He has simply reached the stage where he prefers to use his nose rather than his legs — his nose and the intuitions that are the legacy of a good dog grown old.

Presently Judge stopped short, lifting his gray muzzle as if to test some vagrant cross-current that piqued his interest. Then he abruptly right-angled the path, stalked forty or fifty paces, and planted himself behind a wind-blown lap. As I called to Henry, the vigilant little Sally Anne, who had evidently taken the hypotenuse rather than the leg of the triangle, brought up on the other side of the fallen lap, her merry tail aloft.

A covey erupted from the leaves and went scudding through the tops of the scrub-oaks. I let go at two portsiders that swerved my way, and then "howmanyed" Henry.

"It's bad manners to holler 'How many did you get?' You should say, 'Did you get that one, old man?' Matter of fact, I missed clean as a hound's tooth, and no wonder! Those cock-eyed hellions didn't fly right!" he announced in an injured tone.

"Didn't they?"

"You know blamed well they didn't. I waited for them to rise above that low thicket and straighten out, but they never did. Shot off low, smack through the oak tops, like a bat free-wheelin' out of Hades. You'd have to wear bifocals to pick out one of those jungaleers."

"Maybe," I said, holding up a bird.

Sand-hill quail seldom behave like normal birds, but there's no use in disillusioning a fellow. They all get up that way — not above the oak tops, but straight through them. Picking these quail out from the neutral-colored branches is not exactly to be recommended for astigmatism. The birds have learned the difference betwixt discretion and valor, if you ask me. They have also learned that shot follow a straight line.

And where did the covey go down? They didn't go down. When a bevy of these sand-hill bushwhackers takes off, it breaks to pieces like a bombshell. It's every man for himself, and the devil take the hindermost. Not only that, but these sand-hillers are great skulkers. And your dogs are disadvantaged by the barren sand and tinder-dry leaves. The result is that once you have raised a covey, singles are apt to burst from the leaves anywhere and at any time. They are a great bunch of opportunists. Let a skulking bird catch you off guard, and it's a ninth-inning rally. They have a positive genius for popping up at awkward moments.

We hunted the surrounding area for perhaps fifteen minutes without raising a single bird. They were there, all right, but it was a game of hide-and-seek. Suddenly one materialized out of a stump just behind me. I must have passed within five feet without flushing him.

Pivoting about for a snap shot, I succeeded only in jabbing an eye against a prickly bush. The bird scuttled away through the interlacing tops. For a few minutes I was in excruciating pain from the jab on the super-sensitive pupil. But to Henry it was funny.

"First time I ever saw a full-grown man cry over missin' a shot!" he chortled. "Actually cry. Or maybe you only need one eye to beat me shootin.' Generous of you to handicap yourself that way, old sand-hiller."

Within ten minutes I had my revenge. It convinced me that in shooting bushwhackers he who laughs last laughs best, but it's best not to laugh at all. A string in one of Henry's boots had been working loose. "These blooming rawhide strings!" he muttered, placing his foot on a log.

Just as he leaned over to tie the offending boot, a bird shot up from beneath the very log. Henry made a frantic grab for his gun and sheared off the top of a bush ten feet from the rocketing bird.

"No excuse for a bird's behavin' like that — no earthly excuse. Why, I had been standin' by that log for five minutes doing nothin', yet he had to wait till the precise second I bent over to tie my boot!" he complained ruefully.

"These sand-hill birds have a strong interest in self-preservation, Henry. You can't gallivant around all night and expect to do much with 'em the next day. But you said half a chance — "

"Half a chance, my foot! These freakish varmints don't give you any."

A few minutes later I spied Sally Anne on point in the brush a hundred yards away. The high-stepping setter was a statue in black and white, her patrician head high, her tail up and out.

Two birds, perhaps a remnant of the dispersed covey, shot up from a pile of leaves and straightawayed down a narrow aisle between the oaks. It was the sort of shot that warms the cockles of a harried hunter's heart, the sort of shot you get in the sand-hill barrens only now and then — mostly then. The left bird crumpled to Henry's gun, the right to mine.

"That was right elegant, wasn't it?" Henry grinned. "These little sockdolagers are beginnin' to behave normal. A shot like that calls for a smoke. Reckon it's safe?"

Just as Henry sucked at the cupped match, a bird rocketed from the selfsame pile of leaves and went side-slipping to safety through the oak tops. We looked at each other stupidly.

Then Henry proceeded to enrich the incident with a few manly comments.

"Can't even tie a boot or light a pipe in this dad-blamed stuff. Why in the name of Jehoshaphat didn't that bird get up when the other two did? Answer me that. When you look for 'em, they ain't there. Just turn your back, and they bounce out hell-bent-for-election. That's what is known as perfect synchronizin'."

"Didn't I tell you that these bushwhackers had a strong interest in self-preservation?" I goaded.

On the second ridge we located another covey. Both dogs went down in an almost impenetrable thicket of pygmy oaks. It was to be snap-shooting or nothing; so we inched our way in as cautiously as possible. A big covey exploded almost under our noses. I emptied both barrels at a scuttling brown body. Henry, who is a pretty competent hand with a repeater, kept up the serenading. It must have sounded like Bull Run. The one bird that fell my way I attributed to providence.

"Got half the covey that time, I guess," announced my companion. "I caught 'em just as they teetered through that mass of tops. Look how I mowed those bushes off. Put the dogs in there and let's see how many."

I saw a single cock lodged in a low bush. If Henry got any others, I didn't see them fall, but you couldn't tell much in such a messy growth. Judge and Sally Anne subjected the thicket to a thorough sniffing without result. Finally Judge ambled out and squatted on his haunches.

"I'm bound to have killed more than one bird. Shot four times. There simply wasn't room enough for me to miss 'em all. Law of averages, you know. Sally Anne is still lookin', but your dog has gone back on me."

I ordered the old pointer back into the thicket. He obeyed, but with an air that told me as plain as day it was wasted effort. Judge has a well-nigh infallible nose. If he gives you a negative report on dead birds, you can take him at his word. When he emerged a second time and squatted, I knew the verdict was final.

"I told you to find those birds, you old backslider. Go on! Dead bird!" ordered Henry, nettled by the dog's apparent indifference.

Judge's only response was to lift his patriarchal muzzle and stare at the speaker.

"Go on, you hard-headed old scalawag! Didn't I tell you that there are dead birds in that thicket!"

Whereupon the old pointer emitted a single bark, yawned cavernously, and settled down on his fat haunches. It was a picture worth framing.

"That's the first time I've ever been called a liar by a dog!" Henry laughed, fondling the big muzzle. "And if it weren't for your gray hairs, sir, it would be coffee for one and pistols for two. Well, that's that. Let's scrimmage around a bit. Some of those singles dropped pretty close, I'm thinkin'."

Some of them did. In a small honeysuckled ravine we raised four, two of which got up without giving us a shot. The other two we managed to bag in spite of their unorthodox and baffling flight through the oak tops.

"What about the bill of fare of these sand-hillers?" Henry reminded. "You promised to refer to that durin' the program. These unrighteous barrens are full of fat birds, but where do they get their vitamins, if any?"

"We have five or six birds. Suppose we take time out for a little amateur dissecting," I suggested.

Sitting on a log, I proceeded to remove the crops from the birds I had bagged. The contents, which were all alike as I had expected, I poured into the outstretched hand of my companion. He looked incredulously at the exhibit.

"Acorns! Of all things! Do you mean to tell me these birds eat acorns, and nothin' else?" he demanded, as if suspicious of some chicanery on my part.

"Think I'm shell-gaming you? Examine one for yourself."

Yanking out a crop, he emptied it into the palm of his hand and fingered the contents: four acorns, two half-acorns.

"They must have the democratic tastes of a billy-goat to eat such things. I've heard of queer diets, but this is the first time

I've ever been in the witness box, so to speak. Maybe that's why these sand-hillers are so rambunctious — such an outlandish appetite."

The quail inhabiting the oak barrens apparently live almost entirely on small acorns from the dwarf oaks for a good part of the year. Last season I examined the crops of twenty-five denizens of the sand-hills during the hunting season. Every one contained acorns or fragments of acorns. Most of them were stuffed with whole acorns. One crop contained seven. The fragments observed in some were presumably cut by squirrels or roving hogs, and comparatively easy to swallow. But many of the whole acorns collected were as big as small marbles and almost as hard. How they swallow them is beyond me.

Acorns were, of course, an acquired appetite with these birds. It is merely another illustration of the remarkable adaptability of the Southern partridge, an adaptability that includes food as well as habitat. Making the best of a bad bargain is bob-white's long suit. Otherwise he would have succumbed long ago.

The territory adjacent to these oak barrens is rather heavily shot, and these harrassed birds have taken to the sand-hills as a last stronghold. When the rent got too high, they simply got out. A doubtful sanctuary, one would say, but they seem to have found it satisfactory. It is not such a bad place for a last stand either, when you consider that their presence is suspected by few hunters; that food, such as it is, is plentiful; and that their behavior when attacked is erratic and disconcerting to the attacker. At any rate, most of these sand-hillers attain a ripe old age, which is evidence of the first water.

Late afternoon found us meandering slowly back to our car. For half an hour nothing had happened to relieve the tedium of white sand, dry leaves and pygmy oaks. Judge loafed indifferently ahead as usual, deigning only an occasional excursion to right or left. Busy little Sally Anne left no possibility unprobed, prying into every likely thicket or brush pile. When her quest was finally rewarded, both of us were delighted. Judge dutifully backed her, and we confidently edged in behind them.

We were in a comparatively open area. Hope ran high. If a covey would take off here — But nothing happened. Both dogs relaxed point, warily advanced, and pointed again. We maneuvered behind them, but as we brought up even, they nervously crept forward and pointed farther up the ridge. The birds were running ahead, of course. It had already occurred to me that a covey rise in such open area was not "in character" for sand-hillers.

When they did get up, a hundred yards and half a dozen "points" from where they started, I was so flabbergasted that I got one lone bird. In spite of his enthusiastic cannonading, my companion did no better. But we had another alibi besides nerves: the covey had stubbornly refused to take wing in the clearing where we found them. They had hugged the shore until they regained the snug harbor of a native thicket.

"Why in the pluperfect heck didn't those birds get up back there where we had a chance?" Henry snorted.

"Didn't I tell you these birds — "

"Wait a minute," he interrupted. "Are you goin' to say anything about self-preservation? If you pull that crack again, I'll — Hold your horses! That old Methuselah of yours says he's found a single over there."

Henry walked up behind Judge and kicked the leaves. Just as he did so, the old pointer, with an unsuspected agility, pounced upon a luckless cock skulking in the brush. Surprised and a bit chagrined, Henry pocketed the proffered bird.

"So that's the way you feel about my shootin', is it? Not takin' any chances, are you? Can't say I blame you much. Let's go," he called to me. "When a bird dog insults Henry Massengill twice in the same day, Henry Massengill quits."

"Have a good time?" I asked as we climbed aboard.

"Well, the other team got the breaks, all right, but I can't say I'm regrettin' much. These acorn-eatin' sand-hillers of yours are great little guys. Can't say I'd like 'em as a steady diet, though," he added reflectively. "They've got too many habits. Apt to give a fellow an inferiority complex about his shootin'."

# When It's Crappie You're After

IF THE number of nicknames a fellow has is any indication of his standing, the crappie will poll a plurality in almost any election. Few game fish are so widely distributed and so variously named.

In Louisiana, Texas and thereabouts he is a sacalait or chinquapin perch. In the Ohio valley he goes under the name of bachelor. In Kentucky, southern Indiana and Illinois, he crops up under crappie, newlight, or campbellite, while in northern Indiana and Illinois he becomes tinmouth, tin perch, or paper-mouth.

In eastern Virginia he is esteemed as a freckle, in central Virginia as a silver perch. In South Carolina and Georgia he is plain crappie to the fly-fishermen and goggle-eye to the literal cane-fishing sand-hillers. He is also crapet, bridge perch, speckled perch, freckled perch, goldring, suckley perch, strawberry perch, timber crappie, white perch, fresh-water shad and john demon, depending upon what part of the map he elects to call home. Surely fate didn't try to conceal this fellow by naming him Smith!

In some localities he is erroneously called calico bass; but while these two sunfishes resemble closely, they are readily distinguishable. They differ somewhat in shape, the crappie showing a more decided S curve in the contour of its back. They differ also in color, the calico bass (*Pomoxis sparoides*) being darker, with its irregular mottlings against the silver background, the splotches extending more noticeably into the fins and tail. Hence the descriptive of "calico" and the occasional name of "black crappie." But since the color of the same species may differ markedly with habitat, the easiest and most infallible way of distinguishing the two is by counting the spines in the dorsal fins. The crappie has fewer such spines, normally six, while the calico bass has normally seven or eight.

But to revert to the crappie. As if not satisfied with such gobs of nomenclature, bookish people call him *P. annularis*. The *P.* is supoosed to stand for *Pomoxis;* but if you ask me, it stands for "particular." And the best place to catch him is where you're most apt to get your hook hung.

With a small boy's admiration for competent old age, I used to follow my grandfather a-crappying. Well do I remember one particular spot in a neighborhood mill-pond where crappie would "bite to beat the band." It was a mystic hole alongside a giant tupelo stump, where he would always catch a mess of freckles — if he didn't get his hook hung. To me there was something preternatural about that hole. I entertained vague notions that my grandfather had it conjured. Later I learned it wasn't conjury, but crappie. The lesson should have stuck.

A few years ago a friend and I decided to forego bass fishing for a day and go a-crappying in a large power reservoir. My friend complacently paddled by a number of lovely cove-tips and eventually brought up over a "harricane" of half-sunken tree tops. Interlacing branches were as thick as witches' hair.

"Of all the places in the lake, you would pick such a mess as this!" I protested.

"The place to catch crappie is where they are at," he answered laconically. "Besides, I've been here before."

Adjusting his light cork at four feet, he scooped a three-inch "brass-head" from the minnow bucket and delicately suspended his hook over a small pocket. Before I had my own hook into the water his cork dipped smartly and up came a shining two-pounder. A crappie day, I reflected, dropping my own hook gingerly into another part of the pocket.

Within fifteen minutes my companion had four. Fishing with similar tackle, at the same depth and with the identical bait, I had not had a strike. Experimentally I dropped my line into other spots. The little cork lay inert on the water.

"Trouble with you, you're not fishing at the right place," my companion volunteered. "Drop your hook into that pocket beside mine."

"Ought to be as good in one place as another. All looks alike," I demurred.

"Ought ain't," he said succinctly. "If you want crappie, drop your hook — " And he pulled up another shimmering beauty.

"I don't see any superior virtues that hole has over any other. I won't give you that much pleasure."

I didn't, and I took one forlorn crappie during the whole afternoon.

"Why do you reckon they bit in that one pocket and nowhere else?" I asked, perplexed, as we weighed anchor.

"Ain't a crappie. Can't say," he answered. "But I discovered that precious little pocket years ago, and it seldom fails me."

"Luck!" I begrudged.

But the very next day I went back — alone — and took a baker's dozen from the selfsame spot when I couldn't get a bite anywhere else in the cove. So I say that *P.* stands for particular.

It's that way with a crappie. He will attach himself to one spot, bite readily enough there, and superciliously disregard your hook everywhere else. He has a natural affinity for dim corridors, darksome coverts and grisly thickets — wherever, to be exact, any circumspect angler would hesitate to venture his hook.

Alongside the boat-house, beneath the overgrown bridge, in the matted fringe of a windfall, near any submerged wreckage, *P. annularis* holds high tryst with his friends. He is one chap who does not suffer of claustrophobia — the morbid fear of tight places. His love of shadowy retreats may be due to the fact that his protrusive eyes are abnormally sensitive to light. They injure easily upon exposure. Or he may love the dark because his ways are devious, or merely because he is a crappie. At any rate, the cunning angler can make capital of this idiosyncrasy of his.

Two summers ago I had spent a live-long afternoon in a crappie-infested pond, with one shriveled specimen for my pains. I had tried flies, minnows, catalpa worms — everything in the book. It was just one of those days, I philosophized. But philosophy is scant solace for an empty belly.

As I paddled dispiritedly toward the landing in late afternoon, I espied an ample-beamed colored woman parked in a blunt-nosed bateau in the middle of the cove. She puffed composedly at a clay pipe as she fished with a coarse hand-line over the side of the boat. I smiled and indulgently called a half-hearted inquiry: "Any luck, auntie?"

"Done cotch a smidgin o' goggle-eye, cap'n." And she lifted a fluttering string that made my eyes bulge.

With fifty dollars' worth of tackle at my disposal, an outboard motor and a lot of expensive experience, I had caught practically nothing. I faced the prospect of returning home empty-handed.

"How did you catch 'em, auntie?"

"Fishin' under de boat, cap'n. Dese here goggle-eye lak dark, sinful places."

Well! I anchored my boat in the middle of the cove, sat still a few minutes, and half-hopefully dropped a minnow over the gunwale with a hand-line. The cork dipped and plunked downward. I hauled in a 10-inch crappie over the side of the boat. I dropped over another minnow, and after a discreet interval the cork smacked down again. In half an hour my reputation and supper were both safe.

Giving my lowly informant half a dollar, I came home and made an entry in my diary: "Fish alongside boat for crappie." It was the cheapest advice I ever got, and I have verified its soundness again and again.

After ruminating on the crappie hang-outs I had chanced upon, I decided last year to devise one of my own. Knocking the heads from two large sugar barrels, I removed every other stave, weighted the barrels, and sank them in a likely cove. Within a few days crappie began to frequent my rendezvous. Effective loitering places may be fashioned of dry-goods boxes smashed in, wired together and submerged. I have one energetic acquaintance who took advantage of low water by driving stakes into the ground and nailing slabs irregularly up the sides. When the water came up again, he had a crappie rendezvous *de luxe*.

The crappie has another personality trait which may be turned to advantage: his gregariousness. He is hail-fellow-well-met, with a strong preference for the society of his kind. One of the best ways to locate a school is to fly-cast or "skitter" from a drifting boat until a customer is found. Then anchor your boat and give his compatriots and fraternity brothers a trial.

Although a strictly carnivorous feeder, the crappie is far from being pernickety about his food. Small fish and insect crustaceans constitute the bulk of his menu, minnow-fishing being the orthodox way of taking him. He will readily take large gambusia, brassheads (*Fundulus*), and small bluegills. Or goldfish. Ah! There is *P. annularis'* secret passion, especially in clear water.

Next to minows on his bill of fare comes perhaps the succulent catalpa worm, certainly in the crappie's Southern habitat. In parts of the solid South the catalpa tree is planted and cultivated for its by-product by connoisseurs of such panfish as the matchless bream, the bluegill, the warmouth and the calico bass.

But when I go a-crappying there is one bait I prefer above all others: the drone larvae of the honey bee. Give me a frame of milky young drones and a springy day. If there are any crappie to be had, I will not take an empty belly to bed. In twenty-five years of panfishing in the South I have never found anything else which my customers will attack with such avidity. Truth to confess, I maintain a small apiary atop my house — three blocks from the state capitol — partly for bait. I have discovered a way of making a hive produce a bumper crop of drones, a blackguardly trick, I admit.

In the absence of choicer morsels, the crappie will not disdain common earthworms, crickets, grasshoppers and — *de gustibus non est disputandum* — cockroaches! Indeed, I have a crotchety acquaintance who raises cockroaches for bait in a contrivance in his own kitchen.

Crappie may also be taken by "skittering" near the surface with a long flexible cane, to the tip of which is attached a tiny gold-plated spinner and a single hook, sweetened with a striplet of bacon rind or perch belly, or mayhap a small bright fly. More game fish are taken from the streams of the Low Country this way — "jiggering," as it is known locally — that by any other method. A home-made bucktail fly, tipped with worm, is probably the most efficacious lure. The *modus operandi* is more skillful than it sounds, and a long slender-tipped cane, soaked in turpentine rags a day or so in advance, has the pliability of a whip.

A similar lure on a fly rod is also a sporting way to take crappie. Because of the fish's tender mouth — hence the nickname of papermouth — landing a large specimen on a light rod requires deft handling and no inconsiderable skill. The crappie is a sprightly feeder and a rather mettlesome chap. A two-pounder on a slender rod leaves you little time for metaphysical reflections. He is pugnacious enough, but short-winded. He won't last for the whole game maybe, but for a ninth-inning rally —

The crappie is one of the most adaptable of the sunfishes. He has proved the very salvation of the power reservoirs that are springing up like Jonah's gourd in the Piedmont South. For the first few clear-water years, big-mouth bass thrive incredibly in these lakes; but as the everlasting hills are eaten away and a ceaseless tide of yellow silt sweeps down into the settling basins, the water becomes uncongenial to game fish. *P. annularis*, however, is in his proper element. The biological balance in such water seems to lean his way.

He is about the only gentleman who can compete with the riffraff of cats, carp and jack that soon infest these bodies. Lake Murray, a 50,000-acre power reservoir in South Carolina, is as full of crappie as a Georgia ditch with gambusia, in spite of the fact that the water is now muddy almost the year round and bass are finding it inhospitable. The power reservoir of the low South was preordained for crappie.

Where conditions are favorable, the crappie will attain a surprising size. I took a three-pounder that was seventeen inches long from Lake Murray this spring. Some years ago, while fishing in an estuary of the James River — on Sunday — I took a three-and-a-halfer. There are four- and possibly five-pound crappie in some Southern reservoirs, although two pounds represents normal growth.

The crappie is one of the most beautiful and most palatable of all pan-fishes. If the ultimate destiny of a fish is the frying pan, he has a lot to recommend him. When a sizable crappie is cleaned immediately and dropped for a few scant minutes into a pan of sizzling fat, he is a fillip for the most jaded appetite. It is hard to "fault" him, as my canny sand-hill paddler says. His flesh is infinitely preferable to that of a bigmouth. Some time ago I tried to swap a five-pound bigmouth to a darky for half a dozen crappie. But all my bargaining was in vain.

"Dese here goggle-eye heap mo' sweeter," he grinned tightly, and he was right. To me a crappie has a finer flavor than his "first cousin once removed," the calico bass.

The crappie's wide distribution, adaptability, rapidity of growth and palatability combine to make him an eminently useful fish. He is a cooperative and dependable fellow, a ready and a not-too-discriminating feeder. Along with the bullhead, he is a boy's best friend — what the rock bass used to be. He is the cane fisherman's mainstay and chief delight. He saves the day for many a weary angler and keeps many a meager-circumstanced Southern family from going to bed supperless. "Us gwine have fish for supper!" And he keeps many a bass fisherman from returning home in utter ignominy, for when game fish are finicky or weather conditions are not what they might be the crappie is an ace in the hole.

If I were asked to name the fish that probably gives more pleasure to more people than any other, I think I should nominate good old democratic *P. annularis*. Then I would immediately move to elect him by acclamation.

# Hell Hath No Fury . . .

"Hɪᴛ ᴡᴏɴ'ᴛ cost you nothin' extry, sir. Dawg an' me both for two dollars," urged the boy.

"Where is your dog?"

A gaunt bitch materialized from an ash heap, apathetically shook the ashes from her blue-black hide, and eyed the inquisitor with passive malevolence. The judge looked wonderingly at the scar-seamed rump, the scalloped ears.

"What kind of — "

"Bird dawg, sir," quickly supplied the boy.

"I see," the judge smiled, forbearing to probe an ancestry that carried the unhappy hint of a bar sinister. "In hunting dogs, it's aristocracy of worth rather than birth that counts anyway, but I guess we can manage without your dog this morning."

"All right, sir. I though maybe since Pedro, since he — " the boy politely demurred. "Well, I thought maybe you'd leave 'im at home today."

"Yes. Pedro." The judge's placid features clouded, as if reminded of something he had been trying to forget. "But I've decided to give Pedro his last chance this morning. His case comes before the supreme court, so to speak."

"Home, Blue!" The boy turned severely on the ash-colored dog. "An' don't go a-gallivantin' around the swamp. If you do, I'm a-goin' to frail hell an' Georgy out o' you when I get back."

Four hours later the judge squatted dejectedly on a log in the pine lands, his imported gun leaning against a sapling. Pushing back his faded cap, he wiped the sweat from his glistening bald head and erstwhile cherubic face.

"The fourth or fifth time this morning he has done that trick, son?"

"Fifth, sir."

"And the same story yesterday and day before. Well, it's nothing new. Ran ace-high at Freeport last year until the same thing knocked his chances galleywest."

"What makes 'im do hit, do you reckon?"

"The green-eyed monster," answered the judge abstractedly. "Jealousy," he added, feeling the uncomprehending glance of the boy. "When he sees another dog with birds, he goes berserk. Rule or ruin, that's Pedro."

"Can't he be cured, sir?"

"Did you ever hear of anybody, dog or man, being cured of jealousy? In nigh onto twenty years on the bench I never have. If a dog can be trained, Jim Merryman, down in Mississippi, can train him. Well, Jim gave him up. If it had been any dog except Pedro — "

Two hundred yards away the subject of the judge's jeremiad was racing through the flatlands as debonairly as if he had been the fair-haired child of his master. The boy idly watched as the big liver-and-white pointer flashed around a bay, dropped momentarily, and began to stalk toward the black-and-white statuette that was Princess Anne on point. Pedro, the boy reflected, was enacting his characteristic role.

The scion of aristocrats, Pedro was the hunter transcendent, the greatest bird-finding machine the judge had ever owned. But even Achilles had a bad heel. As if begrudging the prodigality with which she had endowed the dog, nature slipped into Pedro's make-up an apple of discord. Hunting alone, he was as staunch as the staunchest. It was when his lesser mates found birds that the defect in his otherwise gifted nature came to the fore. In his over-reaching greed, he would stalk inexorably forward, jaws avidly weaving, forgetful of all training. A prematurely flushed quarry was too often the result. The obstinacy of this quirk in the dog's make-up had brought more than one handler to the verge of lunacy.

"I've got an idea," the boy ventured, chewing reflectively on a straw. "Hit might work. Let's try 'em together, Pedro and my — "

"Ideas about Pedro have already cost me several hundred dollars and a lot of sweetness and light, son," said the judge. "I ain't in the market for any more. As for me, I ain't going to be a sentimental dodo and let one dog ruin my vacation. And as for Pedro," the judge pulled himself up from the log, smacked vindictively at the seat of his pants, and stabbed the air with a stubby forefinger, "as for Pedro, he is your dog. Take him."

A wild happiness upsurged in the boy's breast as he started homeward. Once out of earshot of his benefactor, he could contain himself no longer. Calling Pedro to him, he swept up the dog in a swift, bone-cracking embrace. Then he lay in the sunny broom straw while his new acquisition wallowed mightily beside him.

"Pedro," said the boy gravely, "you air my dawg. You belong to me, an' I belong to you. I'm a-goin' to look after you and feed you — chitterlin's and cracklin' bread when I can get hit. I won't sell you an' I won't trade you off. I'm a-goin' to stick to you through thick an' thin. An' you got to hunt for me an' hunt *right*. If you don't hit'll be between you an' me. An' another thing: You ain't a-goin' to go projeckin' around the swamp at night, a-leggin' varmints an' sich with old Blue."

The boy lived with his mother in an outlying swamp district of low-country South Carolina, an ill-defined district known from the days of squatter sovereignty by the not unpicturesque appellation of the "said-lands." By various expedients he "took his living" from swamp and plantation. In the spring, he peddled his catches of bream and warmouth in town, or paddled fly-fishermen over the gleaming and tortuous coves of the swamp. In midsummer he made occasional forays for alligators, collecting bounties paid by adjacent game preserves. Too many prized fox hounds had vanished in the black maw of the swamp.

In the fall and winter he ran a trapline, or worked as handy man about the premises of the Homestead Gun Club, whose loosely bounded domains stretched to the door of his cabin. Sometimes he was lucky enough to be engaged as guide for visiting bird hunters, some of whom had found the boy not only a canny woodsman, but an invaluable ally in the birdy pine lands. The judge, principal owner and chief ornament of the Homestead club, would have no other companion, and the boy loved his rotund benefactor as he loved no other. It was his audacious dream that he might some day accede to the post of dog handler on the wide-spreading plantation.

But first, he continually reminded himself, he must show them he could handle dogs. There was Blue, of course. He had trained her from nothing, you might say, from the time he had found her crawling, more dead than alive, from a hole in the swamp where the unenthusiastic owner of the pups had consigned them. He had made a good job of it, too. Tough as whit leather and unerring, Blue was a matchless hunting dog, in spite of her cross-grained disposition and gaunt unloveliness.

But what rankled in the boy's consciousness was that nobody gave him a chance to show his handiwork. Few visiting hunters could be inveigled into giving Blue a trial. They took one look at her unprepossessing aspect and laughed ouright or found some gentlemanly pretext for rejecting her. Trouble was, he told himself, those men wouldn't have anything to do with a dog unless he *looked* the part.

And Blue didn't. She was in fact the result of a *mesalliance,* half setter and half pointer. A dropper rather tends to be like the little girl who had a little curl. "The best dog I ever shot over was a dropper," one hears again and again in the South, where pedigree in hunting dogs is often a matter of academic interest. For her part, Blue combined the best traits of her dual ancestry, empty solace for her owner when there was nobody to demonstrate her to.

When the boy reached home, his cup was brimming full. He had at last achieved a registered dog, one that perhaps had a blot on his escutcheon, but one that at least looked as good as the best.

"We got practically everything we want now, Ma," the boy gravely announced. "I ain't promisin', but we might have a phonograph an' a sewing machine in the house afore long. Even the judge said Pedro had everything, that is, most everything. Jus' one thing we got to look after, Blue an' me, an' we aim to start on that come tomorrer."

Early the next morning Blue dropped on a favorite covey at the edge of the pine lands. Seeing the dropper on point, Pedro began his inevitable forward march. "This here's a-goin' to be a ringside seat," the boy chuckled, sitting on a stump.

As Pedro brought up with Blue's upraised rump, an admonitory growl issued from the throat of the dropper, as if to say, "Finders keepers. No time for monkeyshines." Nothing daunted, Pedro strode cavalierly forward. The blue-black hair on the bitch's back popped upright. Her lips writhed menacingly, an ominous protest rumbling in her throat. Heedless of the storm signals, Pedro took another step to put himself ahead — and into the very midst of a rocketing covey.

"Now, Blue," cried the boy, "hit's up to you. If you want to chaw up this here thievin' varmint, hit's all right with me."

But Blue didn't wait for an invitation. The first notice Pedro had was a bounding ball of black fury that hit him broadside. Without knowing exactly what had happened, he found himself flat of his back in the broom straw with a searing pain in a shoulder.

Had his assailant been a male, Pedro would have given battle. A good scrap was the breath of his nostrils. During his roistering adolescence he had fought everything on four legs and no questions asked. Now he was troubled by elemental proprieties. This thing of being pommeled by a woman, and a woman of the streets at that, was graceless business. Yet a fellow had no defense. So Pedro did what any gentleman would have done under the circumstances. He cowered and sidled away, the picture of smarting dignity and injured virtue. The boy laughed at his discomfiture.

"So you won't fight Blue because she's a female. Well, Blue's a-goin' to keep jumpin' you till you forget she's a lady, which she ain't much of anyway. You won't git your final lesson till you wade into Blue like a circus saw — an' git your hide hung in the tanyard. Blue, you got to put the fear o' Gawd in 'im when he crowds you on point thataway. If you don't, every 'coon in the swamp will be givin' you the forky-doodle, you ol' hussy."

The following morning he was in the pine lands again, with both dogs racing ahead. With a little maneuvering, he managed for Blue to find a feeding covey first, whereupon Pedro backed for a moment, then started invincibly forward. As he came abreast of the dropper, a forewarning growl announced the imminence of the quarry. But the pointer disregarded the bristling back and dripping mouth of the dropper and strode arrogantly on.

The noise of the exploding covey was lost in the clamor of the dropper's onset. Savagely she threw herself on the big interloper. No dog could flush *her* birds twice!

Pedro picked himself up and cowered ignominiously. But his avenger was not yet done. Sallying in with her punishing teeth, she slitted a luckless ear. She sniped viciously at his flanks, mauling and bullying him about. All of which Pedro endured as the lot of man who is born of woman. But when Blue's teeth nipped the root of his unoffending tail, the pointer forgot his chivalry and snapped back. Then he stood across a log, rumbling throaty anathemas at the black nemesis on the other side, until Blue tired of the game and resumed her hunting.

"Blue, we air gettin' 'im hot under the collar," the boy observed judicially. "Pedro ain't a-goin' to stand for sich bully-raggin' much longer. Ol' Gabriel hisself wouldn't."

During late afternoon the boy was out again, finding two coveys near a strip of beans the judge had planted. The first covey was wasted for his purposes, however, because Pedro found it and held as staunch as a cypress knee, as he always did when hunting alone. The second bevy Blue found and pointed with her characteristic pose, snakelike head extended along the ground and gaunt rump upraised. The pointer dutifully backed. For a moment it looked as if he had learned his lesson, but Pedro was made of sterner stuff. He took a circumspect but determined step forward, jaws a-weave with jealousy.

Anticipating the inevitable flush, the boy began talking to the dropper.

"When you hop 'im this time, Pedro's a-goin' to show fight. I feel hit a-comin.' If he does, you got to jump down his th'oat an' ball the jack on his gizzard. If you can't handle this here citified Yankee dawg—"

Under the relentless goading of the dropper, Pedro's nerves had reached the breaking point. As a bulletlike charge sent him sprawling, his gallantry snapped. At that precise moment he would have licked his chops over the carcass of his own grandmother. The raucous cacophony that followed attack and counterattack was music to the boy's ears.

Pedro rushed to the assault as if his sole aim was to visit final retribution upon the meddling maverick of the swamp. Blue fought as if all the multiplying villainies she had suffered in this world were personified in the arrogant pointer before her.

With a powerful lunge, Pedro sent his smaller assailant hurtling from him. Landing on her feet, the dropper met the onrush with flashing teeth. They stood on their hind legs, fighting it out like men. But, as if realizing she was no match for her antagonist in such a gentlemanly affair, Blue abruptly changed tactics. Down they went into the broom straw, over and over, locked in a savage and squalling embrace, with the hybrid more often on the bottom than otherwise. Blue soon found she had caught a Tartar.

As the tide of battle turned against her, the dropper fought with an abandon born of mortal combats in the pitiless swamp. In a dog-eat-dog rumpus the pointer was too much for her. Desperate now, she reverted to the finesse her doubtful forays had taught her. She parried and sidestepped, warily guarding her head, and exposing to the enemy her less vulnerable rump.

As her head came up from a round of vicious in-fighting, the boy saw a sight which chilled him to the marrow. Blue was blinded in one eye by the gush of blood from a gaping wound above it. As if sensing this sudden advantage, Pedro sprang in on her blind side and cruelly lashed an exposed flank. Momentarily dazed, the smaller dog was at a fearful disadvantage in an already unequal combat. She seemed bound to go down under the fierce onslaught of her heavier antagonist.

Impulsively the boy seized a stick. He would go to the defense of the beloved and embattled dropper. If she got whipped, Pedro would go unchallenged, his ruinous jealousy unchecked. He stopped short, with stick upraised. No. If Blue won by his help, Pedro would never respect either of them thereafter. Was he not intelligent enough to discount human intercession? Weakly the boy dropped the stick.

"You got to whup 'im, Blue. Don't you see you have? 'Coon-fight 'im, I tell you! 'Coon-fight 'im!" he screamed.

Then it happened. The dropper sidestepped the lunging pointer, yanked viciously at a hind leg, and cunningly tripped her adversary. Before Pedro could regain his feet, she was astraddle him. Deftly she gouged for the vulnerable throat, where life flowed close to the surface. She found her throbbing mark. Her teeth sank home. Mightily the big dog twisted and writhed.

"Hold 'im!" shouted the boy. "Hold 'im till the cows come home, you precious old hussy!"

Blue needed no encouragement. She had at last achieved the hold her graceless background had taught her. Freezing her teeth about the yielding throat of her threshing opponent, she resisted every effort to dislodge her. Pedro began to weaken, to struggle less. The boy got down on hands and knees beside them, his heart welling madly within him, tears coursing unabashed down his flushed cheeks. When Blue got hold of a big 'coon thataway —

Pedro lay still in the broom straw, his breath coming in raucous gasps. Still the dropper held with the grimness of death, as if unconscious of all else. The victim's muscles stiffened. His legs kicked spasmodically. Then his muscles relaxed.

"You can turn 'im a-loose now."

Blinking her good eye at her master to make sure, Blue relaxed her jaws and staggered up. Bending over, the boy made a satisfied examination of the prostrate dog. Then he hugged the dropper in a ferocious embrace.

"Old lady, you're the fightin'est piece of machinery this side o' North Ca'lina," he told her.

Shouldering the inert, twitching form of Pedro, he started homeward.

"Come on, honey. We got a good dawg now, if we ain't got a daid one."

A week later, sunup found the boy at the plantation house waiting for the judge to finish breakfast. Finally the judge waddled out.

"Been findin' plenty of birds lately?" asked the boy, doffing his cap.

"Only fair-to-middling, son," replied the judge. "Fact is, I was just saying — "

"That's what I come to see you about, sir. Pedro. Will you hunt 'im?"

"We've settled that Pedro business once for all. Besides, this is my last day here. Going over to the Kotee club this afternoon."

"But you got to see for yourself, sir," the boy urged desperately.

"See what?" demanded the judge.

The only answer he got was a cryptic smile. Swearing volubly that he wouldn't go a step, the judge followed the eager boy down the path.

"Here, Pedro! Blue!"

The puffing judge took one look at the ear-slitted, mangled Pedro.

"Great jumping Jehosaphat!" he bellowed. "What in the devil have you done to that dog? Didn't I tell you beating him wouldn't do any good?"

"I ain't tetched 'im, sir. Ain't a hand been laid on 'im. Pedro must 'a' run into somethin' or nother in the swamp."

An hour later Princess Anne flashed to a point in the pine lands. Blue grimly backed, her snakelike head along the ground. Bounding from the rear came a liver-and-white pointer.

"There he goes again!"

"Hold your horses, sir" the boy defended. "He ain't flushed yet."

Confidently Pedro started forward, jaws nervously working. From the throat of the dropper issued a half-amiable growl. As if his consciousness was suddenly flooded with grisly memories, Pedro froze in his tracks. Then as if to make doubly sure, he gingerly took two steps backward, and planted himself.

"Pedro backing! And I'll be dummed if he didn't get in reverse for good measure."

The three dogs held as statuesquely as if they had been carved from the landscape. And one of them was Pedro the incorrigible, Pedro the playboy. The judge stood drinking in the tableau and shaking his head in bafflement.

"Pedro's behaving like he'd been hair-hung and breeze-shaken over hell," he muttered wonderingly.

He eyed the villainous-looking dropper, now growling softly. He looked at the fearfully mangled Pedro, standing penitently at her rump. Suddenly he understood.

"Hell hath no fury," he quoted awesomely, "like a woman scorned."

Then he walked up and shot a perfect covey rise. For the rest of the morning they hunted together, trying Pedro in varying combinations. Nothing could induce him to appropriate another dog's find, or budge from his tracks when he backed. They tried leaving Blue at home and bringing fresh dogs from the kennels. But Pedro had been cured.

When they reached the lodge in the late afternoon, the Judge's car was packed and waiting, with trailer kennels attached. The judge turned to the boy.

"Son, your methods of dog training may be a little — unorthodox, but you've made Pedro the finest hunter I ever owned, barring none. Now here," he said, taking out a check book, "I want to show my appreciation."

Climbing into the car, he summoned an attendant.

"Put Pedro on the trailer too, Jim. I'm taking him with me."

The boy stood benumbed. His hand limply held the unopened check, a throttling lump in his throat. "My dawg," his lips moved wordlessly. "Pedro. He gave 'im to me, and now — "

As the car started up the hill, there was a sudden upheaval in one of the kennels. Boards crackled and splintered. From the wreckage lifted the muzzle of a big liver-and-white pointer, who somersaulted from the the moving car and loped back to the dropper beside the boy. Pedro bellied down and planted a tentative kiss on the cold nose of Blue who, being a woman, disdainfully turned her head. The judge ruefully eyed the shattered kennel, sulphur and brimstone on his lips.

Then he saw the stricken figure, the check fluttering unnoticed at his feet. He saw Pedro, uprearing against the immobile statue of the boy. A great light suffused the judge's pink countenance.

"Bless my soul, son. I clean forgot, absent-minded old fool that I am. Pedro is *your* dog. Take him quick — quick!" and he turned and panted back to the idling car. "And by the way," he shouted back, blowing his nose prodigiously, "tell my manager I've hired you as handler for next year."

# How To Get Rid Of Chiggers

"What's good for chiggers?"

"You must be from Virginia," the storekeeper answered. "They call 'em chiggers up there. Down here we call 'em red bugs. Down in Alabama they call 'em little red sons —"

"Right now," I interrupted, "my interest isn't altogether scientific. I'm not interested so much in the nomenclature of the species, as in ways and means of bringing about his demise on a large scale. I thought maybe you had something —"

"That I do, son, and it's a powerful simple remedy. Just take this bottle of turpentine here, rub it in good and deep, and every blessed red bug will curl up his toes and turn Republican."

Properly turpentined, I went back to camp. My companions had left for a two-day drive in another part of the swamp, but the prospect of spending the time alone was not unwelcome. With one little thing and another, I'd had a sleepless night. I would just loaf around camp and catch up. Scratching doesn't lend itself to an audience anyway. Like making love and asking a fellow to vote for you, it's a business to be prosecuted in privacy.

But turpentine was not the wonder-worker it had been cracked up to be. Whatever its virtues in other fields, as an antichiggerant it was a washout. In fact, it seemed to spur the enemy on to greater achievement. So an hour later, when a squirrel hunter chanced by the camp, I was again asking:

"What's good for chiggers?"

"What kind are they?" He cocked his head critically, as if the matter called for connoisseurship.

"What kind! For heaven's sake, are there *kinds* of chiggers?"

"Thar's chiggers and chiggers, mister. Thar's North Car'lina chiggers. Thar's Georgia chiggers. And then thar's South Car'lina chiggers. Where did you get yours?"

"In the Santee Swamp," I said.

"Then you've got the South Car'lina specie. Now, I ain't tryin' to belittle another state, but them North Car'lina chiggers is rank amateurs. And a feller can get along with that Georgia specie if he makes allowances. But tch! tch!" he clucked sympathetically and propped his gun against a tree to do the occasion justice, "you've got the South Car'lina kind, than which thar ain't nothin' than-whicher."

"I do not know much about the subject of chiggers," I acknowledged. "I've never done any research in the field. But I had the general impression that a chigger was a chigger."

"Well, I recollect readin' a almanac onct. Accordin' to that feller's figgers, thar's a heap o' things South Car'lina don't rate so high in. But I'll tell you right now, mister, thar ain't no other state can hold a candle to us in the output of chiggers. Yes, sir," he snapped his suspenders with state pride, "the South Car'lina chigger is in a class by hisself!"

"Far be it from me to impeach the quality of your output in that field. I have reasons to believe, in fact, that the confidence you have so feelingly expressed in their superiority is well-placed. But my interest at present is rather on the practical side. In other words — "

"*Exactly* what I am a-leadin' to, mister. Git yourself a onion, a big juicy one, smear it all over you, and watch them chiggers h'ist their tails and head for Texas."

I don't like onions, and I have reason to believe onions feel the same way about me. They make me sick, and if they knew how I feel about them, it would make them sick too. But it is a long-established principle of *materia medica* that no medicine does you any good unless it tastes bad. So back to the cross-roads store I went. . . .

Back at camp and all onioned up, I awaited the promised exodus. But the only response I noted on the part of the chiggers was one of gratitude. It furnished just the *hors d'oeuvre* they were looking for. If I hadn't felt as bad as a human being could feel before, I would have felt worse now. When I ran into a timber cruiser in the swamp, I took him to camp and gave him a drink.

"What," I said, "is good for chiggers?"

"Chiggers?"

"Chiggers," I confirmed.

"Have you got 'em bad?"

"Well, I've got 'em in places where only a contortionist could scratch. Places where the presence of a chigger has never been recorded before. I've got 'em in the precise places where a man could get along best without chiggers. In other words, I've got 'em all over me."

"Well, I've seen people whose fixes I'd rather be in," was his candid comment, "but your case ain't hopeless. I've been pokin' around this swamp for a long time, and I can give you a remedy that's guaranteed."

"Guaranteed?"

"Absolutely. Just get you a hunk of rancid fat meat, the rancider the better, and smear it all over you. If there's one thing a chigger don't fancy, it's rancid fat meat."

Here is a plausible fellow, I said, heading back to the store again.

"A hunk of your rancid meat," I said, never one to haggle over a trade.

"We don't sell meat by hunks," the storekeeper's wife bristled, "and if you mean to insinuate that our meat — "

"I don't mean to insinuate anything," I retreated. "It's for the chiggers."

"In that case," she escorted me to the back door, "there's a piece I threw out last week. It's been lying in the sun ever since. Every dog in the neighborhood has passed it up. Whatever rancid meat is good for, that there piece ought to be extra-fine at," she said succinctly.

All rancied up, I shuffled back to camp. Now rancid meat is no doubt all right in its place, wherever that is. But as soon as I rubbed that greasy salt in, I was assailed by grave doubts as to *this* particular function.

All it did was to redouble my misery, and I was soon longing for a simple case of chiggeritis again. The only purpose it served was what doctors call a counterirritant, which means something that makes you hurt so much worse than you did before, that you forget what you used it for.

So pulling off my britches, I took up scratching as a profession and made a full-time job of it. But in such first-class chigger country, surely *somebody* must know the answer. It was just a matter of patience on my part. After all, I reflected, medicine is an experimental science. Sooner or later, sooner or later — if I lasted that long. So when a game warden came putt-putting up the river, I hailed him:

"What," I asked, "is good for the chiggers?"

"Are you the fellow," he looked at me curiously, "who went to sleep on a deer stand?"

"Reckon so." My fame was spreading.

"And let a big buck waltz by within thirty feet?"

"I do not see," I said with a certain amount of dignity, "that that has any bearing on the case." A certain amount of dignity was all I could manage.

"No offense," he added. "I was just wondering. Now, it's a mighty good thing you asked me about this chigger business. I've got the very thing. Government medicine, in fact."

"Government medicine?"

"Here," he offered. "Take this extra bottle. All us game wardens who work the swamps carry it. You'll find it the very thing."

I pulled out the stopper and sniffed.

"Under whose administration," I asked, "was this put up?"

Two hours later, I began to lose faith in the Democrats. It was undoubtedly good medicine. You could smell it and tell that. But what it was good for was another question. That, I reflected gloomily, is what happens when the government goes into business.

By next morning, the little red wenches had begun to hatch out on me — and a chigger can out-blessed-event anything you ever saw. Wherever the second generation hit, they laid out their homesites and commenced excavating.

A tottering old darky shuffled by camp, his ax on his shoulder. Looking for lightwood knots, he said. Nobody, I figured, could live to be that old in this region and not be a chigger expert.

"Uncle," I asked hopefully, "what do you do when you get chiggers?"

"I scratches," he answered.

"But what do you do when you get 'em all over you?" I pursued.

"I gits my wife to help me scratch," he said.

Well, my wife is pretty useful around the house, and there's a lot she would do for me. I could have done worse, I expect. But you just can't tell another person *where* you want scratched; not the precise, elusive spot. You probably know how it is. Besides, my wife was 500 miles away.

Around noon, an elegant-looking gent came by. A fly fisherman waiting for his boat paddler. A dandified fellow he was, with a professional air about him. Maybe —

"What's good for the chiggers?" I asked, having disposed of the amenities in record time.

"Chiggers?" He wiped his specs and blinked at me. "So you've got chiggers. Well now, that's just fine!"

"What's so fine about it?"

"I can give you a piece of advice, my friend, that will save you a lot of inconvenience. *Whatever you do, don't scratch!*"

"What?" I gasped, arresting one hand in midair.

"If you don't scratch, you won't itch. Scratching is what makes it itch. I am a psychologist, and that is what is known in my profession as the James-Lang theory. I can assure you, sir, that scratching doesn't do any good."

"The devil it doesn't!" I replied in unscientific language.

I found myself wondering whether this fellow was really necessary to society. I have got a lot of advice in my life, much of it somewhat jackassical, but this was about the tops. "The population of this country is too numerous," I mumbled vaguely as I walked away. "What I mean is, there are too many people in it."

In the afternoon three men came by, and I loved them as soon as I saw them. Shaggy, homespun fellows they were, with rough-and-ready manners and mud behind their ears. Professional alligator hunters they proved to be, getting ready for a night's work.

"What, gentlemen, is good for — "

"How bad have you got 'em?"

I pulled off my clothes. I pulled off my underclothes.

"You can see for yourself," I announced, parading shamelessly before them.

"Whew!" said the first alligator hunter.

"Fanciest needlework I ever laid eyes on," admired the second. "Wish my old lady could see it."

"One good thing about this here country. Plenty of trees for a man to scratch hisself on," opined the third.

"Your facetiousness is not especially well-timed," I replied stiffly.

"No hard feelings," said the chairman of the alligator hunters. "Matter of fact I'm an expert on scratchin'. Had the seven years' itch once, and I know what'll fix you up good and proper. Only remedy I've never known to fail."

"What is it?" I asked.

" 'Tain't very highfalutin'," he demurred.

"*What is it?*"

"Asafetida."

"Asafetida?"

"Asafetida," he repeated.

My mind reverted to my boyhood school days in the country. Whenever an epidemic of any kind hit the neighborhood, every mother confidently tied a sack of it around her boy's neck. No self-respecting epidemic ever ventured near after that.

"But where could a fellow get asafetida?" I asked.

"Easy. We carry some in our boat — use it to tetch up the meat we use for 'gator bait when somebody wants a live one. Here, soak this in water and wash yourself all over with it. Your troubles will all be over, and you'll never forget the day you met us."

My companions were full of news when they returned to the camp that night.

"Saw the darndest rattlesnake," announced one.

"Didja?" I answered, preoccupied.

"Bagged a big turkey gobbler," bragged another.

"Didja?"

"Got the biggest buck you ever saw."

"Didja?"

"What are you scratching for?"

"Must be something I ate," I evaded. "Kind of rash, I reckon."

All of us went to bed in the one-room cabin as usual, but after ten minutes my companions began to evince a strange restlessness.

"Kind of warm," said one, getting up and stumbling outside.

"Must be the humidity," contributed another, following him.

"Such a beautiful night," murmured a third.

When the evacuation was over, I got up and went outside too.

They were all lying on the ground, muttering among themselves. As I approached, one of them sniffed and warily eased off in another direction.

"What have you been doing since we left?" they wanted to know.

"Oh, nothing. Just loafing around camp and using stuff on my chiggers."

"What kind of stuff?" they relentlessly pursued.

"Oh, just stuff. Different people told me about it. By the way," I asked as a sudden light dawned upon me, "do you fellows mean you can smell me?"

"We mean to say — since you brought the subject up — that we can't smell anything else. You smell like the first-aid room of a slaughterhouse."

"Whoever says I smell is a bald-faced liar," I challenged. "Hell, I'm closer to myself than anybody else. Don't I know?"

"A man can't smell hisself," succinctly remarked the guide.

"You guys are crazy in the head," I stalked away. "Just because a man uses a few chigger remedies! I'm going to use some more tomorrow, and if you don't like it, you can lump it."

But the next day I was in a hospital. They rushed me there, thirty miles away, in the middle of the night, delirious and with a raging fever.

I'm still alive to tell the tale, but a heck of a lot happened in between whiles. Three days later, when I was feeling and smelling normal again, my companions came for me. They were newsy as usual.

"When we brought you in," said one, "a pretty nurse took one whiff and fainted clean away."

"When I asked an interne what was wrong with you," supplemented another, "he said: 'Complications. No one disease could smell like that.'"

"You ought to have heard the orderly who carried him in," added the third. "He said: 'Cap'n, you sho' do smell fatal!'"

"I'm afraid," interrupted the genial doctor, "that your friends are gilding the lily a bit. But just to satisfy my professional curiosity, what remedies did you use?"

"I'm tired now," I explained. "Ask me some other time. Those chiggers surely did me up, didn't they?"

"It wasn't the chiggers," he said. "They were all as dead as a herring when you got here. It was what you put on them. You had about the worst case of remedies I ever saw. Must have had a lot of friends with favorite chigger medicines."

"Then when a fellow gets the chiggers, the first thing to do . . . ."

"Is to shoot all your friends," he laughed. "There are two things about chiggers: first they are always funny — on the other fellow, and second, everybody has a favorite remedy."

"What is yours?"

"Sulphur will keep 'em off. A nickel's worth, rubbed on your body before you entered the swamp, would have saved you a lot of misery and a $30 hospital bill."

"But *after* you get 'em?" I wanted to know.

"After you get 'em, the only thing you can do is to *outlast* 'em."

What this country really needs, I decided, is a good cheap chigger remedy.

🍁　🍁　🍁

# Damn That Honeysuckle!

NOT LONG ago I read that Hollywood, requiring an old-fashioned rail fence for atmosphere in a movie, was hard put to find the authentic thing, finally procuring the fence rail by rail and paying what our grandfathers would consider a fabulous price. The incident awoke within me a surge of nostalgic recollections, not only because I grew up with rail fences, the passing of which truly marked the end of an era in the South, but because I have persuaded myself that the plenteousness of game in those pristine days was somehow identified with those lazy, meandering fences.

The vanishing of the rail fence from the Southern scene was due in part to the widespread use of barbed wire, that invention of the devil. A bygone regime could look indulgently upon a sprawling rail fence with its innumerable elbows and pockets of wasteland. But modern agriculture, with its emphasis on maximum land utilization, must have fences that are straight, efficient and characterless. The old rail contrivance, they said, was unscientific.

Then there was the devastating blight that killed the chestnuts from which the rails were riven, a blight that swept the entire Appalachian region and was so deadly in its ravages that few, if any, bearing trees now survive. And in all probability we shall never again enjoy the savory bounty of the native chestnut.

But Mother Nature must have loved the old-fashioned rail fence. The friendly elbows and pockets, inherent in its structure, were preordained for the propagation of game. In those cozy retreats quail could nest unmolested by plow and reaper. In them clover and grain were privileged to grow unharvested. Beneath the graying rails countless rabbits found a snug harborage, and countless boys set their traps or boxes by the "gnaws" that marked old Molly Cottontail's lines of communication.

And in the ragged growth of small cedars, sassafras, sumac, persimmon bushes and honeysuckle that marked the zig-zagging progress of the fence, denizens of the wild found ample cover from their enemies. Turkeys, quail and lesser game gleaned from adjacent fields what an indulgent regime had left ungarnered. Surely nature could not have devised a finer sanctuary for her teeming progeny.

And many an enchanted day did the youngsters of another generation spend hunting those old rail fences. When we flushed a covey in an adjoining field, they didn't zoom a mile away, but dived into the inviting recesses of the rail fence. Then you took one side and your companion took the other, or lacking a companion, you sent your faithful dog over as a proxy.

The singles bounced up, and you sent a salvo after them as they zigzagged down the fence. Or maybe you stood precariously balanced on the top rail for a shot at a scurrying cottontail, and were bowled over by the heavy charge of black powder. Arithmetic was simple in those days. The harder a gun kicked, the harder it hit. That was a self-evident fact that went uncontested by even the doubting Thomases among us.

Most rail fences were soon overgrown with honeysuckle, which had much to do with their usefulness to game. Now, honeysuckle has been denounced with equal fervor by farmer and sportsman alike. The populace in general regards it as the devil regards holy water, and he is a temerarious soul who will say a charitable word for it.

But has that lusty perennial of the wayside no redeeming qualities? Is it a nuisance altogether unmitigated? At the risk of being hanged and quartered, I should like to say a friendly word for it. Indeed, in vast stretches of territory, honeysuckle is Bob White's best friend.

In heavy and prolonged snows, a honeysuckle thicket is a haven of refuge for quail and other small game. Four years ago, Virginia had an uncommonly heavy snow — nearly waist-deep, in fact — that became ice-capped and held relentlessly for weeks. Great quantities of quail perished.

Wardens, hunters and rural mail-carriers scattered grain in such likely shelters as were accessible, but we were full of dismal misgivings. Some hunters feared that quail had been virtually wiped out over a wide area, or that their recovery would be a matter of decades. And indeed almost the only coveys that did survive were those within reach of a dense growth of honeysuckle which had had the foresight to hole up before the storm.

The thicket kept the marooned coveys from being buried alive, and the birds eked out a livelihood from the seeds and debris beneath the vines. Within three years we had a normal supply of birds again. In extensive honeysuckle thickets a marooned covey can withstand the rigors of the bitterest winters and the deepest snows.

In such a stronghold, too, birds find a blessed asylum from their enemies. Foxes, hawks, cats, stray dogs and other marauders are not likely to harry them there. Indeed, a covey ensconced in such a viney labyrinth can laugh at its most rapacious foes. I have observed that when a territory is overhunted coveys will sometimes hole up in a honeysuckle patch for days even in fair weather, and defy all efforts to dislodge them, while hunters tramp near-by fields in vain and wonder what is happening to birds nowadays.

Such entanglements are also an effective antidote for the gluttony of pot-hunters. There are still gunners aplenty who are so destitute of a game conscience that they will exterminate an entire covey if they can. But it is well-nigh impossible to annihilate a family that has its headquarters in a dense honeysuckle patch. For that matter, it is hard to bag any of them after they have taken refuge in such a stronghold.

Hunting honeysuckle birds is a snare and a delusion. It requires infinite patience, precision shooting and an allotment of luck. If you have any other pressing engagements, look after them and renounce the embattled quarry. If your time isn't worth much and you have a stout pair of shanks, that's different.

Of course, it disappoints a hunter to be thus thwarted of his bag. Of course, it makes him furious. Of course, it makes him blaspheme both birds and honeysuckle and the whole hemisphere to boot, and he swears he is going to buy himself a tractor one of these days and clean out the whole damned place. But if he reflects a little, he must realize that except for such a thicket there wouldn't have been any birds there at all. And probably few anywhere else. Or that some lucky predecessor would have already bagged them.

A worthy counterpart of Virginia's honeysuckle thickets is the ubiquitous bay of South Carolina and Georgia. In the low-country vernacular, a bay is a branch-head or depression studded with underbrush, giant briers and impenetrable mats of honeysuckle, and often full of stump-holes, fallen logs and quagmires. Not an elegant place for a gentleman, to be sure, but where the singles are sure to go. Almost every covey has its headquarters bay.

This country has been heavily hunted for years, yet because of these small overgrown morasses which dot the flat landscape there are still plenty of birds. Ultimately a fellow learns the knack of bay shooting. Having hunted and haunted these bays for eighteen years, I have learned to take them in my stride. But now and then you hit one so formidable that no hunter with any vestige of intelligence will tackle it.

I have one such in mind now, Bradley's bay in low-country South Carolina. It is, I submit, the champion honeysuckle-and-brier patch in the U. S. and all outlying possessions. Brother, I don't know what you have to offer in the way of thickets, but I'll back Bradley's against your best. It defies comparison and beggars description. From a distance, it is a verdant invitation. Inside, it is pluperfect hell. And no matter which way you go in, you've got to go twice as far to get out.

Bradley's bay is a fifty-acre circle, as flat as a table, with honeysuckle, briers and sundry other vines ten feet high and here and there a soaring longleaf pine. Underfoot is a perfect network of debris, with an occasional splotch of quicksand. It is perhaps the birdiest area I have found in thirty years of hunting. In the outer fringes of the swamp, uncounted dozens of coveys raise, wax fat on the rank peafields which surround it on all sides, and hurtle straight back into the bay at the slightest provocation.

In my younger days I have spent hours fighting Bradley's, to emerge not only birdless but with my clothing in tatters and bleeding from head to foot. And limping on both legs! But within recent years, although I still hunt the surrounding pea-fields, I steadfastly abstain from the bay proper. Last season, during one afternoon, I saw eleven coveys flush and dive into the heart of the bay. At least 125 birds, yet I walked placidly away. If a man hasn't acquired any gumption at forty-five, there's little hope for him.

When I was a youngster, a certain territory in our neighborhood was famed for its hunting. Whenever anybody spoke of hunting, he mentioned the old Cap'n Tom's place. The two were always synonymous. Cap'n Tom's was an abandoned plantation, and a veritable jungle of honeysuckle, locusts and thick pines — hundreds of acres, teeming with turkey, quail and rabbits. A fabulous hunting ground it was, and remained so for a quarter of a century.

But a few years ago an enterprising business man bought the old place with the avowed intention of making it a model farm. Tractors and gangs of workmen were put to work eradicating the honeysuckle, felling the pines, clearing half-forgotten fields and close-cropping all ditches and fence-rows. And he did make it a model farm, as clean as a kitchen — and utterly gameless. Perhaps not a turkey or a single covey survives on the place today.

On our old homestead in Virginia, a dense growth of honeysuckle bordered the lane to the house — perhaps a quarter of a mile of it. It was very fragrant in the spring, and in winter a comforting stretch of green that not even the deepest snows could subdue. My father was a master farmer, looking after his 1,200 acres competently through the years. He always kept the honeysuckle within bounds, but never especially begrudged it the space it preempted for its own.

Half a dozen coveys always raised and headquartered in that dense border; and however hard they were hunted and however rigorous the winters, those birds were there, year in and year out. But when my father died, my mother, who had always had a passion for cleanliness, set to work on that honeysuckle with a vengeance. Now the place, although protected for years, is almost gameless.

Such instances could be multiplied almost at will. Again and again I have seen it happen. Birds can withstand almost any amount of hunting, hardships of weather and the inroads of their enemies if they have ample honeysuckle cover. Eliminate the cover, and Bob and his bevy exeunt.

Throughout the quail-hunting South, the honeysuckle-and-brier patch is perhaps the most used harbor of refuge. More than half the coveys, uncounted hundreds of them, that I have found in years of hunting in the quail states have been based in such cover, to which they doubtless owed their survival.

At times I have clucked complacently to myself, after a careful scrutiny of the landscape: "Well, here's a windfall at last. Here's one covey that hasn't anywhere to go! One covey I've caught with its britches down." But almost invariably it was but a pleasant piece of self-deception. However devious the route, their destination was the same old story.

In fact, you can let a total stranger put up a covey of birds anywhere in the South, and I will lay you even money that when the aforesaid stranger locates the singles he will be in the precincts of a honeysuckle-and-brier patch. How far will a covey fly to get to its base? As far as it *has* to fly. Old birds caught on the outer limits of their range will sometimes fly a mile to get to their habitual stronghold.

The modern passion for clean farming, with its abhorrence of waste, is responsible for the diminishing wildlife in many areas. Maximum land utilization and maximum game production do not go hand in hand. A farmer has got to make little concessions here and there, inexpensive concessions, to be sure.

Social historians and agronomists have long poked fun at the old-fashioned farming of what it pleases them to, call the benighted South. Old-fashioned it was. Unscientific it was, and sometimes inefficient and wasteful. But it was the precise type of agriculture most congenial to the incidental production of game! Let's not forget that.

A farmer who has been an ardent sportsman for fifty years recently unburdened himself to me: "Nowadays they want us to keep our farms as clean as a hound's tooth, and game can't make buckle and tongue meet. A forester told my neighbor to cull out the hollow trees in his woods, and the squirrels left. Advised him to sell his pines to the pulp mill, and the turkeys left. Then they told him to shave his ditches, terraces and fence-rows, and all the partridges were killed out. We are just gettin' too damned scientifical for game."

And another hard-bitten old-timer belligerently demanded: "You smart city fellows can laugh at me all you want, but answer me one thing. When I was young, there were no game laws and plenty of game. Now there are plenty of game laws and no game. How come?"

# Bass Are Dumber Than People

"CAP'N, I sometimes think I ain't got as much sense as I think I has," an ebony boat-paddler of mine once sagely opined.

That's the way I feel about the bigmouth bass. For all his prowess, old *Huro salmoides* can be pretty dumb. But bass fishermen can be dumb too, which sort of balances the books and explains why they sometimes catch each other.

For instance, one day I received the following telegram: "Please rush me three Horse Pistols. Not a single one in Alabama."

If a Horse Pistol has any resemblance to a bass lure, or to anything else on this sublunary sphere, it is purely coincidental. It is the stupidest-looking varmint ever concocted in the brain of a dipsomaniac. I had always reckoned that any bass with little enough sense to strike it would be *non compos mentis* and probably *ex post facto*.

Even the left-wingers of our bassing fraternity in South Carolina hold the Horse Pistol in high disdain. But I bought three dust-laden specimens and dispatched them to my friend in Alabama, where he promptly annexed a precedent-shattering string of bass. Now, I realize that one swallow doesn't make a summer, or a drink either; but things like this have happened often enough to make me wonder whether I haven't wasted a lot of high-grade intelligence trying to outfigure a dumb-bell who doesn't know himself what he's going to do. Maybe I've been trying to out-think something that doesn't think. As a friend feelingly remarked: "Bass ain't unpredictable. They're just so damned ignorant. If they had more sense, you could figure 'em out."

A sporting-goods dealer of my acquaintance had a hundred alleged bass plugs that had gathered dust for years. Peterman's Gadgets they were called, and such silly-looking contraptions nobody ever saw. No native son had had curiosity enough to try them.

The proprietor swore that he had been three-sheets-in-the-wind when he bought them, which was probably a conservative statement of the facts, and that he was going to slit the weasand of the salesman if he ever came back. So he charged the Gadgets off to experience and consigned them to the attic.

A few weeks ago a fellow in the town caught a 12-pound bass on a 10-inch sucker tied to an overhanging willow limb. But, reluctant to admit such a plebeian practice, the fellow announced he had caught the bulgy behemoth while casting. The sporting-goods dealer espied the big bass first and had an inspiration. Resurrecting one of the Gadgets, he called the sucker-setting fellow aside.

"I'll give you ten bucks to hook this plug in that bass's mouth before you start showing him off," he offered.

"I've told lies for less'n that," the fellow assented, being blessed with a flexible conscience.

Three days later not one of the plugs was left and the proprietor was hugging himself with pleasure. "One born every minute," he chuckled, and took another toddy to celebrate the gullibility of the human race. But on the fourth day he wore a somewhat harried air.

"You know what," he spat disgustedly, "that monkey plug proved to be one of the best trolling baits you ever saw. They're catching more bass than they can tote with them. People are worrying me to death for more Gadgets, and here's a telegram saying the factory is closed for the duration. Biggest damfools I ever saw."

"Who?" I asked. "Fish or people?"

"Both," he muttered unhappily. "Only thing dumber'n a human being is a bass and vice versa. Especially vice versa."

I have the questionable fortune of living in first-class fishing country. I say "questionable" because it has at times led me to neglect both wife and profession. I am well-nigh surrounded by hydro-electric reservoirs that are producing fish as well as kilowatts. Fifteen miles to the west is Lake Murray with its fifty thousand acres; sixty miles to the east lie the two Santee-Cooper reservoirs impounding 150 thousand acres; and within easy fishing distance are such legendary bream and redbreast streams as the Edisto, the Combahee, the Ashepoo, the Cooper, the Peedee, the Black and the Salkehatchie Rivers, not to mention the uncounted sand-hill ponds abounding with bream and big-mouth bass.

And I live among the huntingest and fishingest folks in the world, I do believe. South Carolinians don't pick a day to go fishing; they pick a day now and then to stay at home and look after their business or reinstate themselves with their families. Elsewhere fishing is an avocation; down here it is almost a vocation. The state has no closed season on game fish of any kind; so we fish the calendar around. On February 28, while estimable citizens the country over were shivering in their unmentionables, I caught an eight-pound bigmouth.

It is the ultimate ambition of every business man down here to retire, run for the governorship, build a bream pond in the sand-hills, and plant himself a grove of catalpa trees. Not because he admires the foliage of the catalpa, but because of its by-product, the catalpa worm, which was ordained by an all-wise Providence for the seduction of reluctant bream.

But to get back to the goofiness of fish and fishermen. In this city of 70,000 Democrats and 13 Republicans you can buy hundreds of Asiatic wigglers with white-and-green skirts, with white-and-brown skirts, with white-and-blue skirts, but not a single blessed one with white-and-black skirts. Bass fishermen telegraph all over the country for them. They write frantic letters to their friends. They offer extravagant prices for the white-and-black panties.

Why? Because along in March a bunch of fishermen, while trolling with Asiatic wigglers in white-and-black skirts, caught an almost unprecedented string of bass and exhibited them widely hereabouts. The impression got around that some special magic adhered to that particular combination, and a run on white-and-black skirts followed. Harried clerks grew tired of saying: "No. We have no white-and-blacks. We have white-and-blues, white-and-browns, white-and —" but the crestfallen customer had already started out of the store.

While the white-and-black craze was at its dizziest here, I got a letter from a friend in Florida begging me to send him two white-and-*blue* skirts. Now, I cannot persuade myself that a bass can distinguish between white-and-black and white-and-blue, for instance, when they are trolled rapidly across his field of vision. A bass's acuteness of vision is much overrated. He can distinguish overtones, no doubt, but more depends upon the action of the lure and the level at which it is fished than its color.

"Fish have funny eyes," one man explained. "They can see only certain colors." Well, they must have funny eyes — awfully funny. Common sense tells me that if bigmouth bass had very keen vision — and any gumption whatever — they wouldn't strike at half the goofy gadgets offered them. More tomfool lures are made for bass than for any other game fish, and they will fall for more tomfoolery than any other game fish.

For the bigmouth is a gluttonous and undiscriminating feeder. In fact, he is almost omnivorous. He shoots first and asks questions afterward. If he isn't feeding, you might as well cooperate with the inevitable and go on home. But if he is, you can throw almost anything in the tackle box at him. The smallmouth is a more discriminating customer and a more elusive quarry than his blunderbuss cousin.

Tell me something, mister. If you were trolling and catching bass to beat the band, and a luckless stranger hailed you from afar with: "What are you using, brother?" would you tell him the truth? Now, don't quibble or equivocate, and don't get sanctimonious with me. I'm not insinuating a thing. I know that you go to church more or less regularly, that you contribute to foreign missions, and that you are a pillar in your community and all that; but would you tell that fellow the truth? Or would you hold up for his edification the unlikeliest plug in the whole tackle box? Now, don't let your dander rise. I'm just asking.

This is not an abstract question. I don't know of anybody who has as many opportunities for lying as a bass fisherman. For instance, while trolling in the Santee last year, Bill Stetson and I discovered the ace of all bass lures. In an hour we had taken eight four-pounders, and we were vowing by the eternal never to reveal the identity of that precious plug to man, woman, or child.

Our pat-me-on-the-back session was interrupted by a hail from a passing troller who had seen us boat two fish while rounding a point.

"What are you using, gentlemen?" he asked.

I looked at Bill. Bill looked at me. I looked back at Bill. "It's your turn," I said.

"We're using a Jackson Jumper," Bill lied with alacrity.

"Thank you, gentlemen. Luckily I have one," and he dived for his tackle box.

That was right original on Bill's part, for neither of us had a Jackson Jumper. Among the 100-odd alleged bass lures in our collection, the aforesaid species was conspicuous by its absence. In sheer disgust we had given our Jumpers to a 'gator hunter in the swamp the year before. He didn't have any reel, so we figured it wouldn't do him any harm. We considered the Jumper the most distinguished dud that any manufacturer ever turned out. It was the unlikeliest plug that anybody's imagination ever conjured up. So Bill was enjoying the humor of the situation.

"I'll eat raw everything he catches, feathers and all, and swallow seventeen tadpoles for a chaser," he chuckled.

But after a while Bill got to ruminating. I don't think his conscience was hurting him, because Bill's conscience and Bill were the best of friends. There was what you might call a considerable *esprit de corps* between them. But he got to moralizing anyway.

"That gent is going home fishless and down-in-the-mouth. And his war department will probably bawl him out. And he's probably got guests for the week-end and no red points, and all because of that lie I told him. Still," he said, shaking his head indecisively — "still . . . "

When we got to the landing that night, the fellow walked up to us. Bill turned bilious-looking and began tinkering with the motor. You never saw a fellow so absorbed in his work as Bill was. But the stranger was unabashed.

"I want to thank you gentlemen," he said. "It's pleasant to meet an honest man. There are people, I'm afraid, who wouldn't have told the truth under the circumstances. I put on the Jackson Jumper and took five handsome fish, one of them an eight-pounder."

When the stranger had left, I turned to Bill. "Well, what do you say to that?"

"Damn," said Bill.

And the next time he went to the swamp, Bill looked up the 'gator hunter and got his Jumper back. He was like the fellow who listed his home with a real estate agent and was so entranced by the glowing description in the newspaper that he went down and bought it himself.

I saw this situation in reverse, too. While casting in the Santee-Cooper reservoir, Henry Estill and I began taking bass on a Jesse James. Five other boatloads of casters in the cove were throwing their arms off in vain.

"What are you using, brother?" one of them called.

"A Jesse James," Henry promptly answered.

Every caster within earshot grabbed for his Jesse James, whereupon Henry calmly reeled in and replaced his own with another plug.

"Why in the heck — " I protested.

"There are now nine Jesse James in the water. Mine would have been just another one — so many the bass won't hit any of them. Reckon I'm not a very good Democrat. I want to be different," he said, and unperturbedly reeled in another fish.

Down in Georgia I saw a 13-pound behemoth encased in a block of ice in a drug-store window — with a Boll Weevil hooked in his mouth. The result was a run on Boll Weevils that swept the town and the surrounding area. Whether the bass was actually taken on a Boll Weevil the druggist declined to say.

The point is that hard-headed business men could be so naive and unsuspecting as to fall for a possible plant. But even the most astute citizen can be an unmitigated sap about fishing lures, his judgment about what to buy being compounded alike of superstition, hearsay and experience. What other people are so credulous? We are prone to forget that a bass is the ultimate consumer, and we succumb to the blandishments of some garish gadget that intrigues us. Plug buying is highly contagious.

"What are they biting?" I asked a tackle dealer.

"Who, people or fish?" was the reply.

Nearly everybody has a favorite casting or trolling lure. Maybe it is better than all others; maybe it's better because he thinks it's better and consequently fishes with it oftener and harder. I have a friend whose favorite bass plug is a pock-marked topwater that he shot out of a tree with a shotgun. To him it is Miss Seduction in person. He thinks he can always catch fish with it — and he usually does.

I'm superstitious too. I have a battered and embattled old wreck that I have taken one hundred bass on. The old girl is knock-kneed, bow-legged and blind, but just try to swap a modern glamour girl for her! The old jade knows her stuff. Haven't you an old standby that you are sentimental about too, some battered heirloom that even a Philadelphia lawyer couldn't talk you out of?

Along in March I lost my Tennessee Runt while trolling. A big bass inconsiderately snatched it when I was off guard. That runt was unrivaled in my affection. Although I have a bucketful of trolling lures, and some so similar to the adored runt that only the closest scrutiny could detect the difference, I spent half a day looking for my little lost sheep. And to date I have spent $3.78 in postage and telegrams trying to get another one.

All of which leads me to the conclusion that bass are saps, that bass fishermen are saps, and that you are probably as big a sap as I am. Fish are funny, but people are a lot funnier.

🍁 🍁 🍁

# I'm A Sucker That Way

I HAVE never bought the Brooklyn Bridge or the Washington Monument, although I was once offered the latter at a bargain. Nor have I bought any hypothetical gold mines, ostrich farms, or the phony gilt-edged. I don't play poker, and I don't follow the ponies. If you should ask me to go your bail, I would wag a moral forefinger and give you a who-so-goeth-surety-for-another look. And if you tried to high-pressure me, I would let fall an edifying precept or two and show you the exit. As you can see, I am a man of considerable moral fiber and high sales-resistance.

But mister, have you got a dog to sell?

Even the mighty Achilles, quoth the legend, was vulnerable in the heel, the mighty Siegfried in the back. There is one vulnerable spot in the armor of my sales-resistance, one weakness that has brought me within two-whoops-and-a-holler of the poorhouse and threatened to loosen the blessed ties that bind; that has at times warmed the cockles of my heart and at times filled me with the bile of disillusionment. I can't help buying bird dogs.

I am a highly specialized sort of sucker. I have bought more bird dogs and know less about buying bird dogs than any other man in seven counties. It's a good thing the thou-shalt-not-covet commandment says nothing about dogs. I don't give a darn about my neighbor's ass, but how I do envy him that high-stepping pointer!

Whenever I see a good-looking dog, only utmost restraint and the inhibitions that come from living with a good woman prevent me from running up with my hand in my pocket and a mister-how-much-will-you-take-for-him look on my face. Even then I sometimes get myself into situations which appeal to my wife's peculiar sense of humor. For instance:

Once while hunting I came upon a handsome Irish setter on point.

"My friend, I'll give you fifty dollars for him as he stands," I offered in a burst of wild enthusiasm.

"That's thoughtful of you," the man answered with quiet amusement. "I just paid a thousand for him."

The fellow's hunting coat was nearly as shabby as mine. How was I to know that I was watching a famous dog, owned by a man whose income-tax refund was bigger than my salary?

I have bought old dogs on their last legs and young dogs that were all legs. Any gangling, big-footed, friendly eyed puppy who looks at me the right way can find a niche in the family budget. I've had my share of impressively papered patricians too, including three great-grandnephews of Muscle Shoals Jake, five great-grandsons of Doughboy (what a man-about-town that old rake must have been!), and a lady-in-waiting to a niece of Hard Cash, if my memory serves me right, a cousin twice removed of Smada Byrd, which I got from a Virginian.

And a lot of others that were just sons and daughters of the people, whence the geniuses come. Some with blots on their escutcheons and some without escutcheons on which to have blots. And one, to confess to the unvarnished, that turned out to be part July hound. That was the time my wife gazed at me fondly and said, "What you need, honey, is a psychiatrist!"

I have accumulated some good bird dogs and a lot of expensive experience. I have owned incorrigible flushers, shot-breakers, egg-eaters, rabbit-runners, chicken-chasers, bird-chewers, intractable hellions and just plain congenital idiots. And one flashy little debutante that never outgrew the profound conviction that her sole mission in life was to point butterflies, which she did with a nicety of technique that would have disarmed the most captious critic. I have had dogs that were gun-shy, bird-shy and car-shy, and that isn't all. Will you pardon the painful particulars?

Once I was dickering for a pedigreed setter wench. The owner, with becoming honesty, confided, "She ain't got but one fault, mister, and that's — "

"Don't tell me what it is, if you don't mind," I interrupted. "Might as well hang a dog as give him a bad name, you know."

It's fun buying a dog sight unseen — sometimes.

So I paid the man his money and took the dog home. When I took her in the field the next morning, she hit a bee-line for nowhere in B flat. At the rate she was going she reached Timbuktu by four o'clock, any standard time. Curious, I went back to the seller.

"I ain't complaining any," I said, "but what was the only fault that dog had?"

"She was man-shy, sir."

"She was what?"

"Man-shy," he repeated, without any elaboration.

"Well," I said, "I've had dogs that were gun-shy, bird-shy and car-shy, but I'll be hanged if you haven't sprung a new kind of shy on me. Right sure she wasn't brain-shy too?"

Why do I do it? Well, whenever I bring a dubious acquisition home, my wife asks me that too, and I always begin: "Honey, you just can't tell. That puppy might turn out to be — "

"I know," she says with Christian forbearance. "He might turn out to be another Manitoba Rap, or Alford's John, or something in disguise. Black diamonds. Acres and acres of diamonds. Some day the ugly duckling will turn out to be a princess. The old refrain, 'some day.' It's reformin' a dog that's fun. You want to see what you can do after the other fellow gives them up. You love an unsolved equation.

"Oh, I know all the answers, after these eighteen years! It's the gambler's instinct in you, dear, plus your natural ego. If you had gone in for poker, you'd have been terrific. Why don't you quit experimenting, take your money and buy two or three good dogs, and stay put?"

And why don't I? Well, just because I was either born that way or got that way since. I'm just a sucker that way.

I've got a remarkable wife, as you can see. Sometimes she is more remarkable that at others. Perhaps most women are that way. Once when I brought a new pup home, she met me on the porch.

"Darling," she said, "you are about to tell me a lie. How much did you pay for that dog?"

Now, what would you do with a wife like that?

Then she propped the broom against the door, put her hands on her hips and began to catalogue my alibis.

"Let's see," she said, checking them off on her fingers. "You have bought dogs for the following reasons: Number one, because he had a fine head. Number two, because he had a fine tail. Number three, because he was a grandson of his grandfather, or something. Number four, because his color would make him conspicuous in the field. Number five, because he had such possibilities. Number six, because you felt sorry for him. Number seven, because you wanted to see how he would turn out. Number eight, because he would make such a fine companion — a man's dog. Number nine, because the man you got him from sounded so honest. Number ten, because the fellow practically gave him to you. Number eleven — "

"Hold on," I protested. "That ain't ethical. You've used up all your fingers."

On another occasion, when I sneaked home a half-starved diamond-in-the-rough, she eyed him narrowly.

"Now I would really appreciate enlightenment here. Why did you bring that son-of-the-people with you?" she asked.

"Well, I'll let you in on something, honey. Most people wouldn't notice it, but do you get the width between his eyes? You can always judge a dog by that. Know what it means? It means brains!"

I glanced up to catch her amusedly surveying the distance between my own eyes.

"What did you say it means, darling?" she archly inquired.

Then she went into the kitchen and put the finishing touches on her quince jelly. And speaking of her quince jelly, well, 'tis the chiefest of my sublunary joys. After all, I reflected, a man might have done worse by himself at the high and aggravated art of wife-picking. The next moment a window lifted for a Parthian shot.

"Is that another *but* dog?" she asked.

"What do you mean, *but* dog?" I returned, all unsuspecting.

"You know. Would be a great dog but for something or other."

It was when I bought a whole litter of puppies and brought them home to my amazed helpmate that the plot really began to thicken. My entry into the wholesale puppy business precipitated something of an incident, diplomatically speaking, and helped to usher in a new household regime. Pointing successively at each puppy, she slowly intoned: "One — two — three — four — five — six — seven — eight — nine — ten — eleven!"

Having taken the census, she folded her arms and gazed at me with quiet martyrdom in her eyes. Watch a woman when you see that martyred gaze in the offing. Then she shook her head resignedly and favored me with one of those with-all-thy-faults-I-love-thee-still looks, following it with one of the but-I-wish-to-heck-I-didn't variety. Her attitude, I gathered, was that when the Lord in his inscrutable goodness gives a woman a husband, her gratitude should be so boundless as to overlook a few motheaten spots in the fabric. Don't look a gift horse in the mouth, you know.

That was the only time the old girl went literary on me. Nothing less than Shakespeare would relieve her mind.

"What a piece of work is man!" she mimicked. "How noble in reason! how infinite in faculty! in form and moving how express and admirable! in action how like an angel! in apprehension how like a god! the beauty of the world! the paragon of animals!" Then, finding that Shakespeare did not go into particulars enough, she added with ardor, "And what a remarkable idiot!"

Obviously things were getting in a parlous state. I would either have to take measures, or take the consequences. Either reconcile my wife to my doggy transactions, or reconcile myself to a dreary and dogless existence. I went to a friend who had had a course in abnormal psychology. He was sympathetic and helpful, having had Belgian hare troubles of his own.

"Encourage your wife in some extravagance of her own," he began. I winced, and he considerately amended: "Some minor extravagance, of course. One of the lesser vices, you understand. If she follows the graph, she will become too absorbed in her own hobby to bother yours. That is what is called checkmating the enemy."

The advice sounded sensible. That spring therefore, my wife received a gorgeously illustrated flower catalogue and a credit slip for ten dollars' worth of flower seed, to be shipped as she selected. She laughed unsympathetically, threw out a general remark about stupidity-running-in-families, and turned the credit slip over to a garden club.

Undaunted, I went back to my adviser. Surely two men should be able to outfigure one woman.

"Have you tried to interest her in collecting stamps?" he asked.

I hadn't, but I would. I promptly ordered a stamp catalogue, a classy magenta album, magnifying glass, water-mark detector, tongs, hinges and what-not, and had the whole business shipped to her. From a junk dealer I ordered a job lot of unassorted stamps.

Well, brother, the vaccine took. Her philatelic ardor now knows no bounds, and my dog-buying troubles are all over. I haven't had money enough to buy one for months. It all goes for stamps. Whenever she rapturously opens up a new lot, I say: "Honey, why do you buy all that junk? Why don't you take your money, buy what stamps you need, and get it over?"

"Run along now, darling," she dismisses. "Some day I'm going to find a rare United States Provisional or a cock-eyed king or something. You never can tell."

And that's the way it is with a woman.

# How To Hunt Quail

BIRD finding, of course, comes before bird shooting. Birds, like gold, are where you find them. They may also be in a lot of other places. Given the same dogs and the same territory, one man may put up twice as many birds as another. An inexperienced hunter finds his game by accident or the process of elimination. An old hand, seemingly by instinct.

"Damned if you can't almost make game!" reverently remarked a friend of mine to a certain guide. "Why, you can take one limpsy old dropper and find more birds than I can with three good dogs. How do you do it?"

The easy-going guide relighted his pipe and whimsically drawled: "Mebbe I just say to myself, 'If you was a covey of birds, where would you be at this time of the day, this season of the year, and this kind of weather?' And I just go there, and there they be. Reckon it's just knowin' the how-come."

Bob White is not only a home-body, but a great creature of habit and lover of routine. No other game bird is so regular and so predictable in its habits. Under normal conditions, a covey will follow the same itinerary from day to day. Learn the schedule, and you meet the train. True enough, the schedule may vary with such factors as time, weather, temperature and feeding conditions, but it will vary predictably. As our guide significantly remarked, you've got to know the how-come. Bird finding is indeed a pretty respectable art in itself.

But it is mainly with the other half — quail shooting — that we are concerned at present. I well know that only a hardy soul will undertake to prescribe a list of don'ts for the bird hunter, and that any man who sets down his observations on the subject is apt to have his life made miserable thereafter by his hunting companions. But with all my sins on my own head, here I go.

Don't try to head off a covey by getting between the birds and their customary refuge, with the fond hope of making them light where you want them. Don't try it for three reasons: first, because it can't be done; secondly, because they will swerve around you and present a really baffling shot; thirdly, because it will "upset your equanimity and make you mad," as I once heard a fellow express it. 'Tis a folly I was most reluctant to abandon as a boy.

Birds are going where they are going and there is precious little you can do about it — except to adapt yourself accordingly by getting behind their habitual line of flight and giving yourself a conjectural straightaway. If they won't accommodate you, accommodate yourself to them.

Most coveys have a traditional refuge which they make for whenever disturbed. Even in new territory it is often possible to determine a covey's flight — simply by figuring out the most unshootable place they could possibly fly to. When dogs are staunch and cover is adequate, a knowing gunner can often maneuver himself into a good shooting position, regardless of natural barriers.

Don't hunt in a hurry. You will overlook birds and break down yourself and your dogs to no purpose. If you have anything important to do, stay at home and do it. If you are in birdy country, forget all about accounts collectable, bills unpayable, your wife's parting remarks, the fugaciousness of time, and the seductiveness of the next field. The finest bird hunter I ever knew seemed to fiddle aimlessly around as if he had nothing else in the world to do.

And never, never run to a point. The surest way to ruin an unstable, over-anxious dog is to run up whooping and yelling to him to be careful. What a jewel of inconsistency — a man hurdling the landscape like a scared cross-countryman and bellowing "Careful! Steady!" at every stride. Not only will it eventually ruin a dog by making him nervous and distrustful of himself, but when you get there you are so out of breath and emotionally off balance that you can't hit anything. Besides, a grown man looks silly doing it.

Don't hunt with a more experienced shot — one of those chivalrous cusses — who cockily announces: "Now I'm going to give you the first shot on every bird that gets up. I'm not going to shoot until after you have finished. Just take your time."

How in the heck can you take your time when the courteous thing to do is to get your shooting over as soon as possible so that your benefactor will have a chance? When I first began to shoot quail, I hunted a livelong day under just such conditions without getting a single bird, and came home that night feeling lower down than the left hind heel of a hound dog.

However fatherly and considerate the other fellow may be, the mere knowledge that he is waiting to shoot, and will get your bird if you don't, will so disorganize you that you can't hit the state of Texas. No one but a hardened campaigner can stand such generosity.

Only good shots — or gentlemen — should hunt together. Learn leisureliness alone. The beginner must work out his own salvation, and the fewer spectators present to witness his infamy and psychoanalyze his failures the better.

Don't shoot singles competitively. When a point is made and the probabilities indicate a lone bird, let your companion take the shot with complete confidence that you are not going to lift your gun, regardless of the consequences. Hit or miss, that shot is his, to be handled as leisurely as he pleases. When the next single is pointed, your companion should show you the same consideration.

When two men stand with itching trigger fingers, each anxious to beat the other to the draw, the effect is ruinous. Both will fire prematurely, often tearing up the bird or missing altogether in their over-anxiety, and sooner or later bickerings will ensue as to "who shot John." Besides, such unseemly competition begets the worst fault there is in quail shooting — overprecipitancy.

Bird hunting, when it is done right, is a gentlemanly and leisurely pastime. In shooting singles, turn about is not only fair play, but the only way. True enough, a companion may sometimes stand in readiness in case a full house instead of a lone jack is raised, but this assurance of non-interference is prerequisite to satisfactory singles-shooting.

If you have a good dog who knows more about hunting than you do — and many dogs do — or one more familiar with the territory than you, give him his head. Let the dog take you hunting. Some gunners unwittingly keep their dogs from prying into gamy places, where judgment and instincts would naturally lead them, by interposing their own preferences. If you have a really good hunter who knows his business, the fewer instructions you give him the better.

Observe your dogs when they are making game so that you will recognize the symptoms thereafter. The posture of a pointing dog is as diversified and as unstandardized as a golfer's stance in putting. A dog's reaction to the proximity of game is equally unstandardized.

One dog registers interest in one way, another in another. One lifts an unobtrusive muzzle, delicately tests the air currents, and proceeds unerringly. Another noisily gulps down draughts of air. One advertises the imminence of the quarry by an undue cautiousness of demeanor. Another contents himself by freezing his tail and sloping forward, while an uninspired groundling may lower his muzzle to the earth and snort prodigiously.

With some dogs, the reaction is almost imperceptible. Some have to be knocked down with a hint, like some people. But to an observing hunter there is always some telltale mannerism that screams aloud. "I think I have something here. Stand by for further orders."

Time and again have I stumbled unprepared into a rattling bevy because I had failed to recognize the symptoms in my own or another man's dog. A study of your dog's individualities in this respect will reward you handsomely later.

When your dogs are making game, keep close behind them. Running birds will sometimes take wing with little provocation. Early-season coveys, or others that haven't been shot, flush easily, often refusing to lie for the point. It is especially important to keep up with your dogs when they are experiencing trouble in pinning a skulking covey down, when the ground cover is scant, or when they are trailing in dry leaves or noisy underbrush.

The gunner who keeps up with his dogs under such conditions assures himself at least 10 per cent more shots during the day's hunt. The percentage fluctuates with such variables as the terrain, ground moisture, rankness of vegetation, and nose and workmanship of the dog, but in any case it is sufficient to justify a little extra-alertness on the gunner's part.

Take your dog seriously. Whenever there is any chance whatever of his being on game, honor his point. Not to do so is to befuddle him, encourage him to discount the importance of advertising his discoveries, and now and then to deprive yourself of a beautiful shot.

Because you never can tell. Birds are often found where, by all reckoning, they shouldn't be. Who of us has not had the experience of ordering a puppy in to flush a suppositional sparrow — and watched in deep chagrin as a thundering covey erupted and sailed away to safety, catching us, metaphorically speaking, with our breeches down?

It is especially important to honor the workmanship of a young recruit. Can you expect a puppy to take himself seriously unless you take him seriously? And if he does a little practice pointing on a skulking rat or a stink-bird, don't embarrass him too much or berate him too severely. That pestiferous stink-bird can fool the canniest of bird-dog noses for an instant.

Not all false-pointing is false. Mayhap an erratic single has decamped from the exact spot just before you came over the hill, or a nervous covey has just scurried into an adjacent thicket. 'Tis best to be charitable. No dog — or no hunter — is infallible.

The time to find a dead bird, or capture a wounded one, is the instant it falls. Unless you have a perfect retriever, not only mark the exact spot where the bird fell, but proceed to the spot immediately. With every minute that passes, the body scent of a dead bird or the trail of a disabled one diminishes and the enthusiasm of your dog wanes.

But before you budge from your tracks to do anything, reload your gun. If you don't you'll feel awfully silly when some laggard pops up and sails insolently away. The easiest shots seem to come after you've wasted both barrels on the initial flurry, anyway.

Don't bawl your dog out for failing to find the bird you thought you killed. If he is a good retriever, he will probably find enough birds you didn't know you hit to make up for it. And, of course, you wouldn't try to pull the wool over the eyes of your companions by yelling "Dead bird! Dead bird!" at your dogs with great moral earnestness, when you know darned well you missed clean as a hound's tooth. But you might know some hunters who are not above it.

Be sure your bird is dead. It is so easy to administer the *coup de grace* to a disabled one by snapping its neck or cracking its head over the gun barrel. An inert bird is often only stunned, and will sometimes regain consciousness and escape. Have you ever had the experience of relieving a dog of an apparently dead one, only to have it suddenly come alive and slip from your hand?

I recall two amusing episodes that may find some sort of parallel in your own experience. A young nephew of mine was highly elated over getting his first bag of quail — twelve in Virginia, where he lives. Summoning the entire family to the back porch, he began removing the birds from his coat and tossing them to the floor as he impressively counted. "One — two — three — four — five — six — seven — eight — nine — ten — eleven — twel —" But the "twelve" stuck in his throat as the last bird swerved suddenly upward and, in the words of one of the onlookers, "sold out like a bat out of Hades," leaving the boy with a sagging chin and a firm resolution.

The other episode involves two friends who got into a chivalrous argument as to who had killed a single which they had shot together.

"Here's your bird," said one, tossing it to the other.

"No. You killed it," replied the other, tossing it back.

"Beg your pardon, I missed him a mile," and back the bird went again.

"But I swear I didn't touch him," protested the catcher, passing it back.

They would have worn that bird out, I guess, had not the corpse terminated the argument by suddenly coming to life and executing a perfect incompleted pass by hurtling off half-way between them. Alphonse and Gaston looked stupidly at each other.

"There ought to be an Aesop fable to fit that," one of the hunters sheepishly grinned. "Just goes to show it doesn't pay to be too magnanimous."

During the twenty years I have been following dogs in Virginia and the two Carolinas, I have asked many crack quail shots the question: "What is the biggest mistake the average bird hunter makes?" With a oneness indeed surprising, they all replied: "Shooting too quickly."

Hardly one dissenting vote!

I have not the least hesitancy in saying that 75 per cent of poor quail shooting is due to just that — shooting too quickly. It looks like a fault easily correctable, but many of us can testify to the contrary. These past masters whom I questioned were all, significantly enough, deliberate shots, some of them seemingly over-deliberate. Their comments reflect the judgment of men who have learned leisureliness. Some of the comments are especially quotable.

"Aim fast. Shoot slow," advised one old-timer. "It is never as far as it looks down your gun barrel."

"Wait until the bird quits his didoes and settles down; then let 'er fly," suggested another.

"Get your gun on the target as soon as possible, keep it there until you think he's clean out of range, then cut loose," offered still another.

"If you'll wait long enough, chances are you will get a straight-away shot after all," was the discerning comment of the finest wing-shot I ever knew.

It is a fact that, in reasonably open shooting, that dizzily careening target is pretty apt to straighten out in time — and there you are. There is one beautiful dependability about Bob:

once he has cut his capers and bought his ticket, he loves a straight line. Holding your fire not only increases the probability of a decent shot, but allows your shell a chance to pattern itself effectively.

Except in snap or brush shooting, where no holds are barred, perhaps the soundest procedure is: Don't make up your mind until the bird has made up his. And don't be so intent on getting a double that you forfeit an easy single.

"Most folks shoot too fast because they think a partridge is flying faster than he is," a versatile and observing quail shot once remarked. "As a matter of fact, a partridge is not an especially fast bird."

And that is true. It is the noise rather than the speed of flight that baffles the beginner. If you don't believe that, aim at a decamping covey with an empty gun. You will be surprised at the comparative slowness with which they fly and the number of easy shots the rise offers — if your gun is empty.

"They fly so fast I can't get my gun on them," bemoaned an amiable New Englander with whom I once hunted.

"The speed of Bob White is partly an auditory illusion," I suggested. "If you don't believe that, stop your ears up before flushing a covey. Ulysses plugged the ears of his sailors so they wouldn't hear the songs of the sirens. You might try it on quail."

The suggestion had been joshingly offered, of course. But when I came in that night, my friend, who had been missing so badly that he had almost become a fatalist, met me jubilantly.

"It worked, old man. It worked!"

"What worked?" I asked innocently.

"Your recipe — plugging my ears. They don't fly half so fast when you do that. Did it on two covey rises today and got a double each time."

"Well, I'll be damned!" was the only comment I could make.

I have often thought of that estimable New Englander and his Plymouth Rock determination to learn quail shooting. And always I chuckle at the picture of a portly gentleman halting proceedings in mid-field, with all dogs on point, and summarily ordering: "My ear plugs, Watson, my ear plugs!"

There are less heroic expedients, however, that might be recommended for slowing down the too-ambitious hunter. Some over-anxious fellows resolutely count a certain number before triggering the gun. I knew one who would curb his haste by saying to himself, "Well, I'm not bound to have this one, anyway." And one ingenious gent there was who bargained with a darkey to "tote he gun for him," surrendering the weapon only after the flush.

Still another way to check premature firing, though at times impracticable, is to observe the sex of your bird before shooting. A large number of hunters can tell you the sex of their birds before the retrieve is made. If your vision is no better than mine, however, you had better skip this. I'm always too busy looking for the bird down my gun barrel to notice whether he belongs to the white-collar class or not.

The best method I have ever found to steel oneself against over-precipitancy is to hunt with an empty gun for a while. But after all it is an individual matter, and nearly everybody has his own recipe.

# Thank You, Sheriff!

IT so happens that the habitat of that gallant little gamester, Bob White is also the habitat of the Southern darky. In the deep South both find their most picturesque as well as their most congenial setting.

In South Carolina, for instance, whose quail hunting is unsurpassed by that of any of the unreconstructed sisterhood, Negroes have been in the numerical ascendancy for 120 years. The colored population is most concentrated in the famed low-country, where bird hunting is at its very best. Here one may hunt for an entire day, encounter perhaps fifty darkies, but not see a single white person. Indeed, during the eighteen years I have hunted in South Carolina, most of my quail shooting has been within a few hundred yards of some "cabin in the cotton."

It follows, therefore, that if one expects to do much hunting in the lower South a knowledge of Negro psychology is as important as a knowledge of bird-behavior. If he makes the wrong approach, the inquiring hunter may be met with a wall of reticence, stolid evasiveness, or what seems to be unaccountable ignorance on the part of the colored natives. If he makes the right approach, he may find the Southern darky a diverting and resourceful ally.

I had my first lesson, an unforgettable one, in this matter of approach years ago. Having been directed to a certain locality for birds, I catechized a passing darky as follows:

"Are there any birds around here?"

"Naw-sir, cap'n," he replied promptly.

"But I understand there are a number of coveys hereabouts. Haven't you seen any of them?" I persisted.

"Naw-sir, cap'n."

When I was about to direct my steps elsewhere, my companion, a native white hunter, came up.

"Uncle Jed, where is the covey of birds you told that man about the other day?" he demanded.

The darky stopped short, wrinkled his brow in an effort at recollection and grinned confidently.

"Oh, dat covey! Right down yanner by de rice patch, sah," he indicated.

And they were. Yet "the covey of birds you told that man about" was an utter fiction invented by my companion.

On another occasion, while I was still in my novitiate, I approached an amiable-looking old fellow who was plowing a field with a steer.

"Have you seen any birds around here this season?" I asked.

"Naw-sir, boss."

"Sure you haven't? There were a good many here last year."

"Naw-sir, boss."

I had every reason to believe there were birds about, yet I knew the old darky was not intentionally misrepresenting the matter. Obviously something was amiss with my technique. I bethought myself a moment and approached the subject from another angle.

"Uncle Pete, where was it you stepped into that covey of birds awhile back that scared you so bad?"

"Lawdy, boss, dey did for a fack!" he answered immediately. "An' old as I is, too. Didn't know you mean dem birds, sah. Dey bees over in de pea patch. An' a sluice of 'em dar, too."

At still another time I had the lesson reimpressed on me while I was trying to locate some baffling singles. In prying about I came upon two colored boys digging up a pine stump for lightwood.

"Did any of those birds come this way?"

"Naw-sir, boss," they answered, doffing their caps.

My dogs had subjected every other spot to a thorough questing. Surely those singles must be hereabout. They couldn't have made themselves into thin air or somehow been transplanted. I resolved to finesse the enemy, and tell a lie to boot.

"Where did that bird light that I saw fly over this way?" I asked hopefully.

One of the boys straightened up, scratched his head quizzically, and pointed toward a sawdust pile.

"I t'ink him light dar, boss."

And him had, several of "him" in fact.

Hundreds of times have I verified this method of approach. It is, in fact, so orthodox with me now as to become second nature. One may ply the average darky with any number of general questions and receive the same non-committal or unthinking replies. It takes a specific question to elicit specific information from him.

The darky is so pathetically anxious to please that he is curiously vulnerable to a leading question. This vulnerability sometimes results in an unwitting misrepresentation or an unintentional misstatement on the darky's part. Should an unwary hunter say, "There aren't any birds around here, are there?" the answer is almost invariably "No," irrespective of actualities. If, on the contrary, he should say, "There are plenty of birds around here, aren't there?" the reply is unfailingly "Yes," whether there is a covey within miles or not. There is no intent to mislead — merely courtesy and overanxiety to please.

But the approach that seldom fails to click is: "Where are those birds you told that man about?" or "Where was that covey you stepped into?" It requires a specific challenge to awaken their power of recall or set up any mentation on their part. The darky, like some of his white brethren, won't think if he can help it. Rare indeed is the country Negro who can't produce a covey of birds for you if properly challenged.

Such a technique works where largess fails; it talks when money is silent. "That covey you walked into" is well calculated to leave an impression on the mind of the low-country Negro, whose subconscious mind is forever listening for the awesome whir of a rattler. He is always unnerved by the unannounced explosion of a covey of birds about his legs. And who isn't? It's a panicky moment for the best of us.

The incautious hunter is misled not only by the colored man's overagreeableness, but by his inherent fear of committing himself. He subscribes to the Biblical adage that a man's speech betrayeth him; that it is hard to convict a fellow who keeps his mouth shut. "If'n de squirrel don't stick out he haid and bark, he mout not git shot," he observes shrewdly. And the black man hates to disillusion the white man.

The fear of self-committal makes a darky demur at estimating the number of birds in a covey. He will evade with "several," which may mean from five to twenty, depending on whether you are in North Carolina, South Carolina, or Georgia; or perhaps with "not so many," "some," or "a few."

If a hunter should ask, "How far is it to the river, two miles?" he normally gets an affirmative reply, although it may be four miles to the river and the darky knows it. He seldom gets an answer in miles, but is assured "It ain't so fur" or "It's on'y a leetle piece," which is comparable to the mountaineer's vague but formidable "two whoops and a holler."

Should a hunter ask a group of darkies: "Boys, is this the right road?" he is apt to be met with a chorus of deferential yes-sirs, without a single member of the group bethinking himself to ask the questioner just where he wishes to go. This psychic kink is a familiar phenomenon to students of darky behavior and is readily verifiable.

"Shet-mouth" policy becomes second nature with them. The fact is that the illiterate Negro is darkly suspicious of the white man's motives in general. He is extremely reticent, for instance, about giving his name or his exact age even when he knows it, or revealing his identity, a racial trait which proved an almost insuperable barrier to census-takers in the lower South. He feels in some vague way that when he gives a white stranger his name he lays himself vulnerable to possible entrapment. He simply "don't trust to no mistake."

The darky's reticence about revealing his identity sometimes takes an amusing turn. Last year I went down to the plantation which I lease for hunting to see Uncle Leben, my game-toter and companion. On arriving, however, I learned that he had moved into another cabin with a new tenant family. I saw Uncle Leben enter the cabin as I approached.

"Is Uncle Leben in?" I asked courteously of a very black and ample-bosomed woman who came to the door.

"Naw-sir."

"Doesn't he live here?" I asked.

"Naw-sir."

"Do you know him?"

"Naw-sir."

"That's too bad," I said. "I brought him some smoking to-bacco, and now I'll have to give it to somebody else."

"Oh" — the ample-bosomed one brightened visibly — "you mean Uncle Leben. Sho, he live here!"

Not only is the Southern darky suspicious by nature, but super-stitious, and superstitious to a degree that alternately amuses, provokes and stirs the compassion of the visiting hunter. For instance, there is the mystery of the blue window-sill. In the more remote habitations the wayfarer will time and again come upon forlorn and ramshackle cabins with every door-sill and window-sill painted a vivid blue. There may be no paint else-where, no other evidence of household pride, and the cabin itself may be in imminent danger of collapsing on the heads of its luckless occupants; but those door- and window-sills must be a resplendent blue.

Blue, you must know, is taboo to wandering ghosts. They dare not cross a threshold so doctored. It is a curious and, for aught I know to the contrary, an effective means of ghost-in-surance.

A thoughtless act on my part once brought grief to an old colored friend of mine. On a piece of land that I had hunted for years lived an ageless, half-mummified crone by the name of Teenie President. Whence Teenie derived such a cognomen baffled her as it did me, but there she was in her spick and span cabin, a living landmark in the ancient eroded fields. Having decided last year to lease the land on which she lived, I went down on a Sunday to tack up posted notices. Finding Teenie away from home, I unthinkingly nailed a notice on her cabin, which struck me as a strategic place for one.

Imagine my mystification when I returned a few days later to find the cabin empty, with every evidence that the evacuation had been accomplished in great haste. A passing darky told me that Teenie had moved into another cabin.

"Why?" I asked.

"Teenie house been conjured," he owlishly informed me.

"What do you mean?" I asked, bepuzzled.

"Conjure-man on de do.' Lef' he sign dar," he explained, pointing toward the abandoned cabin.

Then the uncomfortable truth dawned upon me. Poor Teenie President had misconstrued my "Keep Out" sign, her imagination investing it with some dark significance, and had sought shelter elsewhere.

Although they live in the finest quail country in the world, comparatively few back-woods Negroes have any idea of what the inquiring hunter means by "birds." The quail shooter who asks, "Where is the best place around here to look for birds?" may be directed with equal probability to a rice patch for blackbirds, a savannah for killdeer, or a pea field for doves. "A bird is a bird. It is folly to waste shells on any of them; so what's the difference?" your informant reasons.

If you ask for "quail," you may promptly be assured there is no such thing in the country, although a covey may be feeding in the back yard. If you ask for "Bob White," you may get a fair percentage of rises from observing darkies who associate the bird and its call. If you ask for "partridge" or "pattidges," you are talking Southern and entitled to a better response still. But to be sure, you must dramatize.

"Do you know where any birds are?" the smart hunter asks. "I mean the kind that gets up under your feet when you're thinking about something else, goes br-r-r-r-r-r-r! and makes you jump out of your skin." If he phrases his question in such a fashion, adding a touch of drama for good measure, he will almost unfailingly draw an appreciative and sympathetic grin.

There is one score that the man who leases hunting rights in the deep South may rest easy on: the Negros will not molest his birds. For quail hunting the average Negro has only sovereign contempt. He can't hit them, is uncomfortable when he inadvertently steps into them, and reckons the bird not worth the shell it takes to get him. Just bad economics any way you figure it.

He saves his precious ammunition for more formidable and pot-filling quarry, and he is discreetly amused by the white man's prodigality. In my whole experience I have known only one Negro who hunted birds with any effectiveness, and he was white-man-trained. Rabbit hunter he is by heredity, and sometimes necessity. Opossum hunter he may be by aptitude and appetite. But bird hunter almost never.

The darky does have one puzzling and incurable habit that inconveniences Bob greatly. When midwinter comes, he simply will set fire to the fields. The burning-off destroys cover and food and forces the birds to take refuge in the swamps and bays, where they are well-nigh impregnable. I have never encountered a Negro who accepted the responsibility for such burning. They profess utter ignorance of the origin of the fire or deal out evasive answers.

I have sometimes wondered whether there is something primordial about this. Perhaps the real reason is the darky's desire to rid his premises of "varmints," a category which in the lower South may include snakes, mosquitoes, polecats or anything else whose companionship the Negro does not relish. Certainly the practice of field-burning is exasperating to hunter and dogs alike.

Once his crotchets are understood and respected, the darky makes a canny guide and faithful retainer. He is always ready to quit what he's doing and go with a white man to "tote he game" — and garner up any rabbits that the boss may shoot for him. And if he is an unspoiled child of the South, your game-toter may prove a diverting companion.

In spite of the stark circumstances in which nature sometimes places him, the darky is a humorist after his fashion. The shrewdness of his observation and the homeliness of his philosophy will beguile the time between coveys and temper the hardships of the trip.

I shall never forget Uncle Sessions, that wily old rabbit epicure and game-toter extraordinary who for so many years was my doughty companion, and whose naive drollery redeemed for me many a fruitless hunt. A great realist was Uncle Sessions. On a certain hunt, for instance, he was greatly puzzled by my sympathy for the underling in a dog fight.

"Cap'n, how come you side wid dat leetle dog dataway?" he asked.

"I'm always for the under dog, Uncle Sessions," I explained, thinking to drive home a moral.

"Huh!" he defended promptly. "I'se always for de under dog too, lessen I'se de top dog, sah."

Ethical preachments fairly ricocheted from his shining black pate.

Northern hunters are sometimes highly diverted by the titles that Southern darkies confer upon them. The deeper one penetrates into the old South, the more lavish the darky's salutation becomes. A few years ago I chanced to be with a Northern gentleman during his first hunt in the South and his first experience with Negroes. When I introduced him to Uncle Sessions, our game-toter, he pitched the old darky a shiny dime. Whereupon wise, pious and scoundrelly Uncle Sessions bowed and said, "Thank you, Cap'n!"

The Northerner gave him a quarter.

"Thank you, Colonel!"

Delighted with so rapid a promotion the Northerner produced a half-dollar.

"Thank you, General!"

The visiting gentleman, curious as to what kind of magnifico he would become next, took out a dollar bill. Uncle Sessions looked at the bill, bent in a back-breaking bow, and intoned with fervor:

"Thank you, Sheriff!"

# Puppies, Incorporated

WHOEVER lavishes his affection on a puppy gives hostages to fortune. Things happen to pups. The good die young. Your blue-blooded scion lies down and turns up his toes like a proletarian. Your most promising pupil turns out to be a dumb-bell without brains enough to get through a wire fence. Few businesses are so subject to the arrows of outrageous fortune as that of raising and training puppies.

It ruins your shooting, wrecks your temper, and upsets your digestion. It's a short-cut to the primrose path. Bird puppies chew up the upholstery in your mother-in-law's sedan. They masticate your wife's Easter bonnet. They lay waste the household. A bird puppy, in fine fettle, is worse than the Four Horsemen of the Apocalypse.

Each time you train one you say: "Never again. It's cheaper to buy them trained." But a fool returneth to his folly, sayeth the Proverbs, and back you go again. When your soul is in the slough of despond, a wayward tike gallops up and drops dead on his maiden covey. Then your heart with rapture thrills, and hardships are forgotten. The pleasure of watching the personality of a puppy unfold itself is, after all, the better part of bird hunting. And what else can make hope spring so eternally in the human breast?

In some previous existence, the soul of Mister Zipp must have resided in a hawk or a mink. He had the most prodigious passion for chicken-chasing I ever saw in a puppy. Three weeks after I brought him home, nothing on the place had any tail to speak of. My father said that that spring was the only time he had ever had enough fried chicken to eat. But chicken-chasers make good bird dogs, he said.

Every feathered denizen on the premises soon learned that the familiar ground was now a *terra incognita,* to be ventured upon only at great and moving peril. Chickens took to the trees and house-tops, emulating the guineas. It almost broke Mister Zipp's heart that he could never quite achieve a guinea.

My mother whipped me, and I dutifully passed it on to Mister Zipp, but it did me more good than it did him. One day he celebrated in earnest by killing a whole flock of Rhode Island reds at one fell swoop. Mother had sent all the way to Des Moines for those eggs. She just had to whip something. Since she couldn't catch Mister Zipp, I went with her to the smoke-house myself, hoping it would ease her feelings. When she finished, she laid down the Magna Carta: the puppy had to go.

With my soul sagging to the bottom of my shoes, I walked five miles across country to see my grandmother. She was the only woman I ever saw whose advice was worth much to a boy.

I came back toting Grandma's recipe in a box. It was a fussy little bantam hen, with her uncountable brood darting about her like sleek bumblebees. Mister Zipp had cleaned up everything on the place, including a long-spurred and embattled old Wyandotte rooster and a bullyragging old gander; so I didn't have much faith in Grandma's recipe. But I followed directions by emptying the little hen and her chickens in front of the watchful Mister Zipp.

The puppy sidled up, the old love-light in his eyes. The bantam hen lifted her head, ferociously ruffled up her feathers, and stridently hissed at the intruder. Contemptuous of so puny an adversary, Mister Zipp pounced upon a chick. With a shrill crescendo, the short-tempered little amazon charged.

With flailing wings, gouging beak and raking feet, she swept over the luckless puppy like an epidemic. The suddenness and ferocity of the assault quite unmanned the mighty Mister Zipp. Giving me one bewildered and aggrieved look, he turned tail and fled ignominiously. But it was to no avail.

Verily, hell hath no fury like an outraged bantam hen. With a squalling accompaniment, she went after him like an avenging fury. Into his kennel ducked Mr. Zipp. Into the kennel ducked the irate bantam, like a mongoose after a snake. But there was not room enough for host and guest. Out bolted the puppy, the frame of the kennel door dangling from his neck. Out popped the little hen at his flank.

Self-respect meant nothing to Mister Zipp now. All he asked of this world was a hole to hide in. Wildly he scampered for a chicken hovel that providentially offered itself. Into the entrance he thrust his badgered head, presenting to the enemy his less vulnerable rump. Up she pounced on his back and went at him with a whirlwind of beak and wings, while Mister Zipp shamelessly bawled his lungs out for the benefit of an unsympathetic world.

Thereafter Mister Zipp evinced not the slightest interest in chickens. In fact, he seemed to be somewhat embarrassed in their presence. A week later the chickens were all growing tails again, and the swashbuckling little bantam hen was the boss of the premises. As for Mister Zipp, my father's prediction came true. He did make a middling-good bird dog, the first I ever owned.

It was my misfortune to grow up in a respectable neighborhood. The nocturnal serenading of my dogs was frequently the subject of delicate negotiations between my parents and the neighbors.

I had one puppy in particular, a gangling and big-footed pointer by the name of Jack the Ripper, who made the night hideous with his vocalizing. He was the self-elected guardian of the neighborhood, and a vigilance committee all by himself. Nothing could move about the premises after nightfall without eliciting a raucous commentary from the Ripper.

I was in the Don Juan stage at the time, and I sometimes returned so late at night that prudence dictated a silent entry.

But a flock of guineas and Jack the Ripper made my life miserable. Just as I was about to congratulate myself on my circumspectness, those everlasting guineas would invariably begin to holler "Got back? Got back?" and the Ripper would tear the night into remorseless tatters.

My outraged and long-suffering family was continually laying down ultimatums on the subject of the Ripper's barking, and I was continually racking my brain for some new expedient to try upon him. Many a night did I crawl out of a warm bed, shuffle out in zero weather, and bullyrag and lambast the Ripper into silence. He would always observe a discreet reticence until I got back in bed, then open up hostilities afresh. I used to lie in bed in an agony of anticipation, praying that the Ripper would hold up on his renditions, but the efficacy of prayer was lost on him.

Finally my harrassed brain evolved a way of mitigating the nuisance, an idea that even now seems little short of brilliant. Cutting a rubber band out of a small inner tube, I slipped it over the Ripper's muzzel and attached it to a harness about his chest and neck. Then I hid to await the blissful result.

Pretty soon the Ripper decided to open up on a lusty obligato. But when he opened his moth, his jaws snapped violently together. He tried again. Again the strong rubber band snapped his jaws together. It was about the most comical procedure I ever saw. After twenty years, I still think it was funny.

And it was effective, too. For a week thereafter Jack the Ripper was a model of midnight decorum. With the sword of Damocles thus lifted from above me, I slept the sleep of the reprieved. But my triumph was short-lived. One of our neighbors, hearing of the ingenious contraption, threatened to report me to the S. P. C. A., as if there could be any cruelty in anything I did to the Ripper.

In the end the Ripper had to be banished. The disapproval of the neighbors became so vocal that I had to send him to an uncle fifteen miles out in the country, where Jack the Ripper broke his heart and stopped barking at night because there was no audience to protest.

Toby was born in the objective case and cut on a bias. Not only did he show sovereign contempt for my wishes, but he took a gloomy delight in doing whatever I didn't want him to do. He would never concede, for instance, that he did not have the same right — and a better chance — of catching a bird on the wing than I had of shooting it. He stubbornly refused to be disillusioned. Seldom did he fail to pounce helter-skelter into the very midst of a covey and go on a wild stampede for a low-flying bird.

I tried to get Toby to rationalize about it, but there wasn't much rational in him. And he was too much of an outcast to be soft-soaped or soothing-systemed. I tried trouncing him, but to no avail.

I tried check-ropes on him. When he went after a covey like a plunging full-back, I would jerk him somersaulting backward with an ardent hope of snapping his fool neck. But not all the discomforts of the check-rope were on his end. Once I tied the rope to my belt and prepared to shoot a covey rise. At an unhappy juncture Toby made a terrific lunge, and I sprawled belly first in a clump of thorns. At another time I unwrapped myself from a jagged log with a cracked rib.

Nothing could deter Toby from his determined flushing. He was as stubborn as the laws of motion. Had he not been in other respects a promising puppy, I should have administered the *coup de grace* and counted it a bargain.

One day while ruminating on the matter, I recalled the Yankee trick by which Tom Sawyer got his fence whitewashed. I also remembered how, during an anemic boyhood, my mother induced me to consume enormous quantities of the lowly and despised greens by pretending they were tabooed by the family doctor. Boys and puppies are enough alike, I figured, for the same psychology to work.

The next time Toby found a bevy, I didn't try to break his neck. Creeping prayerfully toward him, I removed the check-rope entirely. Then, bending over, I placed both hands against his rump and shoved him gently toward the birds. Toby tensed and resisted the pressure. I pushed harder. Manifestly puzzled and not a little indignant at this new sort of jockeying, he sat down on his haunches and dug his hind feet into the ground. Throwing my weight forward, I pushed still harder. Toby put on his four-wheel brakes and stubbornly planted himself. With a droll look of reproach and incredulity on his face, he held while I shot the rising covey.

I tried the same maneuver every time he pointed, until he took to squatting on his rump and digging his feet into the ground whenever he saw me coming. After a few weeks he would emit a warning growl whenever he saw me approach, as if to tell me that he knew his rights in the matter, that he was not to be bulldozed or mollycoddled into flushing, and the least cooperation I expected from him the better. Thus Toby's perversity was used to his own advantage.

During the halcyon days of his puppyhood, Trouble, a blue-black Swedish pointer, was a most indefatigable retriever. As acquisitive as a raccoon, he insisted upon bringing me the most useless and outlandish things. In particular he developed a passion for collecting terrapins. It became with him a business rather than a pastime. He went about it tirelessly and methodically, as if he were paid so much per head. It was not unusual to see seven or eight crawling around his kennel after a rain, a tariff he had levied on neighboring fields.

Trouble could never understand why nobody else shared his enthusiasm. He would follow me around for hours with a terrapin in his mouth, plainly puzzled that so precious an offering failed to elicit my unbounded admiration. Wherever I went, there was my *Fidus Achates*, everlastingly at his unique collecting.

As he grew older he began to retrieve birds. The puppy proved to have an unusually good nose, and my hopes ran high. One day, while hunting with friends for whose benefit I was anxious to demonstrate his fine retrieving, I dropped a wounded bird in an almost impenetrable thicket. The other dogs nosed the thicket thoroughly without results. I called Trouble, who straightway began to trail and pump up the earth in his characteristic fashion. Presently he dived under a log, pounced upon something, and started toward me.

It warmed the cockles of my heart to see a wayward child delivering the goods with such gusto. Pridefully I called to my friends to watch the performance. Trouble galloped up to me and, with rapturous delight, handed me a scrawny terrapin.

Trouble's over-enthusiasm finally brought about his undoing as a terrapin collector. One spring morning, when I was "graveling" suckers down in the creek, I saw the puppy energetically sniffing at something behind a hammock. A passing mink, I idly guessed. But suddenly Trouble made a pass at something under the debris. Then he rebounded and, squalling like a stuck calf, headed for the untrammelled spaces. As he scrambled madly up the bank I caught a glance of a brown object dangling from his jaw. He had at last caught a Tartar. The pitcher had gone to the well once too often.

Retribution had overtaken him in the shape of a snapping turtle. Thereafter Trouble was strangely uninterested in his former pastime. Show him a terrapin, and he would stalk stiff-legged and virtuously away.

Then there was precious little Winnie, the puppy I couldn't give away. She was the black sheep of a litter of five young Llewellins. From the very hour of her birth, Winnie was misfortune's darling. Every ill that canine flesh is heir to found her a ready victim. Worms ravaged her. Distemper wore itself out on her. Pneumonia left her practically done for. Like a runted and under-privileged foundling, she permitted everything on the place to tyrannize over her.

Having more than I could say grace over in the four other pups, I gave Winnie to a neighbor. The next day she was back. Repeatedly I gave her away. Just as repeatedly she came unobtrusively back. She was such a negligible and unoffending little creature that I decided to let her hang around, but I gave her no attention at all. She seemed to be destined for an early demise anyway.

In the meanwhile, the imp of the perverse seemed to hit her four promising litter mates. For the puppy raiser, misfortune never comes single-handed but in battalions. A vicious mare kicked one of the four into Valhalla. Another threw down the gauntlet to a rattlesnake and lost. The third yielded up his ghost to a passing truck, and the fourth proved to be as wild as an Afghan and totally unmanageable. It looked as if I had nothing for all my pains. With the hunting season in the offing, I had nothing to hunt with but a rheumatic, wart-covered old dame with one foot in the grave.

During the third week of the season, I chanced to find the unassuming little Winnie on point. My joy was unbounded. I had been unaware of her presence. In fact, I had given her no attention whatever. With my heart in my mouth, I walked up and shot over her. Little Winnie was as staunch to wing and shot as if she had been cut in alabaster. Then and there a new star swam into my ken. I gave my heart to the happy little thing and thanked high heaven for her homing instincts.

The despised little Winnie had a heart of gold. She was always a sedate, unselfish and nun-like character, always hanging out in the penumbra of things, always hunting singles with infinite patience, yet never reminding me of her presence. The wizened little gyp became for me a perfect hunting companion. How she had managed to train herself I never understood. Maybe it was simply bred in the bone, as my grandfather used to say of both dogs and men. Blood will tell in the end.

Playboy started out like a wonder dog. Only a prodigy could have shown such progress. At the age of five months he was pointing stink birds and larks. At six months, during the last week of the hunting season, he found seven coveys and a number of singles for me. He seemed to have skipped puppyhood altogether.

When the next season opened, Playboy was still a wonder dog. He kept me wondering what fool thing he would do next. It looked as if his promise had been a flash in the pan. Every recollection of the previous season had apparently been erased from his brain, and he backslid into puppyhood. During his second season this scion of Muscle Shoals Jake became the most harum-scarum and unguessable madcap I ever saw. Only a lover of martyrdom would have put up with him.

Many of Playboy's antics are impossible to recall or recount. He still hunted like a house afire, but he hunted for everything in general and nothing in particular. All was grist that came to his mill. When he pointed, anything in Noah's ark might emerge — a mangy cat, a rabbit, field mouse, grunting pig, weanling calf or a guinea. He would just as lief — just a little liefer — point a billygoat as a bird, and his enthusiasm for cats was unbounded.

Whenever he saw other dogs on point, he would gallop up and launch himself like a catapult into the dead center of the covey. Or mayhap he would playfully ram a pointing dog broadside and bowl him ignobly into the broom straw. Then he would streak ahead, take great pains to flush every single before I got there, and meet me half-way, expecting to be congratulated. Once he ran down and garroted a prized bronzed gobbler that cost me ten dollars. Never was there a dog who so loved to hunt and who found so much to hunt for.

But age is a sure cure for the enthusiasm of youth. Even Playboy finally outgrew his wild oats. Toward the end of the season he began to take things more seriously, and with the third season he put away childish things altogether.

Playboy is now a grave and corpulent gentleman who has a horror of doing anything that's not exactly Emily Post, and whose chief concern is for the irresponsible antics of a harum-scarum grandson, who in at least one respect is a chip off the old block.

# *Fiddler*

MY GRANDMOTHER was a sweet and obliging soul who spent most of her life convalescing. I say obliging, because in the *materia medica* of our household there was a fixed idea that little convalescing could be accomplished without the aid of squirrel broth, and squirrel broth meant squirrels.

With the advent of September, my grandmother would always get porely, nibble lackadaisically at her food, and murmur with an air of saintly resignation: "Couldn't tetch a thing but a mite o' squirrel broth, but o' course the boys are busy and. . . ." Whereupon my father would glance solicitously up from his plate and reckon he could let us off "about an hour be-sun." A remarkable woman was my grandmother, the unfailing coincidence of her poreliness with the squirrel season never once exciting the suspicions of my father.

"Us gwine a-huntin'! Us gwine a-huntin'!" Jeems would skip about and sing-song. The "us" was a triumvirate made up of myself, Jeems, and little Fiddler, our squirrel dog. Jeems was a small darky of my own age who was attached to our household, and my *Fidus Achates* and undetachable shadow. On the old homestead in the foothills we worked and frolicked together, got into and out of escapades together, with the careless democracy of boyhood. His allegiance to me was that of liegeman to lord, and I was more resplendent in his eyes than I have ever been in another's.

His loyalty to me was often in inverse ratio to my deserts, and sometimes accorded under unheroic circumstances that would have baffled a less valiant spirit.

One day I had been thundering away ineffectually at a squirrel in the top of a soaring poplar when my grandfather came along in his sagging buggy. Sensing the situation at a glance, he got heavily from the buggy and preemptorily demanded my gun.

Now my grandfather was not only aged and infirm, but he was afflicted with the palsy, which Jeems frugally but not disrespectfully referred to as the "shakes." Taking the heavy gun, he pointed it in the general direction of the tree-top, the long barrel describing a wide and wobbling arc in his agitated hands. After an eternity of wobblings, the gun cracked and down plopped the squirrel. It was verily a humiliating experience for me, but as soon as my grandfather had climbed into his buggy again Jeems restored my self-confidence and explained the accomplishment to my satisfaction:

"Shucks! No wonder he brung 'im down. A-shootin' all ovah de tree lak dat!"

Nor was his allegiance untested when, during a neighborhood epidemic, my mother tied a sack of asafetida around my neck to ward off disease. I can't testify to the efficacy of the remedy, but I didn't take diphtheria. Certainly no self-respecting germ with a social standing to uphold would willingly affront so potent a talisman, but at the time I would have infinitely preferred the disease to the remedy.

The stuff assaulted my nostrils and overwhelmed my entire civic consciousness. The whole mundane sphere was suddenly rotting under my very nose. I felt and doubtless smelled like the Ancient Mariner with the defunct albatross about his neck. But the first day I wore it to school was quite a success — for everybody else. As I entered, every nose in the room sniffed an indignant questionnaire. Eyes turned toward me in wild surmise. My mortification was complete when the teacher hovered anxiously above me and asked whether I felt entirely well. I trudged home in wet-eyed martyrdom and a welter of self-pity. When I met Jeems I confided my wretchedness to him.

"Lemme smell you oncet," he judicially invited.

After inhaling two or three gargantuan draughts of the stuff, he settled back on his haunches with the air of a connoisseur.

"Dat stuff stinks good. John Brown effen hit don't! Axe your ma kin I have some."

I straightway dismissed my elaborate plans for self-destruction. A week later everybody, including the teacher, was wearing a sack about his neck, and nobody could smell anybody or anything. Asafetida had a quorum, so to speak.

It never occurred to me that I could go squirrel-hunting without Jeems. And it never occurred to either of us that we could go without Fiddler, whom we admitted into our darkest escapades and most esoteric society on an equal footing.

Fiddler wasn't much to look at. He was an unobtrusive little dog of a nondescript mustard color. Of undetermined lineage, he belonged to that vague and inclusive breed known as "feist," which in our section was used as a descriptive rather than a derogative. For all appearance, he might have been compounded of equal parts of Boston bull and fox terrier, with a few atavistic traces thrown in. But with country boys, pedigree in dogs is largely a matter of academic interest. Pretty is as pretty does. When you went squirrel-hunting with Fiddler you forgot about credentials.

Fiddler was first brought home by my father as ratter to the household, an ignoble pursuit from which Jeems and I soon redeemed him by tying a few selected victims around his neck and enthusiastically holding our noses and hollering "Rats!" whenever he came near. Thus we appealed to his better instincts. After a few such edifying treatments he was content to turn his energies into other channels. Toward rabbits and other animals he exhibited a supercilious disregard, for Fiddler was a specialist rather than a general practitioner.

When an hour "be-sun" arrived and we could quit work, I would send Jeems home for our gun. I say *our* gun because we had only one between us, and because it sometimes took both of us to shoot it. It was as formidable a weapon as a boy ever owned, that ten-gauge, 32-inch choke-bored hammer gun that had come down as an heirloom from the turkey-hunting days of my grandfather. It had about all the specifications a weapon could have. Its stock, what with its successive layers of varnish, wrappings of banjo-wire and intricate splinting operations, presented a wonderfully-and-fearfully-made appearance. One barrel sometimes misfired at the most critical junctures, an eccentricity that greatly enhanced the sporting uncertainty of using it. We ardently maintained that no other gun was ever made with quite its deadly range, a theory I still find myself subscribing to a quarter of a century later.

Jeems and I also subscribed to another theory: that black powder was more powerful than the white variety just then filtering into our neighborhood. A shell shot harder at one end. *Ergo*, it shot harder at the other. So we disdained smokeless powder. Any boy who used it was a smart-aleck and a sissy, probably combed his hair in the middle, and was regarded as fair game.

We got our shells by the simple expedient of selling anything that anybody wanted to buy, under the broad ethical system that the end justified the means. Selling the chinquapins and chestnuts that Jeems gathered was one source of revenue. Egg-swapping at the cross-roads store was another. All eggs laid out-of-doors, as well as all blue chickens, were incontestably mine by family patent. Whenever Jeems found a hen's nest we went on a shell-buying spree. That little scion of Ham was the most astute finder-of-nests I ever saw, so astute in fact that my mother complained that for some unfathomed and unfathomable reason most of her hens took to laying out-of-doors every fall. She even suspected Fiddler of some subtle complicity in the matter.

But egg-pilfering was only a minor accomplishment with Fiddler. His long suit was killing snakes and hunting squirrels. Toward snakes he exhibited a savage enmity, a hang-over perhaps from a fearful snakebite he suffered during puppyhood. Or maybe there was something primordial in it. Certainly he hunted them down in cold vengeance, never failing to visit deadly retribution upon their heads. He would trail a snake as unerringly as another dog trails game.

His method of attack was calculating and deadly. Most snake-killers will duck in, grab a reptile by the mid-riff, and shake it to death. Not so with Fiddler. He was too small for such rough-and-tumble tactics, and too much of an artist. Having forced his adversary into a defensive coil, he would begin pirouetting giddily about him, keeping up a furious accompaniment the while, as the snake's head writhed in a tortured effort to face its attacker. He would continue such maddening antics until the snake, seemingly half-mesmerized, lashed out blindly. Then with the rapier thrust of a mongoose, Fiddler would flash in and clap his antagonist just back of the head. There his teeth would freeze inexorably as Fiddler, oblivious of the whole world, would manfully shut his eyes and let the racking body of his enemy flail and writhe about him at will. When the writhing ceased, he would scornfully drop the limp carcass and switch over to us to be assured that he was the champion "snaker" of sixteen states. Then Jeems and I would dutifully hang the dangling carcass on a bush to make it rain, which it always did — sooner or later.

But if Fiddler was adept at snake-killing, he was a master-hand at squirrels. To an unusual degree he had the canny faculty of putting himself in his quarry's place and forestalling his ruses. I once asked an old darky how his dog found so many 'coons. "Well, Cap'n," he replied, "old Red say to hissef he do: 'Was I a coon, whar would I go?' and he go dar, and dar he is!" It was that way with Fiddler.

To begin with, his mottled, brownish color and his diminutive size effectually camouflaged him. He went skulking through the woods like a disembodied brown shadow, and almost as silent as one. He barked only when he had put his man up a tree or in a hole, and then only to guide us to him. If Jeems and I were slow in locating him, there would follow another yelp or two after a discreet interval.

Nor was he content merely to tree where a squirrel *had* been. To whatever aerial gymnastics a squirrel resorted, there was Fiddler following him like an unshakable shadow. When he did plant himself under a tree, the presence of a squirrel was a foregone conclusion. Not even the cagiest old boar could out-maneuver him. And Fiddler never lied. He never knew how.

When we approached the tree, Fiddler would not squat supinely on his haunches and let us do the work. Scampering to the opposite side, he would raise a pluperfect ruckus to drive the beleaguered quarry our way. Once we toppled a squirrel, our responsibility was over by tacit understanding. Almost before it hit the ground Fiddler would scuddle after it, administer the *coup de grace,* and take it to Jeems, who was self-appointed game-toter on all our safaris.

When a squirrel holed up in a log, we would leave Fiddler on guard while we went for an axe and a cross-cut saw. When we got busy at one end he would alertly plant himself at the other, with forefeet braced, ears pricked up, and head warily cocked. And woe to whatever came out of the other end! Common honesty compels the admission that the size of our bag was due more often to his finesse as a retriever than my own marksmanship.

When conditions dictated a stalking game, Fiddler was always counted in. Sometimes no other tactics were feasible. On our farm there was a giant walnut that in late fall was sometimes overrun with feeding squirrels. But it stood in a field, and the only way of getting within shooting distance of it, without putting the squirrels to chattering flight, was by crawling for perhaps a hundred yards. Many the time Jeems and I would slither forward, dragging our naked bellies through beds of stinging ants and over chigoe-infested rubbish, with Fiddler skulking stiff-legged and circumspectly behind us.

Sometimes we would inaugurate the season a trifle early, or surreptitiously slip into the woods during an unwatched hour or two. For such purposes we often deemed it prudent to cache our gun in a hollow log. Our little obliquities were seldom discovered, but I would be in a parlous state that night when the red-bugs started perforating my epidermis. Sitting before the fire in exquisite agony, I was afraid to scratch lest any undue activity in that direction prove my undoing. When the seven years' itch broke out in our family, to the insupportable chagrin of my older sisters, I bore up gallantly under the ordeal. It gave me *carte blanche* to scratch without having to explain.

Fiddler was so fond of hunting that whenever anybody said "squirrel" he would bark, prick up his ears, and the tail would wag the dog. It was his favorite parlour trick. Sometimes he would try to swindle us into hunting by trotting up on the hillside and treeing vociferously, but the way he "tore a passion into tatters" always told us he was bluffing. He would put on too good a show.

Early one morning Fiddler set up a terrific commotion down on the branch below where I was working. I idly dismissed it as a piece of chicanery on his part, but a few minutes later when he trotted shamefacedly up to me I knew that he hadn't been bluffing. He had come into what the dictionary calls "bodily juxtaposition" with a polecat. Decidedly he had come out second-best in the *rencounter*. As he brushed against my leg a wave of devastating nausea swept over me. Everything I had ever eaten in my whole life uprose in hot and acrid rebellion. In practically a dying condition I hit ignominiously for home, with the penitent Fiddler at my heels.

To be met by a brandishing broom handle in the hands of my horrified mother. A declaration of hostilities followed, and Fiddler was declared contraband. Any overture on his part became the signal for a barrage of flying dish-pans, pie-plates, stove-wood or whatever missile came handy to any member of the household.

I avoided him as I would have the plague, menacing a stick and bellowing "Go away!" whenever he hove in sight. Repulsed on every side, Fiddler became a forlorn and misbegotten bit of brown dog, skulking about the shadows like a lost soul. Mystified by the sudden and inexplicable perfidy on my part, he watched me from a distance, a haunting plea for sympathy in his eyes. I felt sorry for him, but I felt a lot sorrier for myself.

When Jeems returned the next day I communicated the status of things to him, as the bedraggled and woe-begone Fiddler eyed us from afar. To my consternation Jeems walked undismayed into the yard and called Fiddler to him. Picking him up in his arms, Jeems hugged and petted him as if he had been bathed in myrrh and aloes instead of *putorius putorius*. The light of the world crept back into Fiddler's eyes. Here was a friend indeed, a haven of understanding. He never forgot Jeems' kindness. Thereafter he was ready at any time to die for his ebony benefactor, as in fact he did.

It happened the following summer while we were up in the mountains picking huckleberries. Jeems was along, with the everfaithful Fiddler dancing jealous attendance upon him. As Jeems was straddling a dead chestnut log in an effort to reach a clump of berries, my idling glance caught that which caused my faculties to congeal with terror.

An enormous rattler lay within a few inches of the naked black foot of Jeems who, heedless of the waiting death, was carelessly chattering and reaching about him. The venomous flattened head was upreared, the arch of the neck weaving, a premonitory gleam in the beady eyes. I pointed toward the coiled horror and opened my mouth to scream a warning, but my voice died in my throat. I stood soundlessly pointing as if in the clutch of a hideous nightmare that turned my very marrow into water.

As Jeems' foot squirmed, the sinister head drew ominously back. A brown shadow, seeming to materialize from nowhere, suddenly hurtled by me. It was Fiddler, who had caught the dread import of my pantomime. At the same instant the weaving head flicked outward. It was not in the naked black foot that the fangs had found their mark.

Fiddler had not waited for his customary opening. Seeing Jeems in great peril, he had cast discretion to the winds and thrown himself headlong in. Only after two or three grievous miscues, did he manage his characteristic hold, and the snake was so powerful that the body of his tiny nemesis was mauled pitilessly against the log. At every second he would inevitably be shaken loose or buffetted into insensibility.

Our Anglo-Saxon forbears had a saying: Fate never deserts a man as long as his courage holds out. When I recall that, it is of Fiddler that I think, little Fiddler at death grips with the huge rattler down in the huckleberry bushes, stricken and alone, alone because we found it impossible to hit the heaving reptile without striking Fiddler.

All we could do was to watch impotently, in the throes of a corroding fear. Eventually the mad thrashing subsided. The coils of the convoluted body gradually straightened, corded convulsively, and straightened again. Only the subborn tail twitched fretfully. Fiddler tentatively relaxed his jaws, opened his eyes, and feebly wagged his tail. Then he was dead beside the mottled horror, silent in death as in life.

We picked up the warm body and tried to hug life back into it. Then we toted it home, crying. The next day we buried it, grim and silent, fearing to trust ourselves. Then we sawed off a plank for a head-piece. I played hooky that day and Jeems and I carved an epitaph with my barlow knife. We took the inscription from a graveyard. It was in Latin and we didn't know what it meant, but we figured that if it was good enough for people it would do for Fiddler.

# Just Cover It With Gravy

I HAD rather hunt quail than do anything else in the world. Well, almost anything anyway. It is then that my spirits are buoyant, my disposition amiable, and my language more or less chaste. And my gastric juices flow along with a sweet unawareness.

It is the sequel to bird hunting that gets me down. My matronly mate makes me pick all the birds I bring in. When I say *makes*, I don't mean to be taken too literally. I'm not henpecked. I'm just uxorious. As a matter of fact, Alice and I get along nicely together. There is never any disagreement between us. She does what she wants to do, and I do what she wants to do.

But the prospect of picking a jacketful of birds is not a pleasurable one. There are any number of things I had just as lief do. A little liefer, in fact. I might go so far as to say that to one of my age, station in life, and manly attributes the prospect is highly repugnant.

I was brought up with the medieval notion that the menfolk were the providers and foragers, and that the womenfolk belonged to the order of Skinners and Scalers. To be more specific, that the conversion of game from feathers to *a la carte* was distinctly a distaff duty. But Alice is quite modern in some respects.

Skinning a rabbit is a small scimption. During my boyhood in Virginia, I was a rabbit-catcher by profession. I sold my catches for 15 cents apiece and became a man of my own means. And I was adept at rabbit-skinning. I could hook a cottontail's shanks over two nails and have its skin off before you could say O. P. A. But partridge picking is different, and I am not above resorting to devious and dilatory tactics when confronted with a dozen feathered bobs and an uncompromising spouse. In short, I have made procrastination one of the fine arts.

"I'll pick them after supper," I tentatively offer.

"You'll do no such thing," says Alice with considerable force. "When you have something unpleasant to do, do it at once. You are always telling your students that. Besides, we are going out after supper. Besides again, fish are easiest to clean when fresh caught, before the scales set and harden. You said so yourself in one of your articles."

"Shucks, I wrote that for the other fellow. And these ain't fish. They're birds, my truelove."

"Same principle. You always balk at picking your birds promptly. You're a great one for putting off the evil day, yet when it's over you are always thankful to have it behind you. Every man requires a certain amount of bossing. You've got to make him do what's good for him. I would help you pick them myself, but you know it always upsets my stomach."

I have often wondered whether her squeamishness is *bona fide* or a genteel fiction and a piece of adroit malingering. It's a thing you can't disprove. After all, you can't take a woman into court and say, "Your Honor, her stomach ain't really upset, is it?" So she gets by nicely.

"But I don't have to pick these birds at all," I say with a flash of inspiration. "Just happened to remember. I'm giving these to the Browns. They gave us that squirrel pilau, you know."

"Do you mean to stand there and tell me you'd give anybody unpicked birds?" demands Outraged Womanhood. "I can't imagine anything more impolite and illbred. Why, such behavior would be a serious reflection on your upbringing."

"Let it reflect all it wants to. Damned if I'm going to give birds away and pick 'em too. That's too much to expect of anybody, much too much. The Browns can jump into the city reservoir as far as I'm concerned."

That tactic sort of backfired on me. Clearly this matter calls for some high-class cogitation, so back goes the old thinking cap. Ah, methinks I've got something plausible by the tail this time.

"Well, I'll just let 'em season for a day or so. All game should be allowed to season, you know. Any epicure will tell you that. An interval for ripening, you might call it. Why, those million-aire preserve owners down at Charleston wouldn't think of cooking a duck that hadn't . . . "

"Is it seasoning you suggest?" · says Alice with a reminiscent gleam. "Yes, I know. When you were a boy, the Yankee quail hunters who visited your father always suspended birds by their tails, eating them only as the tails pulled out and the birds dropped one by one, like ripe apples. I also remember those woodcock you allowed to season, my love."

The woodcock incident is a delicate affair in my household. Three years ago the ramshackle house at 803 Sumter Street became the abode of a very remarkable odor. I tried to brush it off as a thing of no consequence, a kind of mind-over-matter psychology, but it refused to cooperate.

There are odors and odors, but this was the most malodorous odor you ever odored. Alice ransacked the house. When Alice ransacks a house, it stays ransacked. Finally she pinned it down to something between the walls — a rat, opossum, kangaroo or something in an advanced stage of defunctness. A carpenter prepared to make what doctors call an exploratory incision.

But while he was unpacking his tools, I bethought myself of a minor item: the brace of woodcock left in my hunting jacket 10 days earlier. The incident was not altogether conducive to household harmony, and my ideas about the seasoning of game have not been exactly hailed with enthusiasm since.

"Well, I'm a bit fagged tonight, so I'll just skin this batch instead of picking 'em," I suggest as a forlorn hope. "Picking and singeing to pass your inspection would take me 15 minutes apiece, but I can skin a bird clean as a hound's tooth in one minute by Eastern time. The people we are giving 'em to won't know the difference."

"You will do no such thing," she announces, placing her hands on her hips, which is always a preamble of things to come. When a woman pulls that akimbo act, it's past the appeasement stage. An orderly retreat is all you can hope for.

"Giving a neighbor skinned birds would be an insult. Worse than giving 'em away unpicked. Skinning a bird is the laziest thing imaginable, and nobody but a blackleg would do it. A skinned partridge is not a partridge at all. It loses its precious essences and vital juices or something. I read that in something you wrote, with my own eyes."

"That was written for the edification of the other fellow too," I answer lamely.

I'm smart enough to know when I'm outsmarted. When a man puts himself into print, it rises like Banquo's ghost to haunt him thereafter. So I resignedly hump myself over a washtub and begin the unhappy business of plucking my birds pluck by pluck, meditating the while on the pros and cons of wedlock. And I ponder at length, especially on the cons.

"And don't pour scalding water over them either," Alice fires a Parthian volley. "That takes the sweetness out of them. Always dry-pick a partridge. I read that . . . "

This domestic scene is re-enacted almost every time I go hunting. Sometimes the anticipation of the sequel haunts me during the hunt. When I get a lovely double and Old Black Joe gravely fetches them in, my pleasure is sometimes marred by an untimely recollection:

"Heck, two more to pick tonight."

Do you dislike picking birds and cleaning fish as much as I do? Maybe you are one of those Upper Bracket boys who can delegate such chores to a nyloned maid. Maybe you have a doting spouse who does it for you. My own spouse is more or less doting, and she no doubt has her points, but she stands stoutly on her you-catch-'em-you-clean-'em platform.

Of course, she is right in her fundamental thesis. There is only one time to scale a fish, only one way to prepare a partridge. And all game should be eviscerated before ripening. I don't hold with those epicures who consider their game properly matured only when it is pleasantly putrescent, who cannot distinguish between rotten and ripe. I have tasted duck so fragrant that. . . .

A dry-picked partridge is incomparably better than a skinned one. Indeed, it has a savory richness unmatched by any other game bird. It really ought to be against the law to skin a bird, unless mutiliation makes picking impossible. But a tedious job it surely is.

When preparing a quail dinner for guests, I always start out with the stoutest intention of picking them all. But toward the end, the weakness inherent in my character shows itself, and I sometimes wind up by skinning and sort of job-lotting the last few. And when Alice is away, what I do is my own sovereign business. You probably have a stronger character than I have. You never resort to the barbarous practice of skinning quail, do you?

I also cook all the game and fish brought to the Sumter Street menage. Menagerie would be a more apt description, my neighbors doubtless think. But don't get the impression that I am a paragon of all husbandly virtues, that I am a many-sided genius, or a sissified kitchen scullion with housemaid's knee. I just love to tinker around a kitchen and potter among the pots.

When I'm cooking, I don't want any woman in the kitchen. At such times, a woman is a source of irritation and a fly in the ointment. She wouldn't understand all the things I do. Sometimes I don't myself. But I definitely do want somebody to wash the damned pots and pans and clean up the wreckage after one of my culinary sprees. Nothing in the world can take the place of a woman when you really need one.

Alice keeps me cooking by feeding my vanity. There is nothing a man likes better than having his wife brag about him. It saves him the necessity of bragging about himself. And Alice is an expert in this department.

"All the famous chefs are men," she says. "Whoever heard of a woman chef, darling? They just haven't the touch of genius it takes. I'd be glad to help, but I'd just get in your way. Call me when it's ready, Oscar," and with that lump of sugar she retires.

It is possible that I am not so good a game cook as I think I am. It is within the realm of possibility that I am being played for a sucker. I'm not saying that mine is a double-dealing dame, but experience has given me a wholesome respect for her resourcefulness.

Our guests praise my cooking too. Of course, this may be nothing more than common courtesy and share-the-food gratitude. Or the artful Alice may be in cahoots with the aforesaid guests. Anyway, it surely warms the cockles of my old and impenitent heart to hear a guest say, with the air of a gourmet:

"I declare, I never tasted anything so delicious. How in the world do you impart such a flavor to them? *Do* give me your recipe. You should have been a chef instead of a schoolteacher. Now, George, why can't you. . . . "

Cooking gives free rein to my love of experimentation. There are so many different ways of doing things in a kitchen, especially when a man has a free hand. It is said that architects cover their mistakes with ivy, that doctors cover theirs with sod, and that brides cover their mistakes with mayonnaise. Well, I cover mine with gravy.

It is commonly said that no one can eat a quail a day for 30 days, that after a prolonged quail diet the too-rich flesh becomes unpalatable, and the eater becomes conscious of an effluvium therefrom. Having never tried it myself, I am unable to testify firsthand. I suspect the statement is no more applicable to quail than to other foods. Regularity can make any dish monotonous and unsavory. And the richest foods pall on us first.

Certainly quail will never become unwelcome in the dining room if any imagination is used in the kitchen, if they are cooked and served in different ways. For variety is the spice of any cuisine. It is in the department of imagination that men excel as cooks.

Edgar Allan Poe insisted that a good detective should be half mathematician and half poet. The cook books, I fear, were all written by mere mathematicians. If their authors had more poetry in their souls. . . .

I am half-minded to risk putting my quail recipes into print, but on second thought I am forbearing to do so. Some of you experts would be sure to chuckle and chortle over the expedients of a kitchen piddler and tinker such as I am. I am already regarded as half-cracked by many people. Then, too, I am deterred by the force of Alice's remarks:

"Darling, I think you are a grand cook, but I shouldn't attempt a treatise on game cooking if I were you. Your concoctions are too unorthodox. Some of your dishes are silly but delicious, if you know what I mean. They taste good, but they wouldn't look good in print. Your methods wouldn't stand too much publicity. Besides, you might get yourself sued by somebody."

Women are just too law-abiding and precedent-respecting to become the best cooks. Recipe-worship, one might call it. They lack inventiveness and daring. A woman begins and ends with a recipe. A man begins with a recipe, and improvises as he goes along. It takes a certain amount of recklessness to invent a new dish.

If it is the lot of you husbands to be Skinners and Scalers, why not go the whole hog and cook your own game? And put some poetry and imagination into it. If you don't like the result, just cover it with gravy.

# I'm A Top-Water Man, Myself

I AM an addict of the top-water plug, especially of the so-called injured minnow. Not under all conditions, of course, but fully half the bigmouth bass I've taken during the past twenty years have been via the top-water route. If any of you gentlemen share my predilection for this lure, maybe we can hold a tete-a-tete about the injured minnow in action.

This lure requires a technique of its own. It is grievously mishandled by many of our bassing brotherhood, who overlook the fact that its effectiveness depends upon the adroitness with which it is fished. It is definitely not a lure for the novice, or for the angler who lacks imagination. Neither is it for the bustling burgher whose primary concern is to see how many times per minute he can cast. If you're in a hurry, don't fish the injured minnow. In fact, don't fish at all.

The advantages of the top-water plug are many and substantial. For one thing, it is not continually hanging onto submerged obstructions. You are not forever probing the deeps with a refractory paddle while wasting precious time, exhausting your patience, and blaspheming the circumambient ether.

If it does hang, it is on the surface and can be readily dislodged. And a top-water lure may be your sole means of recovering a rod-and-reel which has slipped overboard through some mischance. I shall not soon forget the halo that wreathed the countenance of a certain gent who, having dropped an expensive outfit into deep water, espied his top-water plug resting placidly on the surface, and retrieved his outfit thereby.

Top-water plugging also gives the fisherman more chance to exercise his skill, since the action of the lure is under constant observation. The merest twitch of the rod-tip communicates itself to the little salesman seventy feet away, giving the caster a close-up of the action and reaction.

He studies the wiles of Little Egypt, repeating those that prove most seductive. He is master of the marionette, pulling the strings behind his punch-and-judy show. Into what other kind of fishing can a man inject so much personality?

If a bass strikes and misses, the caster is instantly on the *qui vive*, retarding or accelerating the minnow as his judgment dictates. He can repeat the invitation to the wily prospect, putting a little more glamor into the second cast. With an under-water lure, you can have the narrowest misses and be none the wiser. You can't profit by your mistakes.

Maneuvering an injured minnow is the most dramatic of all fishing. No other kind gives you so much action for your money. All the cards are on the table where you can see them. It's like having a seat in the baldheaded row at a follies premiere, or one on the fifty-yard line at a football game, depending upon your age and politics.

It is a game of chess with an explosive ending. Tell me, is there anything in the world so beautifully *sudden?* Anything that gives one such tingling expectancy? An old quail hunter will tell you that some uncataloged sense warns him an instant before a skulking covey explodes. A keen top-water man may have a similar presentiment before a big bass strikes. But give me credit for inserting *may.* I've admittedly caught some sockdolagers when, metaphorically speaking, I had my breeches down.

There are few thrills in this workaday world like the resounding crack of a big bass at a top-water minnow. Maybe he misses and comes back with redoubled fury, intent on annihilating that brazen brat above him. When this happens, my heart cuts a

pigeon-wing in my not-so-manly bosom and my metabolic proc-
esses do a somersault. I'd rather have a rambunctious bass hit
an injured minnow and *miss* than to land him any other way.
Unless I'm awfully hungry, of course.

The only sport comparable to it is casting with a dry fly or
surface bug. Up in the lily pads a lithe four-pounder splits the
water and cracks his heels in the air as a saucy challenge. You
loop a long one over, and your little harlot does a seductive
waltz right over the spot. Are you cool, calm, and collected?
The stoic was never born who could sit passively on his philosophical buttocks and watch it happen. After all, a fish's chief
asset is a man's imagination.

But let's get back to our knitting. Regardless of how inex-
pertly a plug caster handles his wares, he will occasionally catch
a nice bass. Even a blind hog picks up a good acorn now and
then. But it is the ability to repeat that counts, and the top-
water angler who hopes for any sort of consistency must make
certain concessions to bass brains.

Recently I watched two casters fish the same body of water
with identical injured minnows. In separate boats, they fished
the parallel sides of a mile-long finger. They occasionally
switched sides to equalize any possible shoreline advantages,
and their paddlers were of apparently equal skill.

Neither was there any discernible difference in their casting
ability. Yet one came out with all the bass he could tote, including a six-pounder, while the other came out with three
undersized fish and a bad disposition. I subsequently learned
that one regularly caught more fish than the other.

But I did observe one difference, a difference so marked that
the luckless fisherman should have instantly observed it himself.
He was by far the more energetic of the two. Over the same
stretch of water and during the same period, he averaged three
throws to the other fellow's one. He spaced his casts uniformly,
regardless of shoreline, retrieving immediately and at an un-
varying speed.

Behind him a tell-tale wake of bubbles testified to the
thoroughness and impartiality of his workmanship. As a me-
chanical performance it was flawless, but of course it wasn't
fishing.

Then I noticed the deliberateness of the man in the other boat. He was the most unhurried citizen you ever saw. He surveyed the wooded shoreline, narrowly regarding every pocket and inlet. He looked speculatively at every jutting log and out-cropping of brush. Nor was he unmindful of angles and shadows. Apparently he was interested not in how many casts he could make, but in how few he could get by with. And when he threw, it was with accuracy and judgment.

The secret of injured minnow fishing is deliberateness. *You can't hurry an injured minnow.* It is disabled only when you play it disabled. "You've got to make 'im look sick," a friend of mine aptly observed, "but not too damned sick." If you want to distinguish between the tyro and the adept, time the interval be-tween the cast and the finished retrieve.

The tyro sends his jangling plug ninety feet away, for he is a vigorous lad who brags about his prodigious distances. He throws indiscriminately, one spot suiting him as well as another, for water is water after all. His plug hits with a resounding smash, startling any customers who chance to be near by. Im-mediately he begins reeling in, for time is precious and he has got a lot of water to cover. He who makes the most casts gets the most fish, he speciously reasons.

When the retrieve is half completed, he fatalistically decides that the cupboard is bare. Then our hero puts on an extra burst of speed, and the plug fairly sizzles the last thirty or forty feet. "What's the hurry?" I heard a canny old gentleman ask a youngster. "Afraid he'll catch up with it?"

Of course, our paragon of energy has caught no fish, except maybe an addle-pated moron who wanted to show his school-mates how smart he was. But he has succeeded in putting every bass in the cove on guard, thus queering the area for other anglers behind him. That big fellow lurking under the stump now knows that the ham sandwich he considered bidding on was nothing more than an ersatz hot-dog.

But your old top-water hand proceeds leisurely. Having diag-nosed the immediate area and selected his target, he smartly flips the plug into a graceful arc. He has aimed at a spot a few feet *beyond* where he wishes to deposit his offering. Just before the plug reaches the farther spot, he deftly thumbs the line, making it fall lightly to the surface.

Does he immediately begin to reel it back in? Not on your tintype. Not if he's after the real voters. He knows that the impact is likely to startle a lurking bigmouth, but that his curiosity and insatiable gut will bring him back. So he lets it lie motionless. He lights his pipe. He admires the landscape. He shifts his weight to a more comfortable position. Mayhap he ponders life's imponderables for a moment.

Then with a twitch of the rod-tip, he injects a little life into the tiny wooden ambassador. Not much. An injured minnow has got to act injured. It darts forward a foot, turns sidewise, rolls over and decides to give up the ghost. It braces up a bit, darts frantically forward two or three feet, and repeats its death agonies — *exactly as does a live wounded minnow.*

If the quarry has not succumbed to his best blandishments, the minnow again darts forward and repeats the touching scene. At this point, bigmouth probably decides that our ailing friend is a candidate for digestion and administers the *coup de grace.*

But if nothing happens, there are several maybes. Maybe there ain't any bass there and you've just been wasting your sweetness. Maybe he has already had lunch, thank you, and his gastric juices are still working on that eight-inch sucker he swallowed an hour ago. Maybe he has just got more sense than you and I have.

But don't be too darned sure. Continue to play the minnow all the way in. The big boy may be following the gal home to see where she lives. He may make a belated pass at her even as she enters the door. I've had bass hit close enough to the boat to splash water in my face. Indeed, I had a seven-pounder smack an injured minnow I was actually lifting into the boat, thoroughly baptizing a good Methodist.

Have you ever seen a bass strike an absolutely motionless plug? Some of my fishing friends tell me they have. I've often seen them strike while the caster was disentangling a backlash, but whether the harried disentangler was aware of it or not, the plug was being tantalizingly tickled at the time. I was once in a boat with my young son when he had a particularly vexatious snarl. It was a regular Ph.D. of a backlash. While he was immersed in the undoing thereof, we heard a tremendous splash behind us.

"Gosh, wish I had him on my line!" the boy said.

He did, as he soon thereafter realized. Father and son hauled in a six-pounder hand-over-hand, and got so entangled in loose line that we finally had to cut the Gordian knot. I have also seen bass strike a plug that was dangling from a limb, while the caster was paddling up and berating himself for over-shooting his mark.

The dangling plug was, however, oscillating back and forth. Vigorous movement is not necessary. In fact, everything in my experience, as well as everything that has come under my observation, convinces me that an injured minnow is not to be hurried. It must be played lightly and deftly, with a series of dilatory maneuvers.

I nearly forgot to say, by the way, that our enterprising friend who didn't catch any fish was also standing up in his boat. Now that is decidedly bad manners in injured-minnowing, especially in clear water. Regardless of what fish can see and can't see, I will certify to one fact: they don't need bifocals to see a man standing full-stature in the bow of a boat and flailing his arms like an animated robot at a traffic intersection.

Not only that, but a caster standing in a moving boat is precariously balanced. The boat smacks into a submerged stump, and our fellow citizen does an involuntary Steve Brodie. If he is unlucky, another guy may soon be eating at his table and collecting his insurance. So sit down, brother, sit down. The good casters don't have to stand, and they have too much gumption to stand when surface-plugging in clear water.

When I am fishing in dead water and the bass are wary, I prefer being alone in my boat. I squat low in the bow. Espying a likely hangout, I like to drift up and throw from a hunched position, so that little of my precious torso is visible. An awkward paddler is worse than none. He will be continually scraping his paddle against the gunwale, stamping on the bottom, or blunderbussing around.

Fish have no external ears, and they can't hear in the narrow sense of the word, but how they can *feel!* They are really ears all over. And the slightest vibration in the boat communicates itself to the water and may startle fish some distance away. In heavily-fished waters, bass soon become boat-wise and boat-wary.

The productiveness of an injured minnow depends not only on how it is used, but on when and where. As a rule, it is most effective in early morning and late afternoon. Of course, an angler need not spend the rest of the day playing solitaire, reading Shakespeare and Aristotle, or meditating on the vicissitudes of fortune. If he is a diligent practitioner, he changes to underwater tackle and keeps his office open.

He knows that in very hot weather bass go down to cooler levels in the middle of the day. Switching to deep-running lures, he goes down with them. But if he is a born top-water man, he is continually saying to himself: come twilight or early tomorrow morning, I'm a-going to get me a seat in the front row again — up in the teeming shallows.

By early morning I mean *early*, not after a leisurely breakfast and the morning paper. You've got to get out of bed before the sun does, and be ready for business while yet the mist hangs like a gray ghost over the water. During the first hour of daylight fishing is prime, especially in mid and late summer.

And it is equally good during the twilight hour, and oftentimes after dark. So if you can't go where the other fellow doesn't, you can at least get there ahead of him or out-stay him. Twilight is the most beautiful time of the day to fish anyway. The wind has died down. The surface is as placid as a mirror now. Other anglers are homeward bound. "It is a beauteous evening, calm and free." A cooling zephyr kisses your brow, wafting to your senses the pungent fragrance of the crowding pines.

But the serenity of the evening is punctuated by a great splash up in the cove-tip, as the big fellows head inshore for the nightly round-up. I drift quietly inshore with them. My injured minnow drops lightly at the rim of a half-drowned brushpile, and little Cleopatra puts on her show for the benefit of any Mark Anthony that might be dallying in the depths below.

🍁　🍁　🍁

# Irish

FOR THE old doctor the prophecy of Ecclesiastes had been fulfilled. The grasshopper had become a burden and desire had failed. Doctor Willie had lost his bird dog, and Doctor Willie was about as sweet-tempered as a hornets' nest. Approaching him on any other subject was something like flirting with a circular saw.

"Old Charley's laid up with rheumatism, is he? Well, he's no good when he ain't laid up. Who else called?" He stared belligerently at his wife.

"And Mame Spradlin sent word that mumps was breaking out in the Spring Hill neighborhood."

"Mumps, eh? Well, let 'em break. If you got to have an epidemic, mumps is as good as anything else. Who else called? Anything about the dog?"

"No. Not about the dog. But Jim Henry called and said his wife was expectin' soon and for you to be ready."

"Expectin', is she? Goin' to have another baby. Well, she can't do it. I got to find Irish before I do anything else. Tell her I said she can't. Tell her to wait."

"But babies won't wait," his wife protested. "If you'd ever had one. . . . "

"They won't wait, eh? And if I'd ever had one! You listen to me. If I ain't had every blessed baby in this neighborhood for forty years, you tell me who has. Answer me that. Now let somebody else have 'em for a while. And furthermore," he aimed a bellicose and dumpy finger, "and furthermore, I told that good-for-nothin' Jim Henry that the next time he had a baby in huntin' season he could have it himself. Three years hand-runnin' now he's been havin' 'em the first week of the huntin' season, and I won't put up with it. You tell him that."

Doctor Willie waggled out, slamming the door behind him. Then the door cracked, and his cherubic face popped in for a Parthian shot.

"And if anybody else calls, tell 'em I'm away. Tell 'em I got the rickets. Tell 'em I'm dead. Tell 'em anything. And have that blamed telephone taken out. I'm not going to do a blessed thing till I find Irish."

Down the steps he waddled, a species of locomotion to which a bountiful nature predisposed him. For Doctor Willie, like a certain rotund Dutchman, was about five feet six inches in longitude and six feet five inches in latitude. They did say he was so fat it was hard for him to get close enough to his patients to practice on them, a slander which he would have rejected with explosive scorn.

The amiable old practitioner had one weakness that was known and suffered by the whole neighborhood: his passion for birds and dogs. In the old days, before his latitude had caught up with his longitude, his marksmanship had been a byword in the county. Before the advent of the horseless carriage, his sagging-top buggy had been a familiar sight along the country roads during the hunting season. It had been his custom to let his spavined nag jog along while a red bird dog ranged the fields on each side of the road, and the doctor found few "cases" so pressing as to warrant his foregoing a nicely executed point.

When he finally reached the patient's bedside, it was often with the largess of half a dozen plump birds, which, according to common report, often proved more efficacious than the medicaments extracted from the Mephistophelian black bag he always carried. You never could tell, they said, whether Doctor Willie would prescribe pills or partridges.

Doctor Willie was not so young as he once was, to be sure, but even now he got about surprisingly. The sagging buggy had been outmoded, but in hunting season the asthmatic flivver that took its place often squatted forlornly by the roadside, or mayhap in the middle of the road, while the doctor and his big setter ranged adjacent fields.

Irish and Doctor Willie had much in common. If the doctor knew every chick and child in the neighborhood, Irish knew the habits and habitats of most of the coveys. Man and dog, they were about the same age, considering. Both had arrived at that period in life when judgment succeeds energy. And Irish's uncanny bird sense, and his master's affection for the mud-colored setter, were alike proverbial. The old doctor would help you with your hospital bill, or maybe indorse your note, or give you the birds he killed, but lend you his dog? Never.

A privileged character was Doctor Willie. Like the wind, he hunted where he listed. Posted signs he ignored as blithely as if they were non-existent. And if some bumptious land owner complained, the complainant shortly received that which made him rue his hasty proprietorship — a bill for "service rendered," with perhaps the half-forgotten, hereditary family account included, and a "Please Remit" notation in the bold chirography of the doctor. And since nearly every family in the district owed him money, it was generally regarded as prudent to suffer his petty impositions in silence.

Perhaps that is why I allowed him to bustle me unprotesting into his wheezing old flivver one afternoon.

"Got a clew that might lead to Irish," he explained. "Fellow come into town this evening. Said he heard tell of a big red dog tied up at a nigger's cabin over on Spicer's creek. Thought we'd run over and take a look."

So away we went, banging and buck-jumping over a rocky shortcut to Spicer's creek, with me bouncing about on the back seat. The Falstaffian figure of the doctor pretty well monopolized the front seat. Old-timers will tell you that Doctor Willie drives his car as he drove his horse, and that he always gave his horse its head. At any rate, I was willing to regard our ultimate arrival as a fresh attestation of hovering Providence.

But we were headed for disenchantment. The Negro had a big red dog tied up, all right, but the doctor waxed sulphurous when he saw it — a gaunt, flea-bitten hound that snarled viciously as we approached.

"These blessed ignoramuses!" the Doctor fulminated. "Can't tell a bird dog from a flop-eared, rabbit-chasin' hound. Here I've come fifteen miles to inspect a varmint that looks like he might have been sired by a syndicate. And Irish is the son of Caswell's Red Rambler!"

"How long has your dog been missing?" I asked on the way back.

"What? You don't know, sir? Two weeks today. And I've looked high and low, but not hide nor hair have I found. Nothin' but crack-brained rumors that have kept me trottin' myself to death. Some grand rascal has stolen my dog, sir, that's what happened to him."

"Haven't you got another dog?" I asked. A bird dog was a bird dog to me.

"Got another dog! Whoever heard of such pother? Got another dog! What in the name of the great Jehoshaphat has that to do with it? *Irish* is lost! *Irish!* Matter of fact, I got a twelve-months-old setter, granddaughter of Irish, that he and I have been breakin' together. 'Course, Betty-Jo would never make the dog Irish is, but sort of an understudy, you understand. And now the young jade ups and goes off her feed. Ever since Irish disappeared. The more I feed her, the thinner she gets. Grieving about the old cuss, I guess, yet for the last month Irish had been making her life miserable, tryin' to whack some bird sense into her. Now the little fool drags her meat off and hides it."

The next morning Doctor Willie, bursting with the news of another clew, commandeered me again.

"Tom Pettigrew saw a red dog on the swamp road this morning. Son-of-a-gun had him in a lumber truck," he panted. "Jump in quick. Tom swears 'twas an Irish setter, too. No danged hound this time."

And away we went. Three hours later, during which time I decided that the doctor's Ford was fearfully and wonderfully made, we overtook a lumber truck. Doctor Willie flagged it down and demanded with out-thrust jaw:

"Let me see that dog, sir."

"What you got to do with it? Constable told me I had till next week to buy a dog tag."

"Let me see him, I tell you!" roared the doctor.

The driver wonderingly kicked the truck door open, and a big mud-colored setter jumped to the ground. For one split second, wild elation danced in the doctor's eyes — the surging elation of the hunter when his long-lost licks his hand again. But then his face fell. He apologized weakly to the driver, handed him a dollar bill, and toddled forlornly back to the car. It was a female dog. The doctor looked suddenly old.

In the silence of disillusionment, we started back to town.

"Maybe you'll get him back yet," I tried to console. "Everybody knows Irish, and he's bound to show up sooner or later."

"No. That must be the twentieth trip I've taken, and they've all been wild-goose chases. Never dreamed there were so many red dogs in the country, and none of them worth a durn. Irish ain't red really, you know. He's sort of mud-colored, like all Irish setters used to be when they were real huntin' dogs. Now they seem to be breedin' 'em for color, and most of 'em ain't worth the powder an' shot it would take to kill 'em, except to look at."

"Stealing a dog is about the lowdownest trick known," I offered.

"Well, I don't know so much about that, if they are hounds and lap-dogs and such, but," he spat venomously, "anybody who would steal a bird dog would skin a flea for his hide and tallow."

Three days passed. Doctor Willie was still following will-o'-the-wisps, hoping against hope that the next lead would somehow be the right one. Meanwhile he was growing more morose and cantankerous every day. His practice was forgotten. Even his wife, who ordinarily wrapped the fussy old fellow around her little finger, gave up trying to get him to look after his patients. Luckily for the community, there were no serious illnesses. As a matter of fact, the doctor was in such a mood that nobody who knew about the dog would have risked calling him anyway.

For all practical purposes, the community was without a doctor for the first time in forty years — since Doctor Willie started practicing as a young man. And one evening the doctor's wife slipped out of the harried house with tidings that were calculated to get immediate action if such were possible. The doctor had ordered her to send every man in the county a bill, with a curt notice that he would turn the accounts over to a constable if they were not paid within ten days.

That night Bud Fowler called a meeting in his store and summed up the situation:

"Things have done got to the p'int where we got to get either a doctor or a dog. An' I'm thinkin', gents, that for more reasons than one, it 'ud better be the dog. In the first place we ain't sure we can get a new doctor, and in the second place, even if we could get another doctor in the first place, we would have to pay up the old one first. So tomorrow we're organizin' what you might call a posse to find Doctor Willie's dog."

The next morning the posse went to work. Toward the middle of the day Bud Fowler came to me.

"Go by my store and tell 'em to give you a sizeable piece of steak. Take it up to Doctor Willie's and give it to that young red dog of his. Then get the doctor, if you have to put him bodaciously in the car, and follow me as soon as you can."

Wonderingly, I obeyed. When I got over to the doctor's house, I pitched the steak to the young dog.

"She won't eat, the dumb bitch," the doctor commented un-interestedly. "Gettin' thin as a rail, yet the blame little fool just takes it off and hides it."

Five minutes later, I had bundled him spluttering and pro-testing into my car.

Half an hour later we pulled up behind Jim Fowler's car near an empty cabin in a cotton patch. Ignoring the sputtering profanity of the doctor, Bud led the way toward the cabin. When we got inside we saw half a dozen men standing up and looking at something through a crack in the weatherboarding. Making way for the doctor, they pushed him as near the crack as his bulging abdomen would permit.

I looked. From the edge of the woods trotted a young red dog. It looked like — it undoubtedly was — the doctor's young setter. And she had in her mouth the steak I had given her before I left town. Head down and intent, she made straight for the cabin. But fifty feet away, she stopped, bellied down, crept forward to the edge of an old well, and emitted an inquiring whimper. Then she leaned over the edge and dropped the steak.

The tension in the cabin broke. Men straightened up, with satisfied grins on their faces.

"Now, Doc, since this here business is all over, and the health of the community is back to normal again, in a way of speakin', you'd better go on over to Jim Henry's. His wife, you know is — "

"But I don't understand," protested Doctor Willie, mystified. "What do you mean by all this?"

"I mean that Irish is found. In the bottom of that old dry well there. I brought a length of rope from the store with me, and one of the boys here says he'll go down after him."

"But is he really in there? How did you find him?"

"We didn't, exactly," Bud explained. "Blind luck. One of the boys saw that little red bitch of yours, the one you been knockin', come trottin' across the field an' drop a bone in that hole in the ground — and if you'd care to take a look —"

But the doctor was already gone. Wheezing and panting, he dropped to his hands and knees at the edge of the well. Half afraid to believe, he peered down.

"Irish! Irish! You old hellion. Answer me."

From the bottom of the well came a soft whimper of recognition. The well was shallow and would have been dry, except for recent rains. Fifteen minutes later Irish, none the worse for his experience, was licking his master's hand.

The doctor was soon on his way to Jim Henry's, to dress Jim Henry down for having babies during the hunting season, and to spend the night, and the entire week if necessary, by the bedside of his wife. But it was all over next morning. Jim Henry's wife had had her baby, twins in fact, one of whom was duly named for Doctor Willie in lieu of the usual charge. And when the old doctor got back to town, he ordered a gross of diapers to be sent to Jim Henry's and charged to himself. Then he went home.

"You didn't actually send those bills out, did you?" he asked his wife.

"Yes," she answered, with her fingers crossed. "Didn't you tell me to?"

"Take 'em out of the post office," he ordered. "You always did take me too seriously. Even when I asked you to marry me," he puffed.

That afternoon I met a fellow on the street.

"Old doctor's car parked up yonder in the middle of the road. Must be broke down," he said.

"Must," I assented. But I knew that if he had looked across the field, he would have seen old Irish and his young running mate on a dead point, with a pink-cheeked juggernaut waddling toward them:

"Steady there, Irish, you precious old hellion."

# Sometimes You Can't Find Them

I HAVE read — and written — articles on how to shoot quail, but what I want to know is how to *find* them. For you and I have learned, ofttimes to our chagrin, that birds can be very plentiful and yet unfindable. Two men may hunt precisely the same territory under identical weather conditions. One finds birds aplenty, the other finds precious few. Now I want to know why. Is there a sort of technique to locating birds, a technique based on an intimate acquaintance with their haunts and habits?

I had much rather read than write about this subject, but apparently few writers have had the rashness to tackle it. What I don't know about it would fill a book. On the other hand, what I do know often takes the sag out of my bag and adds immeasurably to the pleasure of the hunt.

With the hope of starting a friendly feud with other hunters who are more competent to testify, I venture to set down a few things I've picked up, often at the cost of embarrassment or long and bootless tramps afield, during the twenty-five years I have been cultivating the acquaintance of Bob White.

Are there a few rules that might be followed with reasonable prospect of success? Well, yes. But I am not guaranteeing that

Bob and his bevy will always conform to the rules. There are non-conformists, precedent-breakers, and plain damn fools among birds as among us who hunt them.

To find birds you've got to go where they are. Not where they ought to be. Not where you'd like them to be. Not where they would be easy to shoot. You've got to go where they are at that particular time of the day, that particular stage of the season, and during that particular kind of weather. You've got to know your quarry as a ward-heeler knows his constituency.

There are times when a wise man refraineth from hunting, when he stayeth at home and regaleth his spouse. For instance, it is useless to start hunting early on a cold, brittle, and heavily-frosted morning. Birds are loth to leave the roost, and who can blame them? They may be caught in bed as late as ten o'clock on such mornings. And they seem to emit little scent when huddled together in such a compact and inert mass.

Dogs may overrun them entirely, or get too close before detecting their presence. So if the morning is of the aforementioned sort, — benumbingly cold and heavily-frosted, — you may lie in the bed an hour or two longer with impunity. Or you may doze about the kitchen stove and give your pancreatic juices a chance to act on your breakfast, with the assurance of forfeiting little thereby.

All you've missed is a fruitless tramp and a sniffy head cold. And a pair of half-frozen ears so sensitive that when a recalcitrant branch snaps back and clips one, well, I've seen it fetch tears to the eyes of manly and upstanding citizens. Be as sensible as the birds you're hunting and stay in bed. Some mornings are preordained for sleeping anyway.

But if, regardless of the precepts of philosophy, the admonitions of your wife, and the dictates of common sense you must start early, be sure to hunt the sunny exposures first, and continually caution your dogs lest they overrun a laggard covey.

If the morning is warm and sunny, you've got to get up betimes to beat Bob. He and his fussy fellows are hustling for breakfast almost at the crack o' day. Indeed, I have found them afield almost too early for good shooting in such weather.

Another excellent time for the quail-hunter to stay indoors is right after a heavy downpour or earth-drenching fog, when the weeds and fields are dripping-wet. Unlike the mourning dove, Bob White has a marked aversion to getting wet. He is not a good Baptist. In such weather, birds will ensconce themselves under overhanging banks, under fallen logs, brush-piles, honeysuckle-thickets, or wherever a dry covert may be found. Certainly they will stir abroad as little as possible, and will feed only when desperate. And they may remain holed-up for days in such weather.

So when the outlook is on the sodden side, bow to the inevitable and stay at home. It is a fine time to reinstate yourself in the good graces of your wife by looking after the household odds-and-ends that you, as a well-meaning householder, have been meaning ever-so-long to look after. Every hunter ought to have a rainy day agenda to fall back on.

I have never found quail-hunting especially good in very windy weather either. A moderate, prevailing wind is unobjectionable. In fact, I like it. Birds circulate freely, and their scent is disseminated so that the dogs find them easily. But if the day is gusty and blustery, with high capricious winds, birds will move about precious little. They are apt to be on the leeward side of things, or holed-up in unfindable places.

And you will get little shooting if you do chance upon them, because a boisterous wind makes them jittery and hair-triggered. They nervously double their guard, as if realizing that the commotion about them renders them more vulnerable to attack. Certainly they are over-tense, flush easily, and fly unpredictably. So if you have that kind of weather, stay at home and play checkers with your grandchildren. And tell them about your prowess at school in the olden days. If they are young enough, they will believe your fireside epics. If you tell them often enough, you'll believe them yourself.

Hunting in extremely dry weather is vexatious business too, as I verified afresh during a recent season. South Carolina and Virginia suffered a prolonged drought that seared all vegetation and left the ground as dry as powder. Under such conditions, you can come amazingly close to birds and miss them altogether, regardless of how sharp your dogs are, or how closely you hunt. Your dogs can pass within a few feet, not yards, of a skulking covey without detecting its presence at all, yet the singles will almost unfailingly flush wild, and you get few decent shots.

On the opening day, I backtracked a few steps to retrieve a handkerchief and stepped into twenty birds, although four good dogs had just passed unsuspectingly within twenty feet of the spot. Birds were capricious, and dogs well-nigh helpless in the bone-dry and dust-laden fields. We had to step on a covey, — and pray that singles would hold until we got there. Surely a man can't rightfully censure his dogs for overrunning birds under such conditions. We finally got a respectable bag by using a pair of rampaging young buckaroos to run them up, and a pair of gingerly-footed old ladies to gum-shoe the singles.

The only suggestion I can offer for drought-hunting is to *stay close to your dogs* and be ready for all sorts of unguessable antics on the part of the birds. Does this jibe with your dry-weather experience?

Another time when the wise man refraineth from hunting is during the middle hours of the day. From around twelve to three, I should say. During that period birds are not moving.

They might have sneaked off to their regular watering place, for a covey follows a schedule in this respect. They might be wallowing and dusting under a fallen log, or beside a rotting sawdust pile. Or they might be drowsing and preening themselves in some sunny spot. Wherever they are and whatever they are doing, they are not likely to be anywhere that will do you and me any good. It's big recess for them. Take a hint and follow suit.

Stretch out in a sunny spot yourself and leisurely eat the snack your thoughtful dame has prepared, giving a morsel now and then to the faithful dog at your feet. Then relax, speculate on life and its imponderables, and doze for an hour or two. Thanks to him who first invented sleep. This is the only sensible thing to do. Don't squander your energies fretting and fuming. Save yourself and your dogs.

To thresh feverishly about during this lull is a waste of effort you will rue during the choice afternoon hours yet to come. How often do our over-anxious fellows fret themselves and their dogs into exhaustion during the dead noon-hours, only to pay for it by lack of smartness and precision later when birds are on the move. So rest, weary wayfarer, and peradventure do a little cat-napping. You will wake refreshed and ready for whatever lieth ahead. And brother, you will live longer too.

Thus far we have been talking mostly about when *not* to hunt. What are the best hunting hours of the day? It varies somewhat with weather, feeding habits, and other local factors. Some hunters prefer the morning hours, others the late afternoon hours. Some say birds feed more actively in the forenoon, having accumulated an overnight appetite. Others insist that they feed more briskly in the afternoon, in anticipation of an overnight fast. Every hunter is entitled to whatever opinion his own experience justifies. What is your preference?

The poet Browning has the peregrinating Pippa wax lyrical about the glories of early morn. "Morning's at seven" she sings. But not for bird-hunters. I'll take the last two hours before dark myself. This is the peak of the day. If undisturbed, birds have worked their way far afield, leaving a leisurely, meandering trail that can be easily picked up. They are apt to be far enough from base to allow good singles-shooting too. Intent on their feeding, they hold well. The air is mellow and resonant the last two hours, the dogs have gotten their second-wind and second-nose too, and likely enough a springiness has crept into the hunter's gait.

Birds are reluctant to leave the fields. They have become separated, are feeding in segments here and there, and there is no concerted action toward leaving. I have seen covies fly straight into the setting sun, and so have you. Pretty, isn't it? Indeed, they often feed so late that they fly to roost.

The last thirty minutes are the best of all. How often have I wearily trudged the fields the livelong day and reached late afternoon with my pockets empty and my hopes a-dragging at my heels, — to have the whole day redeemed by the last fifteen minutes before dark. How it compensates for a luckless day, and sweetens up the hunt, to have a big bevy nicely scattered then! Where is the bird-hunter who has not had a bootless day redeemed in such fashion?

To take advantage of the last precious minutes, you've got to stay afield as late as the birds do, regardless of a houseful of guests, the sanguine promises you've made the missus, or the overdraft bank notice at home. To heck with everybody and everything when birds are feeding and fish are biting. Stay late and lie like a dog if necessary.

In laying out the day's hunt, I always save my best territory until late afternoon. One who prefers the morning hours will prudently do likewise. To "mess up" good territory by hunting it at the wrong time bespeaks the over-eager amateur or the arrant bungler. The number of birds you get depends upon the judgment you exercise rather than the strenuosity with which you hunt.

Birds are astute weather-forecasters. Nature has endowed them, in common with many other animals, with a strange prescience. They carry barometers in their heads. So did man, until he took to carrying one in his pocket. There are no superfluities in nature. And weather, of course, markedly affects bird-behavior.

Have you ever noticed how dormant and inactive birds are, and how perfunctorily they feed, before the advent of a warm spell? And conversely, how active they are, and how protractedly and ravenously they feed before the advent of harsh weather? Especially before a heavy snowfall?

For years I have hunted quail in the foothills of Virginia, a section subject to rather heavy snowfalls. Again and again I have observed that on the day preceding a snowstorm, birds feed briskly and remain in the fields late, as if taking time by the forelock, as if in anticipation of an enforced fast. You have surely observed this same phenomenon.

I do not mean to imply that a good bird-hunter must be a weather prognosticator. But any observing hunter *can* arrive at a few deductions about the weather and bird-behavior, and enhance both his bag and his pleasure thereby. Such deductions, if based on the experience of a practical hunter in his own locality, should be fairly workable.

But all of us know that the behavior of birds may vary from day to day without any pronounced or even perceptible change of weather. There are times when quail are unaccountably inactive and listless, when they feed almost none, and are mysteriously unfindable even in the best territory.

There are also times when, equally without apparent reference to weather, they are extremely active. There are days too, when without any discoverable cause, they are excitable and jittery, flushing at the least provocation and often ahead of the dogs. Evidently there are subtle weather changes which, although unremarked by us, affect birds profoundly.

But one may encounter traits in the most commonplace animal that will baffle the most discerning student. Nobody can safely dogmatize about the conduct of anything. Shucks, we don't know how we ourselves are going to behave until the time comes, and then our conduct is often neither logical nor explicable. So we can guess with Bob White, but we can't out-guess him, and it is this element of the unpredictable that makes the game worth the candle.

Have you ever noticed the similarity in the behavior of quail and chickens? If you want to know whether conditions are propitious for a quail hunt, go into the backyard and consult your barred rocks and leghorns. If they are spiritedly scratching around for ration points, quail are probably doing the same thing. If they are disposed to remain inside, or stand droopily and lackadaisically around, stay at home and eat your chickens, for birds are probably not abroad. But please note that I said probably. I am too old a sinner to guarantee anything.

Some fishermen have the notion that they can likewise gauge the disposition of fish by glancing at their goldfish pools. Is there any substance to this notion? I have no evidence to offer, but it does seem plausible.

Regardless of the weather and Bob's frame of mind, luck favors the hunter who knows his dog and keeps up with him. He has got to know the mental make-up of his dog, his virtues and his limitations, his habits and his mannerisms. What the dog can do and what he can't do, what he will do and won't do. Otherwise, strangers are hunting together.

An alert hunter therefore keeps an eye continually on his dog, regardless of how good he is. No dog is infallible. The best will sometimes overrun, misjudge, or miscue in some way. That's why they have field trials. Even if your dog were infallible, you'd have to reckon with the unpredictableness of the quarry.

The man who stays in close will get many a shot during the day that he otherwise wouldn't get, and you can lay to that.

I like to stay well up in front where I can command a view of operations, where I can instantly detect signs of game-making and field-faults in my dogs, where I can follow the flight of the covey that flushes wild, and where I can get some idea as to the whereabouts of a dog lost on point. Nothing is so pleasure-marring and time-consuming as looking for a lost dog when you haven't the vaguest idea where to look.

I dislike horseback hunting because I'm not on the spot when the unscheduled happens. I believe a man can get more birds by keeping up with an indifferent dog than by lagging negligently behind a good one. So, especially if you're in broken territory where your view is often obstructed, stay with your dogs, and I don't care how good your dogs are.

Now, will you stick *your* neck out a little?

# Muggins

THE FIRST time I saw him, I thought he was dead. He lay sprawled in the middle of the street, his bulging carcass broadside to the mid-day sun. An automobile came thumping around the corner, jerked to a protesting stop, and blew its horn. The big dog lifted his massive head, glared malevolently at the intruder, and resumed his dozing. The driver laughed good-naturedly and detoured. I turned to an overalled stripling leaning against the jamb of the drug store door.

"What's wrong with that dog?"

"Aw, that ain't nobody but Muggins," he answered, as if no other explanation were necessary.

"Won't he get killed there?" I asked anxiously.

"Reckon not. Muggins belongs to the sheriff," he replied laconically.

"What's he good for?"

"Dawg or sheriff?" the boy countered.

"Dog."

"Passes for a bird dawg."

"Sheriff much of a hunter?" I inquired.

"Sheriff don't hunt a-tall, lessen hit's for stills maybe," he laughed shortly. "Don't take no stock in nothin' but coon dawgs myself, Mister; but if Muggins ain't a sight bettern' he looks, I'd say he ain't worth a whoop in hell. From all the argufyin' a passel of these here courthouse spohts do about who's goin' to hunt him, though, you'd think he was a right smart critter. Sort of a take-up dawg. Visits around and hunts to suit hisself, I reckon."

This unadorned and rather grudging description interested me, so I walked over for a closer look. Muggins wasn't much to look at, for a fact. Dropper he plainly was. Although I had owned and hunted droppers, I had never seen anything calling itself a bird dog that remotely resembled this abdominous mugwump dozing in the sun. He was about the oddest by-product nature ever turned out.

Muggins was built along heroic, if unlovely, lines. A huge over-corpulent fellow, he was as heavily jowled and massively chested as a bulldog. A comically bobbed tail accentuated his pudginess. Surely such a misbegotten brute couldn't be much of a bird dog. Still, I was to remain in the little foothills town through the hunting season, and all I had to depend on was a fancy and flighty Llewellin debutante with half a season's experience. If this lazy-looking Falstaff lying in the street was of the "take-up" variety and good enough to be "argufied" about, it might be worth while to cultivate his acquaintance.

"Muggins, old man, how are you?" I prodded him with my foot.

It took a second inquiry to bring any response. Lifting his bear-like head, he blinked at me incuriously with his red eyes, laid his head back on the pavement and sighed heavily, as if to say, "You must have the wrong number, Mister!"

At the little hotel where I was staying I casually picked up a few side-lights on the whimsical old fellow who had so piqued my interest. Mine host, who was garrulous enough on any topic, told me that Muggins was notorious for his visiting, that he was a privileged character in the little courthouse town, and that everybody accepted him and his crotchets as a matter of course. The sheriff, he said, had long ago become reconciled to his vagabond habits and allowed the dog to hunt about with friends of his own choosing.

I also learned that Ned Farrabee, proprietor of the drug store, was one of the group of hunters among whom Muggins apportioned his time; that Muggins himself nightly hung out there to keep himself posted on the doings of the town, and that any of the gang who foregathered there could tell me about the dog. So I made it a practice to drop by the drug store at night for a cigar and an idle chat. I soon found an occasion to introduce myself to the proprietor, jockeyed the conversation around to dogs and hunting, and finally led him to my special interest.

"Funny thing about Muggins," he said. "Nothing seems to happen to him. Old hellion seems to be immune to disease, accidents and what-not. Why, two years ago, when half the dogs in town was dyin' of black tongue, he come through without a scratch. And last year, when an epidemic of hydrophobia broke out and nearly every dog of any account died, Muggins kept gallivantin' around like a country parson, nosin' into everybody's business as usual.

"And the blunderin' idiot takes his naps in the street and makes the cars go around him. Miracle he hasn't been killed, except everybody knows him and he belongs to the sheriff. Belongs to the whole town, really. When good dogs are plentiful, he don't get much attention in huntin' time, but somethin' or other happens, and we fall back on him. Of course, he's as ugly as home-made soap and ain't rightly much of a dog but — Hey, Henry," he called to a clerk. "Give Muggins his cone of cream so he'll go on out."

A few nights later I was lucky enough to run into Punch Dorsey, the town butcher and one of the coterie who hunted Muggins. We fell to chatting about dogs, and before the confab ended my dropper friend cropped up again.

"Never was a dog with less of what you might call style," he said. "Looks like he ain't doin' nothin', yet somehow or other I can kill more birds over him than any dog I ever hunted. But hard-headed and set in his ways as a Georgia mule! You can't tell 'im nothin'. When you hunt with Muggins, you got to hunt his way. And he's notioney.

"About the steadiest dog you ever saw, and won't bat an eye at a county full of rabbits when he's really bird huntin'; but all at once he'll quit birds cold and go on a rabbit-huntin' spree. Why, last year didn't the old son-of-a-gun leave me flat in the middle of the field and take up with a howlin' bunch of rabbit hunters the rest of the day? As I was sayin', sir, in some respects he ain't much of a dog, and I don't reckon no gentleman would hardly put up with 'im," he concluded.

Along in October the druggist, Ned Farrabee, Punch Dorsey, Slim Menefee, the county surveyor, and I fell into a doggy conversation over a game of pool. From a symposium on dogs in general they finally progressed, or retrogressed, as Slim Menefee said, to a discussion of Muggins. There were still a few things about the strange dog I couldn't figure out.

"If Muggins is really a good dog and belongs to nobody in particular, how do you fellows divide him up in hunting season?" I asked.

"Well," answered Menefee, "when the five of us started huntin' him, we asked the sheriff to act as referee, since we were all his friends. But the sheriff said he was hands off, that the Logan-Dewberry feud had started over a dog, and a hound dog at that, and we'd have to settle it ourselves. So we drifted into an arrangement that's been more or less satisfactory.

"As you probably know, Muggins is one of those gregarious fellows who visit a lot. Only five of us here hunt much. Muggins knows that, and he kind of divides his time amongst us in hunting season. We just wait for him to come around. There's a rough sort of equity in the way the old hobo does it, too."

"It's a wonder somebody doesn't pen him up in hunting season, or steal him," I suggested.

"Not such a wonder," answered Ned Farrabee. "In the first place, it's impossible to keep Muggins up for long. Too much dog and too much sense. Two years ago he hobbled into the drug store with a broken front leg and a piece of poultry wire around his neck. We had a kind of committee meetin' that night, and the next day Punch Dorsey went out to see a squatter who had moved in on Troublesome Creek.

"It seems like Punch had a little conversation with the fellow" — here the narrator grinned knowingly and looked at the massive

Dorsey — "and the next day he decided to put the fire out and whistle for his dog, as we say here. Besides, you couldn't make Muggins hunt for you unless he wanted to, anyway. Independent cuss. Why, last year didn't he leave me flat, come back to town and take Will Coffin out huntin'? And for no reason at all. Half bird dog and half damn fool, if you ask me."

"Why doesn't somebody buy him from the sheriff?" I asked casually, and instantly saw that I had stepped off on the wrong foot.

There was a quick, meaningful exchange of glances, and the pool game suffered a momentary lull.

"Sheriff wouldn't hardly sell 'im." The druggist looked at me with cue poised. "And it wouldn't be a very sportin' thing for anybody to do, anyway."

"Ain't very likely," remarked the huge Dorsey unsmilingly.

"Wouldn't meet with what you might call unanimous approval around here, I reckon," added Slim Menefee.

"You have me dead wrong, boys," I put in quickly. "It was an idle question. I hadn't the remotest idea of trying it, I assure you."

The slight tension broke, everybody laughed, and the game continued.

"Nothin' like an understandin' among friends," said Dorsey, and I was pleased at the tacit inclusion of myself. "But tell you what: if Muggins chooses to add you to his huntin' list, ain't a one of us will complain, or hinder 'im, or feel hard toward you, sir. It's up to Muggins."

"That's generous of you, and I appreciate it," I told them. And I did.

So Muggins was not only a town character, but apparently town property. And he really was. When his leg broke, it was Slim Menefee who took him forty miles to a veterinarian to have it properly splinted. At intervals too frequent to suit Muggins, he was put through what the druggist vaguely called "a course o' medicine." Will Coffin and Cliff Walters, the other members of the quintet who hunted him, took turns at paying taxes on him and outfitting him with new collars. For his part, Punch Dorsey fed him enough beef scraps to keep half a kennel, and all five men would have fought a sheriff's posse for him at any time.

I began to wonder where I figured in the picture. It was obviously time for me to do a little friend-making on my own account. Muggins would call on me in due time, they had said, and sure enough he did. One October morning I found him waiting for me on the porch of the hotel. For the rest of the day he attached himself unshakably to me, went where I went, and did what I did. He could not have been more adhesive had I owned him since puppyhood and had a fee simple title to him. And he refused to accept attentions from anybody else during his visit. That was the way Muggins visited.

On the second day I had a carpenter build a comfortable kennel for him behind the hotel. Maybe I could get him into the habit of sleeping there. I also bribed the hotel cooks to pitch him tidbits from the back door. Perhaps a good hefty steak would make an impression on him, I decided. But as we entered the butcher shop and I pointed out an expensive cut to the clerk, Punch Dorsey's voice hailed me from the rear:

"If it's for Muggins, he'd just as lief have that round steak. Do him as much good as that 40-cent stuff. I'm here to sell meat, and I ain't aimin' to meddle; but if you're tryin' to make an impression on Muggins so he'll remember you later on — " He shook his head good-naturedly. "Ongrateful old cuss, sir."

When we went by the drug store and I set him up to ice cream, I came in for more kidding.

"Might as well save your money, Doc!" called out Will Coffin. "It's been tried before."

The whole town knew that I was making up to Muggins, and nobody seemed to mind. For his part, my guest accepted everything I offered him, including the kennel, with great gravity. In spite of the attentions I showered upon him, however, he unceremoniously walked off on the fourth day. The next I heard of him he had taken up with an outfit of wheat-threshers and was following them about the neighborhood. Then I heard that a highway encampment was building a bridge across Rough Creek, and that Muggins was bossing the job for them. A week passed without further report on his peregrinations. One night a farmer dropped into the drug store for some medicine.

"Saw Muggins yesterday," he told Ned Farrabee.

"What was he doin'?"

"Old war-horse was on the prowl, I reckon. Saw him clear over in Buckingham County."

So the vagabond was in another county, with the hunting season only a few days off. The report was a bit disturbing.

"Suppose he'll get back all right?" I asked, trying to sound casual.

"Who, Muggins?" the crowd laughed. "Knows every pig-path and rabbit-gnaw this side o' North Car'lina. Always goes off on a bender about this time of the year, but he'll be strictly business later on. Shucks, that old monkey knows when the season opens as well as you do. Liable to be squattin' on his haunches out there in front and panhandlin' us for ice cream tomorrow night," offered Punch Dorsey.

"Or sleepin' in that $11 kennel of yours," twitted Will Coffin.

And he was. I was overjoyed to find him waiting for me the next morning, looking as patriarchal and grave as ever. There followed a determined campaign to make the dog feel at home. I danced attendance upon him. Enlisting the aid of the hotel cooks, I fed him on the fat of the kitchen. When the day before the opening came, Muggins and I were inseparable. Maybe the old hobo was settling down at last. Perhaps my kennel had turned the trick. The thought of having out-maneuvered Ned Farrabee, Will Coffin and the rest gave me a chuckling satisfaction.

That night I met several farmers, in town for a Masonic meeting, who told me their places were overrun with birds. "We've had a tolerable wet summer," explained one, "and there's plenty of vegetation, which means the birds are in the open fields. More partridges on my farm than I've seen for years. Come out tomorrow and try your hand," he invited.

Arranging for an absence of several days from the office, I overhauled boots and gun, had the cooks pack a substantial snack for Muggins and me, and got everything in readiness for an early start the next morning. Just before retiring I went out to see whether Muggins was in status quo. There he was in the warm kennel, snoring like a trooper.

Beating the alarm, I was up and dressed by daybreak. Grabbing coat and gun, I jumped into the car and called Muggins. No response. I called again. The old codger must be oversleeping. I walked down to the kennel and looked in. For a minute I stupidly eyed the box before the full force of the blow dawned upon me. Muggins was gone!

Left high and dry on the opening day, and a crispy November morning at that, with plenty of birds and no dog. Few misfortunes that can happen to a bird hunter are comparable to that. In chagrin I turned back and changed my clothes and went to the office. I would keep away from those expert kidders at the drug store. But during the day I ran into Punch Dorsey on the street.

"What, you not huntin' today, Doc?" he asked, a knowing twinkle in his eyes.

"No. Something developed at the office, and I couldn't get off," I lied.

"Told you Muggins was a ongrateful cuss. Know how you feel. Was up kind of early myself, thinkin' maybe — but you can't depend on that monkey. Fellow told me he saw 'im at Will Coffin's house at daybreak. Two years hand-runnin' now he's hunted the openin' with Will. Don't let it worry you too much. He'll come around sooner or later."

But he didn't come around. I waited vainly for three weeks, while he took up successively with Will Coffin, Punch Dorsey, Cliff Walters and the rest and hunted several days with each. Then he disappeared. Rumor had him on a rabbit-hunting spree. The old renegade had evidently marked me off his list; so I wired my sister, in Mississippi, to send the Llewellin pup. She would be better than no dog.

Her telegram hardly restored my spirits: "Sally Anne down with distemper. Veterinary doing all possible but recovery doubtful. Terribly sorry."

Whoever invests his affections in a dog gives hostages to fortune, I reminded myself. Not to be outdone entirely, I wired two other friends for dogs, only to pay charges on two wordy "regret" messages.

Well, I would give up and take a long deferred official trip to Washington. I had my secretary arrange for an appointment and packed. But when I went out to get into the car, my eyes must have bulged in their sockets. There sat Muggins, as big as life, in the front seat. I gaped incredulously, my bag dropped to the ground. He looked up and barked a throaty invitation.

"Cancel that trip," I called to my secretary. "Telegraph 'em I'm sick. Got the fever or something."

"What kind?" she called back, with her punctilious regard for details.

"Any kind that'll take about four days to recover from. Walking fever might do," I shouted and changed into my hunting clothes.

The next four days I shall not soon forget. They were everything a hunter could wish, made doubly memorable by the crotchets of my homely but amiable companion. I soon verified what I had heard about him for months: that he had his own way of doing things.

At the very outset he showed me who was boss. When we got out of the car, I started in one direction while Muggins shambled off in another. I stopped and called to him.

"This way, Muggins!"

He stopped, turned his massive head toward me, and waited.

"This way, I say."

Swaggering a few steps farther, he turned and eyed me again. Then he emitted a guttural protest and trotted stubbornly on. He won the argument, as he won most of the others that arose the next few days. He did whatever I wanted him to do — when it was what he wanted to do. Not the scantiest respect did he show for any ideas I had as to where or how to hunt. To be honest, I soon discovered that he knew more about it than I did anyway; so I stopped trying to hunt him, and let him hunt me.

He didn't do anything the way one would expect a seasoned dog to do it. His pointing, for instance. A short distance from the car he sniffed lazily and stopped. Didn't point. Didn't do anything. Just stopped.

"Hi on, Muggins!" I ordered.

He still refused to budge, just seemed to be criticizing the landscape. Indignantly I walked up, and stepped into a thundering covey of birds. He was short on patience, too. If I was a bit

slow in getting up, he would sometimes turn his head toward
me and growl irritably: "Well, what's holdin' you? We ain't
got all day."

Valiantly and vainly I tried to make him retrieve. When the
first bird fell and I insisted that he pick it up, he looked at me
as if to say: "You're big as I am, Mister. Pick 'im up yourself.
My business is to find 'em." And when I got a little rough he
went off and lay down in the shade. Later in the day, though,
he puzzled me by making a prompt and unordered retrieve of
a bird that had fallen across a creek. I soon learned he would
fetch a bird that fell badly, but he refused to encourage my
laziness by noticing one that fell near by or in plain view.

In the field he was the pokiest and most ineffectual-looking
dog I ever saw, waddling along as if he had nowhere in particular to go and plenty of time to get there. He didn't appear
to hunt at all, just fumbled and monkeyed around; yet he could
find more birds with less hunting than any dog I ever shot over.
I would have sworn that he merely blundered into his birds; but
the first day convinced me that, dropper though he was, he combined a really magnificent nose with that prized ingredient known
as bird sense. He simply hunted where the birds were.

Though staunch as you please — if you accepted his idea of
a point — he would not allow himself to be imposed upon. During the second day we somehow got separated. When I located
him fifteen minutes later, he was complacently squatting on his
fat haunches in the shade of a bush, with a covey feeding in
front of him. And he had no apologies to offer. A comical
spectacle he was, and I could not help recalling Punch Dorsey's
remark that "no gentleman would hardly put up with 'im."

On the last day of the hunt, however, an incident occurred
that the old fellow did apologize for. Although it should have
disgusted any self-respecting bird hunter, it afforded me great
amusement. And it was the only time I ever knew the old
gentleman to lose his dignity.

I had gone to the car for shells, leaving Muggins to his own
devices. When I returned, he was not to be found. Calling repeatedly, I fired my gun and circled the field, but without results. Half an hour later, while rambling about alone, I blundered into a tremendous covey of birds. A few yards beyond

them was indisputable evidence that the flesh is weak: there lay Muggins, sound asleep in the noonday sun.

Tired of standing, he had lain down on the job and dozed off. When I prodded him with my boot, he almost jumped out of his skin, and the droll way in which he rolled his red eyes in self-reproach made me instantly forgive him of even so gross an offense.

But it is impossible to review that hunt, or to catalog Muggins' individualities. Certainly he was unlike any other dog I ever hunted with, and the four days I spent with him in those warm Virginia fields will always live in a niche of my memory.

It has been several years now since I hunted with Muggins. Somehow I could never quite manage another trip to the little courthouse town. Likely enough Muggins has been gathered to his fathers long ago, and other dogs, of an ancestry less ignoble, have succeeded him. But of all the dogs I have ever known, it is of that hard-bitten and uncompromising but companionable old dropper that I think most often.

# Give Me A $40 Dog

"WHAT ABOUT her papers?" I asked, singling out a shaggy little setter that had taken my eye.

"Papers? Follow me," was the laconic reply.

Picking up his gun, the owner led the way to a nearby lespedeza field. Ten minutes later the shaggy little beast had found, pointed, and retrieved a brace of birds with a neatness and dispatch that would have disarmed the most squeamish critic.

"Them's her papers, Mister," said the owner with simple finality. "And if you don't like 'em, you know what you can just do."

This little by-play, which added one more dog to my family and one more strain on such connubial felicity as my wife and I enjoy, illustrates the utilitarian standard by which bird-dogs are bought and sold in the South, where a dog is rated on accomplishment alone. Everywhere one meets the pragmatic doctrine that "A good dog needs no pedigree."

"A good dog needs no pedigree, and if a dog ain't any good, a pedigree don't help him none," argued a plausible old-timer down in Alabama while urging on me the merits of an unregistered pup. "A bird-dog's business is to hunt birds, ain't it? If he does that well, hit don't make no differ about his ancestors.

You take a mule now. A mule ain't got no pride o' ancestry nor hope o' posterity, but if he plows cotton all right, you don't hold it agin him because his forbears was jackasses, do you?"

"I ain't a-sellin' his ancestors, sir! I'm a-sellin' him," was the indignant reply I got from an old gentleman in Virginia. "When you find what you want in a dog, what's the use of pryin' into family matters, sir?"

"When a feller gits so he can't shoot, he gits powerfvl interested in pedigrees," philosophized an old codger living near a game preserve in Georgia. "That dudish feller over thar, now, he won't tetch nothin' but a registered dog. But between you and me, Mister, I betcha if you go back far enough, he ain't registered hisself."

And the attitude of Uncle Cephas, that sanctimonious fraud who is my game-toter in the South Carolina low-country, shows the doubtful esteem in which canine genealogy is held in that unreconstructed province.

"Cap'n done bought hisself a new dawg," he announced to me.

"Did he get a good one?" I asked.

"I t'ink Cap'n done bought hisself thutty dollars wuth o' papers and ten dollars wuth o' dawg," he chuckled.

What proportion of the birds annually killed in the South are shot over unregistered dogs? Only omniscience could answer that question, and only a foolhardy man would try. But foolhardiness runs in my family, so here goes. *Over ninety per cent of the quail annually taken in Bob's native habitat are shot over such dogs.*

Included in the ten per cent excepted are, of course, some of the best-bred and most superb hunters in the country. And a sizable percentage of the unregistered dogs are registerable. Southerners are the world's worst record-keepers. The wary dog-buyer soon learns, however, that the phrase "entitled to registration" is used too often to be construed as a polite little fiction. Just an old feudal custom. Most dogs so represented turn out to be nothing more than sons-and-daughters-of-the-people.

I myself confess a lack of enthusiasm about a shooting dog's ancestors. It is over these same sons-of-the-people, who have only their hard-headed practicality to recommend them, that I shoot my own birds. My predilection for such job-lot hunters puzzles some of my friends. Not long ago one of them came to my dog-yard, looked long and wonderingly at what he saw there, then turned to me.

"Why a man of your station and alleged intelligence will keep such a riff-raff is beyond me. Why that shaggy, flop-eared varmint there —

"Is Sadie. Half Gordon," I supplied.

"And half what else?" he pursued ruthlessly.

"None of your damned business," I answered.

"And that rat-tailed Jezebel there — "

"Is Winnie the Wench," I supplied again.

"And that choice brace of ruffians by the gate — "

"Are Miltmore and Mack, and they'd hunt your city legs off in two hours."

"And that misbegotten old gallows-bird in the far corner."

"Is none other than Jericho the Dropper, and a finer dog no honest man could ask," I defended.

"But Doc," he chided, "there ain't a pedigree in a thousand. Why don't you get some respectable dogs, some a gentleman would hunt with?"

"Gentlemen *would* hunt them, — other gentlemen," I replied, recalling the advice given me years ago by a sage of the Georgia pinelands. "Always keep one fine-lookin' dog to lend out, a fine-lookin' one that ain't worth a durn," he counselled. "Then nobody will borrow the hard-lookin' dogs you do your real huntin' with."

To confess the truth, my dogs are not pretty. To an unsympathetic eye, they must look a rather hard-favored and democratic crew. There is not a registered one on the place. Some are respectably descended, as I count descent, but of the parentage of others the less said the better. Some are frankly droppers. But one thing they have in common: they are all hard-headed, hard-hunting dogs who know their business.

When I reflect on the breeding of Southern dogs, I would not be misunderstood. What is a well-bred dog anyway? However negligent Southerners may be about record-keeping, and however indifferent to what may be called abstract breeding, their dogs *are bred to hunt*. Whatever bar sinisters and damaged escutcheons a genealogist might find amongst them, the best of these dogs are matchless hunters. May I illustrate the practical attitude toward breeding?

Last year I chanced to be visiting a friend in Georgia who owned a fine pointer. While I was there a new-comer who had bought a quail preserve in the neighborhood came in with a bitch to breed.

"May I see the papers on your dog?" he asked my host.

Two days later a native hunter came in with another bitch.

"Do you want to see the papers on my dog?" asked my friend.

"Papers? No sir," answered the native. "But I'd take it right kindly if you'd let me see your dog work the field a little first."

This fellow was a pragmatist who didn't give a damn about pedigree. What he wanted was dog.

Not only are my own dogs lacking in lineage, but many of them are problem-children. I have never had — and am not sure I should want — perfection in a bird dog. It's the dog with a streak in his make-up that appeals to me, the archangel a little damaged, the dog that "would be the best you ever saw IF." It's tackling the IF that challenges me. But I am not assured of the unfailing sympathy of my wife.

"Why do all the dogs you get have something wrong with them?" she demands. "One is gun-shy, one won't retrieve, one breaks shot, whatever that is. Why don't you and Junior get a dog that hasn't any faults? Why, you've spent enough time and money curing that pup of gun-shyness to buy a good dog."

"Shucks, Mother," defends my sixteen-year-old son and favorite hunting companion, — "What would be the fun of hunting with a perfect dog, even if you could get one? You'd know in advance what he was going to do. You never will understand about dogs, Mother. It's reformin' 'em that's fun."

Why do I prefer these harum-scarum hunters of mine to fancy patricians and be-papered aristocrats? For several reasons that seem to me good and sufficient. For one thing, they don't represent such an investment. Habitually unconfined, the Southern dog runs a gamut of dangers ranging from rattlesnakes, heartworms, the hazards of the highway, hydrophobia, and other ills of the flesh to which the torrid summers predispose them. In one South Carolina county more than 100 dogs died of hydrophobia last summer. "Give me a forty dollar dog!" exclaims a friend.

"Something happened to every expensive one I ever owned."

I like these sons-of-the-people, too, because they are such a heady, stout-hearted, and companionable lot. How I do love a roughneck! It is written that a man likes a little Devil in the horse he rides and the woman he marries. I don't mind a little in the dog I hunt. These tough campaigners of mine are equally ready for a fight or a frolic, will hunt a man's legs off any and every day in the week, and face any barrier without asking quarter. And though they may be a bit shy on ancestry and manners, their mastery of the fundamentals of bird hunting is so thorough that one forgets and forgives their shortcomings.

Such rowdies, for instance, as Miltmore and Mack, two high-stepping pointers who will out-fight and out-hunt any other pair I ever saw. And old Jericho the Dropper, acknowledged boss of the outfit. As a matter of principle, Jericho never fails to thrash on the spot any dog that crowds him on point, and woe to the over-anxious youngster who flushes the old martinet's birds! Woe also to any dog that tries to enter the car or yard ahead of him, or who tries too hard to ingratiate himself with me. Jericho will turn fiercely — and I mean fiercely — on the upstart and impart a lesson not soon forgotten or invited twice.

Almost every experienced hunter has at some time owned a dropper. "Best dog I ever owned," one hears again and again in the South. A dropper, result of what the dictionary unkindly calls a miscegenation between pointer and setter, is apt to be like the little girl who had a little curl. When she was good she was very good, and when she was bad she was horrid. A dropper may derive good qualities from both sides, or conversely, bad qualities from both, and is usually absolutely worthless or a prized hunting dog. Jericho "dropped" on the right side, and without shame I pronounce him the peer of the best.

I love these roughnecks, too, because you don't have to handle them with silk gloves, as is too often the case with highly-bred, hair-trained dogs. Most of us have known beautiful dogs that were rendered untrainable through over-sensitiveness. Delicately-strung dogs take correction to heart too much. Give me a dog I can bawl out, on proper occasion, without his being mortally offended, — one willing to take part of the blame for my mistakes.

I was once hunting with a very refined gentleman whose very refined dog ingloriously bolted at a rabbit. The old gentleman was visibly put out, in a refined sort of way. "Old man," he chided gently, "I am disappointed in you. Gravely disappointed. I can't understand what made you so completely forget yourself as to stoop to such folly. The next time such a thing happens, I shall have to take measures, sir!"

Take measures! If it had been one of my dogs, I would have bawled out: "Hey you Mack — Winnie — Miltmore, you flop-eared misbegotten-son-of-promiscuity, I'm going to frail the living hell outer you the next time you try that." And I like a dog that can stand that kind of conversation, that doesn't mind a few tri-syllables thrown at him now and then. But I never lend Miltmore and Mack to my friend the Parson. They don't speak each other's language. You've got to be able to plumb the depths of the soul of a mule to manage these bullies.

"I'll admit that Miltmore and Mack and even Jericho are perfect hellions, but they sure have a lot of personality," volunteered a friend who occasionally hunts with me.

They would probably have too much "personality" for most people. Anything is rather more than likely to happen on a hunt, but to me their unguessable capers add zest to the game. As my son stoutly insists: *"It's not knowing exactly what a dog is going to do and watching him do it that makes it fun."* The performance of my dogs ranges from brilliance to stupidity. So does my own. They have a rare capacity for doing fool things. So have I. I love them for their imperfections.

A day in the field with these rough-and-ready troopers is sure to bring thrills, suspense, chagrin, — and a coatful of birds. To hunt them requires a pair of stout legs, lusty lungs, and a knowledge of Anglo-Saxon derivatives. But they have a way of growing on one. After a few days hunting last year with a friend whose beautiful and highly-finished hunters followed the game through with an almost faultless precision, I was glad to get back to my "forty dollar dogs," where I could make as many mistakes as I pleased.

It was like settling back restfully with the home-folks after some ritzy caller has left. Hunting with perfect dogs is too much responsibility, — like eating at the table with people who have better manners than you have. A sentiment in which Uncle Cephas, my aforesaid game-toter, heartily concurs. Uncle Cephas is particular about the dogs we hunt, particular that they aren't too good.

He and I were once captured by a dog-fancier who descanted for a full hour on the distinguished lineage of a dog I had come to see. The recital put me in mind of the endless "begats" of the Old Testament. When it was over, Uncle Cephas, with a harassed look on his brow, called me aside:

"Cap'n, don't you buy dat dawg," he advised gravely. "Dat dawg better bred dan what we is."

## Candy From A Baby

WARILY THE traders squared off. The Judge seated himself ponderously on the running-board of his car, took out a penknife, and immersed himself in the architectural possibilities of a hickory chip. The Cracker sprawled on the sagging steps of his cabin, plucked a turnip from his baggy overalls, and began fastidiously to peel it.

"Supposing I was in the market for a dog," the Judge opened, "what would you want for him?"

"Have a turnip?" proffered the Cracker, digging tentatively into his overalls.

"No, thanks," the Judge declined.

"Air you satisfied he's what you want in the way of dawg? You just hunted 'im one day, you know," the Cracker reminded, taking a bite of turnip.

"Well," the Judge hedged, "supposing I am." As a matter of fact, that one day had been sufficient, quite sufficient, he slyly confessed to himself.

"There mout be dogs better'n him," the Cracker admitted, jerking a thumb toward a big lemon-eared pointer sprawled impudently under the heels of a gaunt mule. "There mout be faster."

"Might be," conceded the Judge, but the concession was purely rhetorical.

The Judge looked wryly at the Cracker's mule. He had ridden him on the day's hunt, while the Cracker followed afoot. Experimentally he straightened his back, half expecting a protesting twinge of lumbago. Might get by without an osteopath after all, he decided.

Flies plagued the mule, and he spasmodically stamped the ground, missing the head of the dozing dog by inches. The Judge winced. "Better call that dog away. Liable to get maimed there."

"Ole Mose ain't a-goin' to hurt 'im, don't hardly reckon," the Cracker dismissed, without looking up.

"Well," resumed the Judge, "what is your figure?"

"I mout have one figger, and you mout have another," he demurred.

"Might," was the terse admission.

The Judge was becoming a trifle nervous. As his gamekeeper had warned, these Crackers did have a sort of native cunning. He had set $250 as his limit. Looked now as if he might have to stretch it to $275, but that, he promised himself, would be absolute tops. Unless he was pushed. Of course, he had brought along $300, but if this fellow thought. . .

"Sure you won't have a turnip?" The Cracker dug out another and industriously brushed it off against his pantlegs. "There's turnips and turnips, mister. Now, this here is a Georgia specie and — "

"No. Neither the Georgia nor the Alabama species, if you don't mind."

The Cracker clucked deprecatingly that one should be so entirely destitute of appreciation.

"Well, mister, a dawg's a dawg, you know."

"I'm not asking you to give him away."

"And hit's right smart trouble trainin' a good 'un." The Cracker cocked his head, a half-section of turnip in his jaw.

This fellow was going to be more difficult than he had thought, the Judge decided. Of course, he had a few loose bills besides the $300. And he had brought along his check-book, just in case. But . . .

"If the dog's for sale — "

"And Tuckahoe's the onliest dawg I got right now, excusin' that passel o' pups. Natcherly, a fellow'd have to ask more when he's disfurnishin' hisself that-away."

"Naturally," assented the Judge.

The Cracker inspected his last turnip, regretfully rejected it, and wiped his barlow-knife with a gesture of finality. "Things being as they air, I don't see how I can take less'n thirty dollars for 'im."

"What did you say?" the Judge asked in amazed disbelief.

"Thirty dollars, sir. A-course, he air only a dawg, but — "

Ten miles away, a car roared to a stop at a big plantation house. The Judge, a gleam of triumph in his eye and his pink cheeks suffused with excitement, waddled across the yard with a big pointer on a leash.

"Come a-running, Jed," he excitedly summoned his game-keeper and right-hand man. "Best dern dog a man ever lifted a gun over! Oh, boy! Oh, boy! Oh, boy! Just heft that hunting jacket. She's plumb full. Honest, Jed, never saw his equal in the field. Sort of got something up my sleeve, Jed." The Judge winked broadly and did his best to look arch. "Just wait till old J. D. and those other buzzards — "

"So you bought him, did you? I was afraid that Cracker — "

"Me have trouble with a Cracker? Me? Why, it was like taking candy from a baby," he chuckled in huge delight. "Got the dog for thirty dollars. Here's the receipt. Fellow couldn't even sign his name. Had to make his mark. And you telling me he was tough!"

"You bought that dog for thirty dollars?" The gamekeeper shook his head with misgiving. "Why last year he charged a man $300 for one not half as good as this one. Somehow I'd feel better if he had stuck you, sir."

"Just had my trading pants on, son," the Judge clucked. "It's bred in the bone with us Carringtons, you know. Why, my grandpa was a horse-trader, my great-grandpa a horse-trader, and my great-great-grandpa a lightning-rod agent. Ha! Who outswapped that St. Louis gang in '34? And who took those Chicago cutthroats for a cool million in '21? And you worrying about a cracker's hoodwinking me! Get me up early in the morning, and have a good horse ready. That blasted mule! Honest, Jed, judging by what I saw today, old J. D. and the Bossy Run boys won't have such a walkover this Christmas, that they won't!"

The Bossy Run trials, be it recorded, were a pretty ritzy affair. In fact, probably the most exclusive in the country, being limited to not more than a dozen rather well-heeled Northerners who owned quail plantations in the same section and who held a field trial of their own every Christmas. Old cronies they were, but competition among them was none the less keen.

In their efforts to capture a ten-cent piece of blue ribbon, the gonfalon of Bossy Run, it is just possible that they had collectively spent enough to establish a small blue-ribbon factory, after the manner of field-trial zealots the world over. Winning meant more to them than a sizable coup on the stock market.

Game old roosters they were, who handled their own entries, took an immoderate pride in their dogs, and crowed lustily over their chopfallen adversaries. All the Judge had won thus far was a deal of ribbing, and his several discomfitures had begun to rankle in his otherwise tolerant bosom.

But the next day the Judge was back at the Cracker's cabin, looking, it must be confessed, somewhat less elated.

"Have you seen that — humph! There he is, sleeping under that confounded mule again. That dog refused to hunt. Left me in mid-field this morning."

"Kind of expectin' you, sir," said the Cracker. "Light and come in."

"No, I'll just get my dog and — You say you were expecting me?"

"Sort of," acknowledged the Cracker.

"Why?"

"Tuckahoe thar won't hunt without that mule is along, sir. He just won't hunt. Nary a step."

"Won't hunt without the mule!" the Judge exploded. "But that's ridiculous."

"Shore is."

"But why didn't you tell me?"

"Why didn't you axe me?" countered the Cracker.

"Why won't he hunt without the mule?"

"Well, mister, hit's thisaway. Tuckahoe thar was give to me as a puppy when his mammy died a-whelpin' over at Colonel Wentworth's plan'ation, and —"

"Wait a minute. Wentworth's place? Was he by any chance sired by that Holiday Jack dog of old J. D.'s?"

"Yes, sir. Tuck was the onliest pup in the litter that lived."

The Judge licked his chops in a very pleased manner, for J. D., as the redoubtable Colonel was called, was his bosom crony and archest enemy, having beaten him five times at Bossy Run. After getting out of his car, the Judge walked over and looked intently at the dozing dog.

"Yes, sir. Holiday Jack's head as sure as shooting. Now go ahead. I'm listening — hard!"

"Well, I put the puppy in old Mose's trough, intendin' to move 'im later. But Mose took a fancy to 'im right away. Kind of adopted the leetle 'un, lak he was a orphan. And the puppy sort of growed up in the stall. When he got about so-high, he took to followin' the mule around. And whenever anything got after 'im, Tuck would high-ball it for Mose, and that old gent would kick the everlastin' stuffin's outer anything that bothered the pup. Tuckahoe wouldn't let another dawg git nigh that mule, neither."

"Humph!" snorted the Judge. "Of all the fool things! No wonder that mule didn't step on him."

"Yes, sir, them two's powerful thick. Kind of sweethearts, you might say. I rode ole Mose when I trained Tuck as a youngster, and he just got in the habit, I reckon. I always hunt on Mose anyway, so hit don't unconvenience me none. No, sir, he won't hunt a tap for anybody without that mule is along. But then he'll out-hunt and out-find ary dawg in the country, as you saw yesterday."

"Humph!" And not finding sufficient relief, the Judge humphed again. "The damfoolest friendship I ever heard of! Absolutely the damfoolest. Well, what do you expect me to do about it?"

"Nothin,' mister. He's still your dawg."

"But Great Jerusalem, man! If he won't hunt without that mule —"

The Judge looked speculatively at the raw-boned mule and shuddered at the implications. Surely, 'twas as melancholy a specimen as he had ever seen, its demeanor reflecting neither pride of ancestry nor hope of salvation. "Well, supposing I wanted to buy that cussed mule — just supposing now — what would you want for him?"

The Cracker fished out a turnip, examined it minutely, then swapped it for another more to his liking.

"Air you satisfied ole Mose is what you air lookin' for in the way of mule?" he asked.

"Supposing he is," the Judge sighed.

"Mose is right smart of a mule. Sort of handed down in the family, you might say."

"You can name your figure anyway."

The Judge looked lugubriously at the mule. The mule looked lugubriously back at him. Five dollars would have been a fair price for him. Ten would have been generous. Fifteen dollars, the Judge appraised, would have been munificent indeed.

"Have a turnip?"

"No," the Judge wearily declined. "I've got to get back."

"Mose thar is the onliest mule I got right now. When a fellow disfurnishes hisself thataway —"

"Yes, yes. I understand all of that."

"Besides, I mout git into trouble with the Gov'ment by sellin' 'im. Me and the Gov'ment air in business together, you see."

"What are you doing for the Government?" The Judge was puzzled.

"I ain't a-raisin' cotton for 'em."

"What are you doing for the Government, then?"

"I just said I ain't a-raisin' cotton for 'em. They pays me so much a acre for all the cotton I don't raise. And how can a man not raise no cotton without no mule to raise it with?" he asked.

It was a species of logic which the Judge, in all his devious enterprises, had never confronted.

"But a-course," the Cracker added, "iffen I could git my figger —"

"What is your figure?"

"Things being as they air, I don't see how I could take less'n three hundred for 'im."

"Three hundred dollars!" spluttered the Judge, springing up from the running board. "You have the gall to ask me three hundred for that — that — "

"Mule," imperturbably supplied the Cracker.

"Can you sit there, sir, and with any semblance of honesty tell me that animal is worth any such price?"

"No, sir. I can't afford to sell 'im for what he's wuth. Some things air natcherly wuth more to some people than they air to others," the Cracker philosophized.

"I won't put up with it, that I won't!" the Judge stormed. "Here, chauffeur, put my dog in the car and let's go home. Why, it's grand larceny. It's high-handed robbery. It's — "

"Shore is," assented the Cracker."

Two days later the Judge was back again, to find Tuckahoe dozing in the customary place.

"That cussed dog chewed his rope off and broke through two fences. Reckon I'll have to take that mule after all."

"Powerful sorry, sir," the Cracker apologized. "Fact is, a feller was here yestiddy a-lookin' at that mule. Seems like he taken a fancy to ole Mose. A-course, I didn't promise the feller nothin' definite, but, things being as they air, I don't reckon I could take less'n three-fifty for 'im now."

The Judge started to protest to high heaven against the infamy of man, but when he saw the Cracker reaching composedly into his overalls he shuddered and resignedly reached for his pocketbook.

The Bossy Run trials excited the keenest rivalry in years. And no end of speculation. Not only by the Judge's showing up with a new entry, a big lemon-eared pointer of mysterious antecedents, but by his riding to his dogs on a raw-boned mule.

When the Bossy Run boys espied his rotund figure, dressed to kill and looking vastly uncomfortable, astride an ancient and sad-eyed plug, they pushed their hats back and looked at each other. Some said this, and some said that.

"There's old Judge Carrington, got more money than Carter had oats, riding to his dog on a ten-dollar mule," said one onlooker.

"There's something peculiar, I tell you. Almighty peculiar!" clucked another.

The Judge, they knew, had plenty of gaited aristocrats in his stable. And when a puzzled rival offered him a mount, the Judge declined, and declined in such a way as to close the subject permanently.

"What did he say?" asked a curious bystander.

The would-be benefactor grinned wryly. "Can't begin to tell you, gents. I ain't gifted that way."

When they learned, by discreet inquiry, that the mule had been hauled fifty miles in a truck, the mystery was hardly resolved. Old Mose, too, remained non-committal.

That night fellowship and mint-julep flowed freely. The Judge, his amiable and convivial self, had the time of his life. In tremendous humor he made life miserable for old J. D. and the rest — and got more than a little tight. For which he might be pardoned, for did he not flaunt a tiny blue ribbon in his lapel? Yes, the show had been all Tuckahoe's. That high-stepping and humorsome bounder had put the whole field to rout — utterly to rout.

True enough, a report got out that the Judge required the services of an osteopath the next morning. But every man has his detractors, and the rumor was no doubt a fiction invented by the Judge's discomfited adversaries.

When, with the advent of New Year, pressing matters called the Judge back to his New York office, he bethought himself of getting someone to look after the mule and the dog in his absence. So he called upon the Cracker again.

Would the Cracker consider boarding Tuckahoe and old Mose for the Judge until the next hunting season? The Cracker would, for a price. A price that even the ebullient Judge considered a trifle steep, and anybody else would have considered grand larceny. But that wasn't all. In winding up negotiations, the Cracker dug out an inevitable turnip and began fastidiously to peel it.

"Now what about exercisin' them two?" he asked.

"Exercise?"

"Funny thing about a mule," he said, as he bit into the turnip with the air of a connoisseur. "A mule will natcherly spile iffen he don't git exercise."

"Hadn't figured on that," the Judge demurred a moment, "but it seems reasonable. What kind of exercise would you suggest?"

"Well, ole Mose is too old and set in his ways for anything new. Wouldn't enjoy hisself none at some newfangled doings. Plowin' cotton, now, and sich as that. . . . "

To which the Judge agreed.

"And Tuckahoe thar?"

"Well, what do you suggest for him?"

The Cracker pondered the matter gravely for a moment.

"A-huntin' with me and ole Mose, I reckon. About lak we always been doing, to keep his nose freshened up. Kind of around the edges of your preserve. Just the edges, sort of."

Back in New York, the Bossy Run boys resumed their weekly session of pinochle at their exclusive club. And, as usual, they often took the Judge for a ride. But when they nicked him for a thousand or two, the Judge didn't seem to mind. Just quietly took out his wallet and held up a piece of faded ribbon.

# Birds Scare Me

I STILL get a bit rattled when I step into a covey of birds. And I have been hunting them ever since the days when a country schoolmaster was forcing certain facts on my consciousness, namely: that eight times seven is *also* fifty-six, that Boise is the capital of Idaho, that the Mississippi River has several tributaries, and that Arkansas is bounded on the north by something or other. In fact, I date back to Fry's Geography. And that wasn't yesterday, my friend.

Down through the years, I have peregrinated around the country considerably, campaigned against Bob White through much of his habitat, and hunted so indefatigably as repeatedly to jeopardize such connubial bliss as my household knows. You gunners understand, I'm sure.

Yet, I confess without shame, an exploding covey still speeds the heartbeat under my scrawny chest, raises sand with my metabolism, and makes the hair stand up on the back of my neck. And I still do fool things.

In spite of this I am perennially advising youngsters. I have been known to go considerably out of my way to instruct them in the fundamentals.

"Now see here," I say, "what is there to get nervous about? A covey of birds is just — a covey of birds. Don't let 'em ruffle you. Just march in confidently and bide your time. The arch-enemy of wing-shooting is tenseness. Relax, my boy, relax, and it'll be as simple as your ABC's. And another thing — "

But I am forced to the melancholy confession that I do not always follow my own advice. Who does? As Shakespeare's Portia so eloquently sighed: "I can easier teach twenty what were good to be done, than be one of the twenty to follow mine own teaching."

I still stoop to the juvenile folly of broadsiding a whole covey instead of singling out a target, as a respectable bird hunter is supposed to do. I still forget to watch the singles down, so engrossed am I in the spectacle at hand. Sometimes, when birds continue to pop up around me, I get thumb-fingered and lose precious seconds in reloading.

And when a big covey explodes under my very garters, I sometimes forget to release the safety catch. I stand with a look of imbecilic ecstasy on my face, dazedly squeezing a dead trigger until the covey fades into the distant landscape. Then I berate myself eloquently for days thereafter.

Here am I, *genus homo* himself, the crowning glory of the bipeds, the masterpiece of creation, the paragon of the animal world, and I haven't got gumption enough to release a safety catch!

Don't let this tickle your risibilities too much, brother. You can probably recall sappy interludes of your own. And these queer quirks of behavior might have something to do with the way you find your birds.

Do you prefer them flushed or pointed? That question is not so witless as it sounds. Can you shoot better when half-a-dozen dogs are statuesquely frozen around a bevy, or when you stumble slapdash into a skulking covey and they fly up from under your feet?

A surprising number of hunters get a better percentage on unadvertised rises.

"Don't tell anybody, but I shoot better when a covey pops up unannounced," one friend admitted.

"But when your dogs are pointing, don't you have more time to get set for the rise?" I asked.

"Yes. The longer the dogs point, the more time I have to get set — and go to pieces!" he replied with a dry grin.

Last season, I saw a man who was usually a poor shot stumble headlong into a covey and get a beautiful triple.

"How did you do that?" I wanted to know. "You've been missing all day."

"Simple," he answered. "I shot before my blood pressure found out about it."

"You mean you shot well because you didn't have time to get scared?"

"That's about it, I reckon."

Not long ago a companion and I were hunting with seven dogs, our aggregate pool. One after another, each in his characteristic posture, every dog came up and froze on a covey. There they stood as immobile as alabaster statuettes in the swaying broom straw. A picturesque scene it was, a tableau such as warms the cockles of the hardest heart. I shall not soon forget it.

Nor shall I soon forget the mortifying sequel: when twenty birds popped up from the tight little circle, we failed to cut a single blessed feather.

"Too damn dramatic," my companion aptly observed. "Let's rest a while. My very bones are aching. I feel as though I'd been sitting in an electric chair and waiting for somebody to press the button."

Too much preamble *is* nervously exhausting. A friend with whom I occasionally hunt is addicted to a habit that, innocent enough in itself, has a ruinous effect on my shooting.

Whenever our dogs point, he spends several minutes appraising their postures, commenting on their crotchets, and admiring them generally. This fellow is quite a connoisseur, and he enjoys the prelude immensely. But for me it is prolonging the agony. When the inventory is finished, I step up — and go to pieces.

I can admire with the best of them, but waxing rhapsodical over four or five pointing dogs when I am already nervous enough is like falling in love with the nurse who is giving you ether. Just not the time for esthetics.

Ground-running coveys can be especially nerve-racking. Yesterday our dogs repeatedly pointed, broke, and pointed again, while I repeatedly prepared for a rise that didn't materialize. After 200 yards of such maneuvering, and innumerable "get sets," I slumped weakly to a stump.

"If this keeps up much longer," I sighed, wiping the sweat from my forehead, "you'll have to get a stretcher for me. Think I've got water on the knee or something."

But please don't get the idea that my wife's husband is a bum shot. I seldom feel the necessity of apologizing to my companions. As a matter of fact, I am a middling-good shot, and you will get quail on toast whenever you come to my house. If you are skeptical, come and see. I am just telling you how scared I am when a bouncing bevy of birds erupts in front of me.

Are you more effective when the rise is a large one or when it is small? Do you shoot best when a big covey or a segment or even a twosome pops up?

Some hunters find a big simultaneous rise an upsetting business. I am one of these. A handful is my meat. When a twosome gets up, I commonly get both. When a covey of twenty bounces up, truth to tell, I sometimes draw a blank.

When a populous covey whirs off in close formation, few hunters seem to miss. But when I face a simultaneous rise of twenty, and every bird instantly becomes a law unto himself and grabs a ticket for a different destination, I often switch my affections from one absconding target to another. Finally, when my shilly-shallying is over, every last bird is likely out of range, and I emerge birdless and a bit chastened.

*Many a man forfeits a certain single by trying to make a dubious double.* I am italicizing that partly for my own benefit. Maybe I will remember it better — but chances are I won't.

What is the largest covey of quail you ever saw? Or more accurately, the largest rise, since coveys often feed together or just go a-visiting. Have you ever lain in a warm bed on a frosty night and dreamed of stepping into forty or fifty birds that flew low and straight away? What poor sinner hasn't? But did you ever actually have it happen to you? I did, and it's not what it's cracked up to be.

It was on our old homestead in Virginia. Our orchard lot was encircled by a rambling rail fence overgrown with honeysuckle. The field, rank with ragweed and partridge peas, was a veritable quail factory. One day, after I had vainly trudged the orchard over, my shaggy setter "stood" at the base of an old sawdust pile. Such sophisticated terms as "point" and "quail" never swam into my ken until years later. Our dogs just "stood" a covey of "partridges."

Several coveys must have been socializing about the sunny slope of the sawdust pile, for fully sixty birds whizzed up and went whirring away, low and straight, through the orchard. Well, I had snitched my older brother's automatic, and I gleefully opened a barrage that must have been a record breaker. When the echoes died away and peace settled in the old orchard again, I realized, with galling humiliation, that I had bagged not a single bird. There were just too many. "Too much sugar for a cent," as our boyhood language phrased it.

It was years before I could contemplate the debacle without chagrin, and still more years before the incident ripened into chuckling reminiscence.

When I first began bird hunting, I hoped — I ardently hoped — that we would find no birds. When the dogs struck a trail, I hoped the trail would peter out. Even when they pointed, I hoped the point would be unproductive, that the covey might flush prematurely, or that some intercession of Providence might keep me from getting a shot.

Such a confession entitles me to a preferred rating in the order of simps, until you understand the *why* behind it. Then maybe something in your own experience might make you a little sympathetic.

It was simply fear of embarrassment. I was hunting with my older brothers, all of whom were creditable shots, and I was afraid I would miss. In fact, I *knew* I would miss. As long as no birds were found, as long as there was nothing to shoot at, I was one of the gang and as good a hunter as anybody else. So I would trudge behind them the live-long day, hoping against hope that I would not be so unfortunate as to get a shot.

Not until I began hunting alone did I overcome my defeatism. There is only one way to learn quail shooting: *go by your own sweet self*. Then if you make a fool of yourself, it's your own business. You won't be embarrassed when you miss. A man is never embarrassed, regardless of what happens, unless somebody else is along to witness his foolishness.

And especially should a beginner avoid the mistake of hunting with some altruistic but misguided soul who insists that the beginner take the first shot. That is the high road to ruin, because the learner's gentlemanly instincts will prompt him to shoot too quickly so that his benefactor will have a chance.

Yes, I still do goofy things aplenty when I am bird hunting. A big covey rise rattles me because it thrills me. I go back the second time because I made mistakes the first time. There is always a *freshness* about a game in which you make mistakes. If the time ever comes when an exploding bevy ceases to upset me, I think I shall quit bird hunting.

Do I envy those nerveless fellows who can walk imperturbably into a covey of birds? Not so much. They are probably liars anyway. Theoretical experts are often disappointing in the field. Let twenty pieces of feathered dynamite explode under their feet and go gyrating and spinning among the tree tops, and these selfsame experts are likely to reveal very human qualities!

In any case, they are not so enviable. They may get more birds, but do they enjoy it as much? Verily, it is more fun to pursue than to overtake, as many an erstwhile amorous swain could testify if guaranteed immunity!

Bob White still gets my goat. I hope he always will.

# Are You Goofy Too?

WHAT IS the goofiest bait ever used to catch a fish? While fishing in the Chesapeake bay, I saw a fellow rip a pearl button from his shirt and haul in a big croaker. While fishing for chain pickerel in Georgia, I saw a guide, who had lost his bucktail, nonchalantly cut a strip from his red flannel underwear and continue fishing. And in Tennessee I saw a Democrat catch a bass on a live mouse — just hooked the ill-starred rodent through the back and shooed him across the pool.

But in each case, it is to be ardently hoped, the fish in question was not altogether representative in his tastes.

It would be interesting if we could all get together and hold a round-table on the wackiest bait we ever caught fish with. But all it would prove is that some fish are as goofy as the people who fish for them. And before the meeting adjourned, somebody would be calling somebody else a three-decker liar. What I want to bring before the house is not some fluky once-in-a-wonder, but a few unorthodox and screwy-sounding baits that are actually very effective in some localities.

Ever use goldfish for live bait? Try them sometime. We often use them, instead of ordinary minnows, for crappie and bass.

They have a lot to recommend them. Goldfish are tough-mouthed, stay alive well, and are hard workers. No pampering is necessary. Indeed, they may be used repeatedly, so much vitality do they have. And sometimes they are the only minnows we city slickers can get on our occasional off day.

We buy the small ones for fifty cents a dozen. A good many naturally escape from the hook, and although their color makes them a target for marauders, some of these escapees undoubtedly grow up. Especially in the semitropical waters of the lower South. They almost never bite, however. But I shall never forget the wonderment on the face of an old darky, patiently fishing for carp, when he hauled in a twelve-inch goldfish.

"Lawsy, Cap'n, Ah done caught myself a gole-plated carp. 'Deed Ah has!"

There's nothing very screwy about using goldfish for bait. But on a hundred-mile stretch of the upper James, in Virginia, they do use a wacky bait, one of the wackiest anybody ever heard of. Last summer, while chatting with a storekeeper in the Blue Ridge, I observed a curious transaction. A gangling mountain lad entered and passed a dozen eggs across the counter.

"Fish bait," he laconically demanded.

The storekeeper handed him what appeared to be two cakes of soap. The egg trader pocketed them and slouched out.

"Pardon my curiosity, but what sort of fish bait do you sell?" I inquired.

"Soap. White laundry soap," the storekeeper answered.

"Soap? Just ordinary soap?" I was incredulous.

"Sure. Everybody up and down the river uses it for catfish bait, especially on trot-lines. Sell two or three cases a week in fishin' season."

"I know catfish are not very fastidious feeders, but soap — surely, mister you're pulling my leg!"

"Gonna bait my trot-line now," he said. "Come and see for yourself."

Cutting the soap into small squares, he baited his hooks, while I watched with mounting skepticism. Two hours later we ran the line — and took off a dozen channel cats, some of them weighing two or three pounds. The channel cat, by the way, has little affinity with the infamous bullhead and such degenerate scavengers. In cool mountain streams, the channel cat is fast and frisky, the gamest of all the cats, and one of the most savory morsels to be found anywhere.

"By and large," the storekeeper remarked, "soap is a first-rate fish bait, considerin' how cheap and handy it is. The travelin' salesman sells more soap on the river than in the rest of his territory put together. And nobody can tell me" — he spat eloquently — "that these here folks is a-wastin' any of hit a-washin' their own carcasses!"

Later, in my peregrinations up and down the James, I verified what he said. White laundry soap is indeed orthodox catfish bait. The discovery gave me a scintillating idea I'm going to try out sometime: I have some highly perfumed soap that my mother-in-law gave me for Christmas three years ago. If ordinary soap is good, that precious stuff should be super-extra de luxe!

In a little South Carolina town, something brand-new swam into my ken. An enthusiastic fellow I met there called me aside. "Doc, I got the cockroach rights on three stores. Three!" He impressively held up his fingers.

"Cockroach rights?"

"Sure. Everybody around here fishes with 'em. And I got exclusive rights on three places. Tell you what," he added confidentially, "I know of another store — "

"But how do you catch 'em?" I asked, waiving all proprietary intentions.

"Cockroach traps."

"And how do you fish with them?"

"Well, you take a big fat roach and — I'll tell you what. Meet me here tomorrow mornin,' and I'll take you to the creek."

I declined with voluble regrets. A previous engagement with a dentist or something. Guess I'm just not the cockroach type. But far be it from me to traduce the characters of you cockroach connoisseurs!

Everybody in that town was daft about cockroaches. The corner druggist proudly displayed two dozen, and critically pronounced them to be ideal in size and disposition. And they told me of some fellow, with more initiative than the rest, who had sent off somewhere and got a special brand for breeding purposes. So help me! Strangely enough, it had never before occurred to me that a cockroach had a family tree.

They also told me of another citizen who, in the prolonged absence of his wife, went into the cockroach business in his own home, on a rather ambitious scale, and who found himself in great domestic disfavor when his wife suddenly returned.

Often, in widely separated sections, I have found cockroaches highly regarded as bait, but I am not able personally to testify to their effectiveness. Nor do I expect to be. For forty years my relation with cockroaches has been one of mutual disrespect, and I don't intend, in the evening of life, to go scraping up acquaintance with such characters. How many of you gents have ever tried them?

Have you ever fished with the cicada, or seventeen-year locust?

In 1928, a year I shall long remember, I was spending the summer in a small-town hotel in central Virginia and fishing pretty regularly in the James river. My chief interest was bass, until the proprietor of the hotel suggested that his guests might like an occasional mess of catfish.

So across the river I set a trot-line, lawful enough then, but since outlawed in Virginia. For bait, I was using long green earthworms found in the false banks, a worm with a peculiar and almost ineradicable odor. On a whim, I picked up a live cicada from the boat and impaled it on a hook. When I ran the line, that hook had a sizable cat on it. Paddling to shore, I captured a dozen seventeen-yearers and tried them again. The results were such that thereafter I renounced all other bait, using cicadas throughout the summer.

That same year witnessed one of the heaviest infestations of cicadas ever known in that section, the insects being so numerous and voracious as to kill large trees. Small boys kept me plentifully supplied — at ten cents a hundred. I have never tried anything that cats would go after so ravenously. They would start gobbling up these cicadas before the line settled to the bottom. Mine Host, and all his neighbors to boot, were well supplied that summer with channel cats, the excellence of which I have already extolled.

It was one plague I was in favor of, and I have been looking forward, I confess, to another visitation. I had not the least compunction about putting the cicada to such ignoble use, although my mother, pious and beloved lady that she was, thought it was something of a sacrilege, and was apprehensive lest some punishment be visited upon my hapless head.

One of my vivid boyhood recollections is of catching tobacco worms for my brothers to go fishing with. In spite of the tobacco grower's most valiant efforts, along in August and September his crop is likely to be infested with ferocious-looking green worms, and any fisherman who stops by a roadside patch to pluck a few for bait is regarded as a friend indeed. Throughout the black-tobacco section, these worms are still highly regarded as an all-purpose bait.

A similar worm prized throughout the South is that which feeds on the catalpa tree, generally pronounced "catawba" down here. So highly esteemed are these worms that there is quite a seasonal traffic in picking and selling them to fishermen. I paid three cents apiece for them this year. Farsighted sportsmen often plant groves of catalpas to insure a never-failing supply. Such voracious feeders are they that they often completely strip a tree of foliage within a few days. But catalpa worms are not without their enemies.

Just recently, a horde of starlings swooped down upon a catalpa near my house and devoured every worm within an hour, to the great joy of the tree owner but to my own dismay, since I had been waiting for days for the greenies to reach fishing size.

As a bait for bream and redbreast, the catalpa worm is one of the very best. It is surpassed, in my judgment, only by the drone larva of the honeybee. Expert breamers often turn catalpas inside out before hooking them. 'Tis a practice hardly recommending itself to squeamish stomachs, and an operation I lay little claim to expertness in.

The common earthworm, of course, is still the most-used bait in the wide, wide world. Most of us are content to use earthworms as they are, without attempting to gild the lily. But there are quite a number of fishermen who hold in disdain the ordinary unflavored species — who go in for medicated worms only. There seems to be little uniformity of treatment. These enterprising gents doctor their worms with an impressive variety of oils, essences, tinctures, and extracts.

When I was a boy I was entranced by two advertisements I found in a discarded magazine. One was of a magic solution into which worms were dipped to make them irresistible — an amazing secret formula only recently perfected. It would enable me to catch more fish than I could tote, as the accompanying picture so convincingly portrayed. It would make me the envy of all my friends.

The second advertisement was of a self-setting automatic fish-hook that caught 'em while the owner slept. All you had to do — Well, it was simple enough. So, in great fear lest the supply be exhausted, I sold my three ducks and ordered both items.

It was the beginning of my boyhood disenchantment. The magic bait proved a humiliating flop. The automatic hook auto-maticked itself around a root at the bottom of the hole, and for all I know it's still there.

Ever since, I have entertained a deepseated suspicion of magic formulas and secret solutions — and automatic hooks. Not that I was permanently cured. In fact, I have done a deal of wondering, and some little experimenting, since I came to man's estate. Medicated bait has possibilities.

A lot of estimable folk wouldn't *think* of going fishing without their particular brand of magic. Last year an old codger called me aside, glanced circumspectly around for possible eaves-droppers, and intrusted me with a solution that would make bream "cut each other's throats" to get on my hook. All I had to do was to perfume my worms with a few drops of the precious essence.

I bought all the stuff the druggist had, followed directions punctiliously, and prepared to gloat over the discomfiture of my companion the next day. And I did get seven nice bream. But my companion, sitting beside me and fishing with unglamorized worms, caught thirteen. So I slyly dumped my secret essence into the creek.

In North Carolina I met a druggist who had almost fished himself into bankruptcy. But he wasn't satisfied. Sweeping his hand toward shelves filled with unpronounceable essences and tinctures and extracts, he announced:

"I'm going to take earthworms and flavor them with every-thing up there, one after another. And, brother, I'm going to find what flavor they like, and hit the jackpot!"

I remain something of a skeptic, agreeing in the main with an uncouth but stout-hearted friend of mine who snorted:

"I'll take my fishin' worms as God-amighty made 'em. When I get low-down enough to squirt perfume on fishin' worms, danged if I don't quit!"

You can't make a silk purse out of a sow's ear, they say, but you *can* take a wooden clothespin — a homely, naked, and un-imaginative clothespin — and make one of the deadliest bass getters ever contrived. Just add hooks, flounce it up a bit, and there you are.

The clothespin plug, already famous in some sections, is relatively new. I saw it first on Lake Murray, South Carolina, nine years ago. A farmer's boy, having seen our casting plugs, allowed he could make one of the dadgum things. And dadgum if he didn't! It cost him, including the fixings, about fifteen cents. Now craftsmen up and down the seaboard are making them for a growing clientele.

A lot of nice people say a fish will bite best what he's most used to, but the exceptions are both numerous and brilliant. Surely, no bass ever yet found an edible clothespin on his menu.

When a boy I often fished with crickets, laboriously moving many a wheat shock to find them, though I had been notably absent when the shocking was done! I've known trap fishermen who used roasting ears in their traps; catfishermen who verily doted on chicken entrails as bait. And one ingenious fellow who, protesting against the price of pork rind, bought a full-size rubber diaper and cut it into strips. This was before the Age of Shortages, of course.

Many an excellent bait has been discovered by sheer accident. Many used regularly in some sections are unknown in others. A lot of baits you and I use seem goofy to the other fellow. And no doubt the other fellow catches fish with things you and I wot not of. Let's hold an anglers' bazaar and exchange opinions.

What goofy baits have you found good?

# When Your Shooting Slumps

Dɪᴅ ʏᴏᴜ ever get so you couldn't hit a barn door? I got that way in the middle of the quail season one year. It was pretty bad, I can tell you. Why, one afternoon I found eight coveys and bagged only five birds. Ordinarily, of course, I would have — But there's scant comfort in post-mortems.

My neighbor, a sympathetic and thorough sort of fellow, came over to diagnose the trouble.

"Sleepin' well?" he began.

"I've always been an expert at that."

"How's the vision? Maybe your glasses need changing."

"No. Eyes all right."

"Maybe you're worried about that note that's coming due. The best gunner in the world couldn't shoot well when. . . . "

"Coming due is no new experience for *that* note," I laughed.

"Then it's more'n apt to be your liver. I can always tell when my liver ain't functionin' well by the way I play golf. What you need is a good . . . "

"Got one of the best livers in the country," I defended warmly.

"Well, then," he sighed, "I reckon your shootin' is just a little off."

And that's about the only diagnosis that's safe in such cases. My unaccountable slump lasted for a week, then just as unaccountably passed off and left me shooting normally again. I have slumps occasionally, maybe once or twice a year, but I've stopped trying to figure them out. And I've stopped worrying about them . . . *almost.*

They are the common lot of all good wing-shots. If you do much quail-shooting, the chances are so-many-to-one that at times, for some obscure reason, you get so definitely and horribly "off" that you honestly feel you couldn't hit a bull in the rump with a $10 spade. No matter how good a shot you ordinarily are, either.

It is also true of our misguided brother who smacks a golf ball up and down the fairways, who plays tennis, shoots skeet, or does anything else that requires the same nicety of coordination — *the sixth sense we have when the other five are working together.* There are days on which we can't do anything wrong. Other days on which we can't do anything right. And the thing passes understanding.

If you've hunted much, you'll know there are days on which you can't miss a bird. You pluck the dizziest customers with surprising ease. And other days when you can't hit one flying straight down Main Street with a 10 gauge gun. As an old darky, one of the few competent quail shots of his race I ever knew, feelingly remarked:

"Dey is times, Cap'n, when dis here ole britches-loader shoot heself. I don't have to do a t'ing! And dey is odder times when de Debbil heself cyan't hit a sassafras wid her. How come dat, Cap'n?"

If you hunt a lot and you never get off, maybe it's because you're never *on!* Maybe you are like a traffic cop I heard about:

"That fellow is undoubtedly the most even-tempered man I ever saw."

"Is that so?" I asked admiringly.

"Yeah. Stays mad all the time."

If you come into court and say you do a lot of wing-shooting, and that you are not subject to an occasional "streak o' missing," you might be telling the truth. Might be. But the probability is that you are allowing yourself to fall into a verbal inexactitude. You can't hit a fellow in the nose for that.

If you do hunt a lot and you really never, never get off, you are just a freak of nature, and I have no sympathy for you. I haven't any use for anybody who is always right.

Dogs are subject to slumps too. Even the best of them have off days, and often without any ascertainable cause. Some times a dog, apparently in good condition, can't for the life of him pin his birds down. You have seen that, I am sure. However hard he tries, he bungles the job, while his master berates him for his maladroitness. The dog's precision just deserts him, and he is often aware that something is wrong and is decidedly unhappy about it himself.

Sometimes such a condition is induced by physical trouble, but just as often no cause is discoverable. When dog and man both get off at the same time, the whole world just ain't worth a tinker's dam and it's right hard to be philosophical about it. When this happens, I love the fellow who can call his dog in and say:

"Old man, you can't smell 'em and I can't hit 'em. We're both off. Let's go home, get us a good supper, and forget about hunting for a few days."

To be consistently good is hardly human, and really not much fun. Most of us ordinary mortals are streaky and freaky. We shoot by spells. Off and on. We make the most of our streaks when we have them, knowing full well they won't last forever. As Mr. John Oakhurst, gambler, pithily remarked in Bret Harte's famous tale: "Luck is a mighty queer thing. All you know about it for certain is that it's bound to change. And it's finding out when it's going to change that makes you."

What is it that makes us sometimes shoot away above our heads? Golfers call it being *hot*. It is an intangible but terribly real something — often the only difference between first-money and also-ran. A hot amateur can whip the stuffings out of a cold professional.

I once asked a famous tournament golfer: "Exactly what do you mean by being hot?"

"You don't know what it is, where it came from, how long it's going to last, or where it goes when it leaves you. But when you've got it you're unbeatable, and when it deserts you it's pluperfect misery," he answered.

Nothing is more surprising than how dumb a man can be at times, especially a bird hunter. I happen to be a reasonably good shot, but I have walked up thundering coveys in the wide open and let them all sail away without shooting. Just stood like a dumb cluck in a brain fog. Should be ashamed to admit it, but it's a fact. Sometimes I don't think I have as much sense as I think I have. I have watched many an easy shot sail away while debating whether it was within range, suddenly deciding that it *had* been within range after all, and getting furious with myself for realizing it too late.

Very often some physical upset underlies a persistent streak of missing. A mean cold, a sleepless night, eating some food to which one is allergic, all may undermine our reserve powers, make our senses less acute, and dull our reactions. A lazy liver is often the *bete noire* behind a slump. A discerning companion of mine often declares: "I can always tell when Bill is constipated by the way he shoots."

It doesn't take much to get a man off, and not much to get him back on. I have a Virginia brother-in-law, a crack shot, who invariably does poorly when he comes down to South Carolina to hunt with me. It's the coffee, he says, and it may be, but I subscribe to the theory that he's worrying over his affairs at home. You can't shoot well when you are divided. You've got to be *all there.*

The trouble may be physical without our being aware of it. A physical state may induce a mental state, although neither obtrudes itself on our consciousness. Neither outcrops. We can just feel bad without knowing it, I suppose.

Here is what puzzles me: all of us can testify that on the very days we have felt our worst, we have often shot our best; and on the days we have felt best, we have often shot our worst. We can remember particular days on which this has happened. There's something metaphysical about this business. You are always safe in calling anything you can't figure out that.

One thing is mortal certain: getting mad won't do any good. Neither does cussing enter into the therapeutics of the case. The more you cuss the more you'll have to cuss. I've demonstrated the futility of this measure myself.

And don't agonize. The more you do the more prolonged your slump is likely to be. In fact, that might have brought it on. *Failure often comes from trying too hard.* Bird shooting, like a lot of other games, is easy unless you make it hard. Trying to outshoot the other fellow is one of the surest ways of inviting trouble.

Such competitive shooting is bad business all the way round. To make a gallant game bird merely a target for marksmanship is hardly a gentleman's pastime. And it will adversely affect your shooting, making you tense and over-anxious.

Trying to outshoot the other fellow makes it too *important*. When you get into a slump, go out by yourself with one sure dog, and content yourself with one shot on a rise. Take it un-importantly and leisurely. Say to yourself: "What if I do miss a few birds. There will be other days. Don't need so many anyway."

If your bad streak is an especially stubborn one, quit hunting for a few days; immerse yourself in something else, something different. It is a prime time to overhaul your boat, catch up with your correspondence, or get back into the good graces of your wife by doing the thousand-and-one things about the house that you, being a promising kind of fellow, have intended doing ever so long. Sometimes the best way to find something you've lost is to quit looking for it. Ever notice how often it will turn up?

Another thing is certain too. A slump period is the worst time in the world to do any experimenting. If you *must* experiment, experiment *inexpensively*. It is the best time known, for instance, *not* to trade guns, or to make any major adjustments. Because as sure as fate and taxes, you'll rue them later.

I know a slumper who persuaded himself that his vision was defective and who enriched his oculist without benefit to himself. Another who spent half the night manicuring the stock of his gun. When he got his shooting pants back on, the gun didn't fit. Still another who decided that his gun barrels were too long and had a gunsmith amputate them, to his everlasting regret. And a melancholy fellow who, always thorough in what he did, turned against his gun and swapped it for a new one.

Two weeks later he was walking his pants off trying to find the man who had his old gun, and he had to pay a premium when he found it. Moral: The gun wasn't in a slump!

When you're in a slump, your judgment just ain't worth a durn. Gun fit is of prime importance, of course, but trading off an old companion with which you have always shot well, or making any major adjustments on it, is not only ingratitude but costly folly. If you feel your gun is suspect, don't buy another one. *Borrow* one and try it first. It may be you and not the gun. If you've simply got to make adjustments, make minor ones.

If you want to switch to another shell, fine. If you think you can shoot better with another you probably can. But be sure you don't do anything you can't undo later.

Nothing is so easy as bird shooting to a man who can shoot birds. Nothing is so hard to a man who can't. If you happen to be one of the latter, don't let it get you down. It may be a compliment to your intelligence!

I have derived a deal of comfort from an observation I once heard an old sportsman make:

"A *smart* man is not apt to be a good shot," he said. "He's got too much imagination. Thinks too much. He misses because he is afraid he is going to miss. Takes a man who hasn't got much on his mind to shoot well. No, sir, a smart man ain't apt to be a good bird shot. Never saw one yet that was."

"Well," I said, "that's the most encouraging thing I ever heard."

And about that time my wife, who is a realistic sort of woman, drifted by and said sweetly:

"What makes you think that applies to you, *darling?*"

# Santee's Gentleman

"SANTEE here?"

"Ain't know where Santee."

"That's funny," I said. "Promised to go bird hunting with me today. We agreed to meet here."

It was unlike Santee to fail me. I drove to the next cabin.

"Santee here?"

"Santee a gennerman now."

"What?"

"Santee a gennerman now."

I would make a gentleman of him if he kept me waiting much longer! Ought to go on without him. Well, hardly. I had tried that once. Two days later I emerged from the swamp with my clothing in tatters, and a profound respect for the accomplishments of my black specialist.

For Santee was the best guide — and the biggest scamp — in the whole swamp. The one tribute I ungrudgingly paid. The other Santee himself modestly acknowledged. Not only was he my guide and game toter, but privy councilor as well. My confidence restorer and alibi concocter when I shot badly, my admiring and voluble gallery when I shot well. Santee, who "kept the census" on certain over-populous bevies of artful dodgers that commuted between the swamp and the wasted fields near-by and might occasionally be caught off guard — if you knew their schedules. And Santee did. Find him I must. I drove to a third cabin.

"Santee here?"

"Santee rich now."

"What!"

"Santee rich now."

"What in the devil are you talking about! I've been listening to this tomfoolery long enough. How rich is he?"

"Santee have $100."

"How on earth did he get so much money?" I demanded.

"Santee have $100," was the only enlightenment to be had, leaving me with the inference that my erstwhile guide had some-how come into unprecedented wealth and was out "pleasurin' heself" amongst the fleshpots.

So Santee had not only turned gentleman, but he had gone plutocratic on me. A Santee with $2 in his pocket would have been of no earthly account to anybody for a week. I will not say that he was the laziest human being I ever saw. But I can say, without trespassing on his sensibilities, that I have never known a man who held any sort of useful labor in such lofty disesteem. Santee, shiftless, harum-scarum, carefree Santee with $100 was just an incongruity. Certainly it was unlikely that he had come by any such sum honestly.

The idea gave me a start. How *had* he come by it? Several times Santee had been in minor difficulties with the local magistrate, and once, when I was desperately in need of a guide, I had paid his fine and relieved the county roads of an indifferent workman. In common with other swamp darkies, Santee had a genius for petty larceny. But no amount of petty larceny in that neighborhood would have netted any such sum. Yet it was an undodgeable fact that Santee had it.

Here was a mystery that needed investigation — and promptly. I went to a cabin occupied by his mother-in-law. Here, if any-where, I would learn the harrowing particulars.

"How did Santee get all that money?"

"Santee *say* he sole he gun," she answered with emphasis. The gleam in her eye told me that she, too, was nursing her wrath to keep it warm.

"Sold his gun? Who in the world was fool enough to buy it?"

"I ain't know. Santee sole he gun." And that was all I could get from the most clannish and uncommunicative folk in the world when a white man comes questioning.

So Santee had sold his gun for $100. And they expected me to believe that, me who knew Santee's gun. I conjured up a vision of that remarkable gun and shook my head dismally.

If my worst fears were confirmed, I might have to get along without a guide for months, indeed for years, depending upon the temper of the judge. Something must be done. I first struck the trail of my quarry at a small crossroads store, where, it seemed, Santee had converted a heroic portion of his newly won legacy into cologne, hair straightener, yards and yards of red calico, remnants of dizzy percale, women's stockings, high-heeled shoes, and other articles calculated to dazzle a dusky belle. Then he had stuffed his bright allurements into a large sack and swaggered out to look for temptation.

"Jest about every unprotected female in this here neighborhood has got herself a brand-new red dress," the storekeeper told me. "And that Santee outsmells a Georgia polecat. Of course, I ain't complainin' none," he grinned at his empty shelves.

So Santee was cutting a wide swath. From what I could gather, he had become a distinct social success overnight. I soon picked up the scarlet trail of his largess. Every woman I met, except his own wife, showed signs of his flaring favor.

I finally found the prodigal — in the cabin of a certain "widder 'oman." There he sat, humped over a table, a big, red handkerchief under his chin, and a baked 'possum in front of him. The 'possum was as fat as a young shoat and piled high with melted butter and sweet potatoes. Behind him stood Delilah, shooing away imaginary flies and ogling her half-stupefied swain. It was much too much.

"Santee," I began, "you unholy cross between a pussy willow and a mud turtle, why didn't you meet me this morning? And what is all this damned foolishness I hear about your selling your gun for a hundred dollars?"

"Hit's de Gawd's troof, Cap'n."

"You really sold that gun for that much? Who bought it?"

"A white gennerman, Cap'n."

"Santee, you are lying and I know it. Nobody would have been such a fool. But I'm going to have you jailed if you actually sold that thing for —"

"Cap'n, hit was worth hit — to dat gennerman," he defended warmly. "Hit wus a bargain."

Whereupon, my entrapped prodigal took refuge in dignified silence. I confessed myself temporarily balked. But I would get the story out of him later, during the day's hunt. And it had better be a good one.

Through the rest of the day, however, he followed along strangely reticent, an air of injured innocence about him. Again and again I tried to inveigle him into casual conversation, to get nothing but guarded monosyllables for my pains. Plainly he was not to be tricked into a confession. But late in the afternoon chance gave me my cue. As a covey of swampers scurried up from the broomstraw and rocketed away, Santee remarked:

" 'Twus right here hit happened. De white gennerman was a-standin' thar and — "

He caught himself quickly, with a look of deep chagrin. Here was business more important than following those singles. Propping my gun against a sapling, I lit in on the luckless Santee. I accused him of everything from battery and assault to multiple mayhem, manslaughter, and malice prepense. I threatened him with everything from spontaneous combustion to mandamus and habeas corpus. It was the habeas corpus, I think, that melted him.

"Cap'n," he finally began, "I ain't tole you 'cause I knowed you wouldn't believe hit. Hit do sound powerful onreasonable, for a fack. But I'm a-gwine ter tell you de troof, de Gawd's troof. You know dat gennerman fum de Nawth dat hired me to hunt wid 'im las' week? Well sir, he wus one o' de greatest gennermen dish here country ever produce, escusin' present company, Cap'n. Dat gennerman had heself a gole-triggered gun, solid gole! An' he name wus writ on de stock in gole. Cost 'im a thousand dollar, I specks. An' he shells wus specially made for him. Not de store-bought shells lak us uses. An' he paid

me a dollar *and a quarter* a day," he said significantly. I paid
him only a dollar. "Yessir, he was one o' de han'somes' gennermen —"

"You've taken care of his gentility pretty well, Santee. Now
let's hear exactly what happened when he was in the field.
Could he shoot?"

"Could he shoot? *Could he shoot!*" he repeated with wither-
ing scorn. "He wus de shootin'est gennerman I ever laid eyes
on, dat he wus. Us hunted for four days — Mossy Crossy, Po'
Chance, Bull Hill, an' all dem places nigh de swamp, an' us
found plenty o' birds. Plenty o' birds, Cap'n. De wedder was
damp and de dawgs work fine. An' whenever dey would p'int,
he would march up des lak a ginral. He would brace heself des
lak dish here, and lebel off wid dat thousand-dollar gun. Den
he holler 'Pull!' and let fly wid bofe barrels. He shoot lak a
millionaire, Cap'n, which I tink he wus."

"How many would he get on a rise?" I asked, enviously.

"Cap'n," Santee answered reproachfully, "Don't ax me dat.
You know he never kilt nothin' on no rise."

"But, you rattle-brained idiot, you said he could shoot."

"Lawsy, Cap'n, he could. He was de shootin'est gennerman I
ever see — an' de no-hittin'est, sah. He had done learn to shoot
dem *skeets,* he say, but quails wus different. Dey don't respeck
de signal an' dey don't fly 'cordin' to de pattern, he say. Dem
skeets is little birds dey shoots up Nawth, but dey don't eats
dem," he explained.

"But surely he got some birds during the four-day hunt," I
protested.

"Nawsir, Cap'n, nary a bird — for t'ree days, dat is. Hit don't
look possible, do hit? But hit de troof. An' on Mossy Crossy us
foun' ten cobeys one day. But my gennerman never complain.
Nawsir, not him. When night come, he would say, des as cheer-
fullike: 'Santee, us had fine shootin' terday. Yessir, fine shootin'.
Us'll get 'em tomorrer. Be here bright an' early, Santee. An' feed
dem dawgs good.'

"Dat gennerman was a great spoht too, sah. Sometimes I
would make out lak de bird I shot wus his'n, but I couldn't
bluff 'im dat erway. He wouldn't shoot into a cobey, neder.
Always pick out he bird. An' he wouldn't shoot 'em in a tree.

When a bird light in a 'simmon bush right at 'im, he back off and say, 'Santee, skeer dat bird so's I kin shoot.' Den he would lebel off and miss 'im ag'in.

"Cap'n, I say dat gennerman never complain, an' he didn't. Dat is, not till de las' day, and den he didn't raly complain, I don't reckon. But atter he had done been missin' all de mawnin', he set down an' open a shell and count de shot. Yessir, counted de very las' one. Den he straighten up an' say: 'Santee, dere wus 600 shots in dat shell. Two o' dem shells has 1,200 shots. Tink o' dat, Santee — 1,200 shots. An' yet I miss dat bird in de wide open wid bofe barrels. Where did all dem shots go, Santee?'

"An' hit don't seem hardly *room* enough for a body to miss 'em so regularlike, do hit, Cap'n? Dar ain't but so much emptiness atter all. But he did. Den he set and look at nothin', wid he chin in he hands. He look at nothin' right hard, and den he say:

" 'Santee, I've done come a long way, and put in near erbout a week a-shootin' quails, an' I ain't kilt a ting. I have never shot quails afore, Santee. I looked forward and dreamed erbout dish here trip down South for a whole year. I am a busy man, Santee, a very busy man, an' I can't hunt again for anudder year. Tomorrer I must return to my home in de Nawth, an' I am re-turnin' empty-handed. What will my wife an' friends tink o' me? I have a new wife, Santee. Must be I ain't cut out fer to be no bird hunter, Santee.'

"I declar, Cap'n, hit wus de mournfullest sight, wid dat fine gennerman a-settin' on dat log and he sperits a-flaggin' an' a-floppin'. Atter while he got up and follow de dawgs again', but he heart wusn't in hit. An' when ole Buck p'int on de hill and I call 'im, he look at me wid a kinder sicklike smile an' say: 'Tain't no use o' me shootin', Santee. You go ahaid.' An' sho nuff, he lebel off an' miss wid bofe barrels again. But I catched 'em on de cross an' drapped t'ree o' dem. Den all to onct a funny look come over he face, an' he jump up an' say:

" 'Santee, gimme dat gun!'

"What! Dish here ole t'ing?" I say.

" 'Gimme dat gun,' he say, 'an' flush dem birds old Buck has got yander.'

"An' he took de gun bodacious he did, an' slipped de wire in place what held hit togedder — de breech lock, you know. Den he walk up an' lebel off — 'twus dat ole chimbley cobey — an' let fly wid my gun. Afore de Lawd Gawd in heaven, Cap'n, *effen two birds didn't fall daid!* Den he swung eround an' let fly wid de udder barrel, an' bless de Lawd effen anudder bird didn't fall.

"Well sir, Cap'n, I wishes you could a-been dar and seed dat gennerman. He was a-standin' dar a-tremble wid pure happiness, he face shinin' des lak a angel's when de dawgs fotch all t'ree birds to 'im. A lump come in my th'oat for to watch 'im, Cap'n.

" 'Come on, Santee, les go atter dem singles,' he holler an' start a-runnin'. De rest o' dat evenin' dem dawgs showed dey self, an' us found t'ree more cobeys. Bless de Lawd, but he mowed 'em right an' left. An' every time, he would slip dat wire back in place an' pat dat ole gun. By night he had done kilt de limik an' he pockets wus a-bulgin'. An' when de las' bird drap, he laugh happy and turn to me and say:

" 'Santee, you have done sole dish here gun, sah.' An' he pat hit lak hit wus de sweetest ting on earth. Which I reckons hit wus fer a fack. 'Hits de greatest natchel weapon I ever see,' he say. An' wid dat he took out a hundred-dollar bill an' gin hit to me. *A hundred-dollar bill,* Cap'n, an' hits de Gawd's troof!"

"And you had the face to take it," I said. "Santee, isn't that the same gun you traded a one-eyed billy goat and a mess of catfish for?" I asked severely. Santee bowed his head in guilt.

"I tole 'im he could have dat breech lock fix so he wouldn't need de wire," he said.

"What did he say to that?"

"He say: 'Have it fixed? I'll shoot in cole blood, sah, any gunsmith what tetches her.' "

"But Santee," I said, "it was still nothing short of grand larceny."

"Cap'n," he grinned. "Hit wus a bargain at de price. When you gits what you wants, you got a bargain disregardless o' de price."

# When Dogs Fight

NOT LONG ago there was a knockdown and drag-out fight in my dog lot. It had been brewing for some time between two lusty buckaroos in adjacent runs. For weeks they had been making uncomplimentary remarks about each other through the fence. For hours they would stand, with backs a-bristle and tongues a-slaver, exchanging epithets and reflecting upon each other's ancestry.

Since I knew that they would have to compose their differences sooner or later, I let them into the lot. In a trice the bounders were at each other. And a third dog, one that a friend had left with me, bolted from his kennel and joined the fracas. What the newcomer's grievances were or where his sympathies lay are matters of conjecture, but he sailed in with great gusto.

The melee writhed raucously and savagely around me. My friend's dog was in fast company. He would surely be maimed if I didn't intercede. Impulsively I kicked at the nearest combatant — and narrowly missed a vicious snap. I could lay my hands on nothing whatever to separate them with, so I did what many another manly fellow has done under the stress of circumstances: I bawled vociferously for my wife.

Now my wife is not a doggy woman. I don't mean that she is lacking in charity or tolerance, or that she isn't indulgent toward her husband's foibles. She is just not a particularly doggy person. But when she heard the racket in the backyard, she glanced out the kitchen window and quickly appraised the situation. Then she came running out with a pitcher.

Of all things to stop a dogfight, I thought! Why would anyone grab a pitcher when surrounded by as many really effective missiles as our back porch afforded?

But that pitcher was filled with ice water, which my puissant spouse dashed vigorously into the brawling melee. The effect was instantaneous. Each combatant broke his hold and went slinking to his corner, yelping in discomfiture. There they sat shivering and disheveled, and looking silly and embarrassed. You never saw a less belligerent-looking trio. Gaping in admiration at the instant effectiveness of the remedy, I perceived that I had married a rather remarkable woman.

"What made you think of *that?*" I asked sheepishly. "I always thought a broom was the only weapon in a woman's arsenal."

"Shucks!" she discounted. "I grew up on that stunt. My father had a pack of hounds that were forever fighting, and my mother always kept a bucket of water ready to throw on 'em. Never saw it fail to break up a fracas. I can't imagine anybody's being so dumb as not to have heard of it. Sometimes I think you haven't got as much sense as I think you have. Now" — and my paragon of resourcefulness turned matter-of-factly away — "come on in and fix another pitcher of ice water for dinner."

Yes, sir, a pitcher or bucket of cold water is a great little peacemaker. I've tried it often since that day, and it's never failed. At its first flourish, the hardiest mutineer beats a shame-faced retreat.

Have you ever noticed, by the way, how a bunch of penned-up dogs soon come to an understanding among themselves? Each dog will set about the business of ascertaining his official status, his relative standing in the community — which means finding out which of his fellow citizens he can whip or outtalk, and which can whip him.

He learns which he can safely bulldoze, and which he must defer to. And once this has been done thoroughly and decisively

— that is, to the satisfaction of all parties concerned — the status quo is not likely to be disturbed thereafter. They will get along more or less amicably together. Nor do they seem to harbor resentment over such a matter-of-fact settlement of their differences.

Sometimes the most sensible and humane thing to do is not to interfere in a dogfight. Let them settle their differences in their own way, especially if they must live and hunt together. The show-down comes sooner or later. If one dog is not permitted to whip the other decisively, they will be forever bickering and wrangling, and old animosities and unsettled scores may flare up in the field to plague you at inopportune times.

If a heavy collar is placed on each combatant to protect the jugular vein, even the most savage encounter between evenly matched dogs may leave no lasting scars. But dogs do not always resort to settlement by tooth and claw. Like people, they sometimes put their heads together and growl it out. One *talks* a better fight than the other, and the other very sensibly concedes the point.

I was once present when ten strange deerhounds were placed in the same inclosure and left to themselves. They were all lithe, seasoned hunters and all touchy about their prerogatives. For the rest of the day pandemonium reigned in that pen, with free-for-alls popping up in every corner. But when I returned a week later, everything was as peaceful as you please. I could hardly believe it.

"What happened?" I inquired of the kennel master.

"Oh, nothing much," he said. "Old Rowdy there licked every dog in the pen, got himself elected justice of the peace, and retired. Rock licked all the others and earned his right to second place. Then Snap, that mild-mannered bitch over there, drubbed the rest of them, and so on down the line. Now they're friendly as can be, for when every dog in the lot knows his place they can live together without arguing. And that's all there is to it. Just like lawyers in a courtroom or politicians at the polls, I reckon."

I have said that a balance of power, once established, is seldom disturbed, for a whipped dog usually stays whipped. A dog is a fatalist. "That guy whipped me once and can probably do it again," he theorizes.

I owned a big pointer who quickly established himself as boss of the kennel, a fact which the others accepted philosophically. Later an insidious malady brought the big fellow to such a state of debility that the puniest of adversaries could have bowled him over. Yet not a rowdy in the pen presumed to question the pointer's position, however irritable and downright bossy he chose to become in his declining days.

Now and then two dogs will be so evenly matched and so self-willed that they do not readily arrive at a basis of settlement. I once had a pair of stalwart young setters — handsome animals they were — neither of which could decisively out-argue the other, although they squared off almost daily. What to do about them was becoming a problem.

But when I returned from a day's absence, I found Billy Boy tipping his hat to High Pocket, and all was quiet on the Potomac. If High Pocket was eating and Billy ventured too near, Pocket just looked around as if to say, "It's the second table for you, bud. Don't you know your betters?" Whereupon the ebullient Billy would withdraw with dignity unruffled. I could see that a business matter had been discussed and settled between them — and what a whale of a conference that must have been!

Some dogs, to be sure, are never able to come to an understanding. Their differences, whatever their nature, are irreconcilable. They hate each other with an unquenchable hatred, and there is nothing the owner can do but keep them apart. Years ago a man practically gave me a fine quail dog for this reason. The owner's extremity was my opportunity.

"There they are!" he said, indicating a pair of stalwart and identically marked setters in separate runs. "Although they are full brothers, no two living things hate each other more than they do. They fight incessantly and inconclusively. Neither can convince the other that he's a better man. They fight even in the field, each taking a malicious delight in flushing the other's birds. So if you want one of the hellions, take him before I go crazy and shoot both of them."

So I brought one home and dumped him into my yard. A shrewish old maid promptly ripped one of his ears open, and after that the big swashbuckler was as docile as you please. His feud was, after all, with only one of his kind.

Although a dog may not harbor a grudge against another that has bested him, he will hotly resent the efforts of another to supplant him in the master's affections. A teacher's pet is held in special disesteem. The fair-haired Benjamin upon whom a doting master lavishes his attentions is cordially hated by the rest of the kennel. And the owner who expects the highest performance from each of the lot must use judgment in distributing his favors, for dogs will sometimes go to unusual lengths to avenge themselves upon a pampered apple polisher.

All trainers know the advantages of bringing up a puppy under the tutelage of a steadfast older dog, since imitation is the handmaiden of instinct. An impressionable pup is a great copycat. To a large extent, he patterns his behavior on that of his seasoned consort. I once had an old spinster, Miss Priss by name, who was such a fine schoolmistress that I was inclined to turn my puppy training largely over to her. But on one occasion Miss Priss did me dirt — and almost ruined a promising prospect.

Dandy was so handsome, starry-eyed, and affectionate that our entire family fell for him. And we made the mistake of praising and petting him in the presence of Miss Priss, who had long been the apple of my eye and the household's darling. Aggrieved and resentful over this turn of affairs, Miss Priss got her revenge in a way that was both unique and exasperating.

I had noticed that, when I was near by, Dandy held his birds perfectly, with the old dowager dutifully seconding at his rump. But when I was not immediately on hand, he frequently bungled the job and looked chagrined and unhappy about it when I came up.

The mystery resolved itself when I covertly watched an entire performance through a hedge. I saw young Dandy freeze on a covey, as stylish as Park Avenue. Then Miss Priss stalked up behind him, glanced warily around — and smartly nipped the pup's stiffened tail. Attacked thus from the rear, Dandy yelped and leaped aside, and the birds exploded. Then pious Miss

Priss straightened out and was pointing like patience on a monument when I came up.

Grabbing a switch, I started after the old fraud with blasphemy on my lips and mayhem in my heart. Then the reason for her singular action flashed upon me. I found myself not only excusing her but confessing a sneaking admiration for her resourcefulness. I straightway took the hint and assured Miss Priss that she had no rival in my affection. Thereafter I praised her whenever the puppy pointed, and she was soon taking great pride in Dandy's workmanship.

Willie and Pluto, two rollicking pointers, were kennel mates and great cronies. But Pluto became ill and had to be brought onto the back porch and nursed for ten days. Whenever the narrow-eyed Willie saw me fussing over the patient, he growled his disapproval. And when Pluto recovered and was returned to the kennel, Willie turned savagely upon him. I discovered the next morning that the outraged Willie had kept his erstwhile crony out in the pouring rain all night.

Entering the lot, I ordered Pluto inside the house, but Willie wouldn't have it. He straddled the doorway, flexed his muscles, and growled uncompromisingly.

"I been nursin' a viper in my bosom," he said. "That two-timin' goldbricker has been tryin' to cut me out, and he ain't a'comin' into this house unless he's a better man than I think he is, which I doubt."

I had to let Willie sleep on the back porch and make a fuss over him before he was mollified. A few days later the two pointers were as thick as thieves again. Poor Willie didn't have much in the upper story anyway, I'm afraid. He never saw the least impropriety in gulping down every bird I shot, and he was always amazed that opinions should differ on such a matter.

And I once had two pointers, who had been in the habit of riding in the trunk of my car, challenge the right of a big setter to ride in the front seat with me. They had quite a conference over the matter right in the middle of the road. The big setter whipped them both, climbed gravely into the front seat, and closed his file on the case. The two vanquished conspirators climbed philosophically into the trunk where they belonged. You can't blame a fellow for trying, they figured.

Dogs, even the most cross-grained, will tolerate all manner of liberties on the part of a pup. He is the privileged character in any kennel — until he attains his maturity. Then the others expect him to put away childish things.

But I once saw a doting mother turn furiously upon her son under circumstances that were quite amusing. I had taken a five-months-old youngster on a short hunt with his mother, who was a very patient and painstaking performer. The mother pointed. Junior pranced up, noted the singular pose, and thought it very, very funny.

He nipped her sportively on the rump. Getting no response therefrom, he yanked vigorously at an outstretched leg. Still not content, he grabbed an ear and began tugging his mother's head from side to side. Although the old dame had not budged an inch, I could see that she was outraged motherhood and that she was nursing her wrath to keep it warm.

Suddenly the covey exploded a few feet ahead — and the mother exploded on that hapless brat of hers. Junior must have thought that the hind wheel of destruction had hit him. Amazed and chastened, he scrambled to his feet and stiff-legged away.

Later in the afternoon the mother pointed again. Again the pup pranced roguishly up — and suddenly bethought himself. He couldn't exactly figure this thing out, and until he could, he sidled behind and remained at a distance which he hoped the Old Lady would consider respectable. Thanks to the rough-and-ready ministrations of his mother and the burgeoning of his instincts, Junior was an awfully earnest young fellow two months later.

# Billy And The Big Boss

ARE YOU sure the big bass you've been telling me about is still in the mill pond?" gravely demanded Billy.

"Well, sonny," replied the miller, "I couldn't exactly give you an affidavit to that effect, but he was sure there last year, and if he's been caught since then I haven't heard about it, which ain't likely."

The boy turned to me. "Dad, what is the biggest bass you ever caught?"

"Seven pounds, I believe."

"Do you think the bass in the mill pond is bigger than that?" Billy asked the miller.

"Appearances are sometimes deceivin', you know, but I'll venture to say your dad never caught anything that would hold a candle to this old fellow. He's been the boss of the pond for years — about the only one left, in fact. He's a right cagy customer, though, and I misdoubt anybody's ever catchin' him."

The boy, who had been listening to the old miller's recital with a rapt expression on his face, announced with grim finality: "Well then, that settles it. I'm going to stay up here with you, Dad, instead of going back with Mother tomorrow as I had planned. I'm going to stay up here and catch the Big Boss of the mill pond."

So the feud between Billy and the big bass was officially inaugurated.

The boy's decision to spend the two weeks with me in the mountains accorded perfectly with my own plans. I had figured that a little Blue Ridge "ozone" and the bounteous table which the miller's wife set would put him in fine fettle for school. But I hadn't insisted on his staying, a father's intuition warning me that too much insistence might provoke the rebel that lurks in a twelve-year-old boy and have the contrary effect.

Now I found myself wondering whether the miller had made him a victim of over-stimulation — whether his ardent pursuit of the big bass might not lead to bitter disillusionment for the boy. I didn't want him to go up against a "cold deck" to start with. So I looked up the miller.

"See here, Will, is there any such bass as the Big Boss, or have you been telling Billy a cock-and-bull story to intrigue his interest and make him stay?" I asked.

"What I told the boy is straight," he answered. "There's a bass in there, right enough, and he's as big as I said he is. How the overgrown varmint got there I can't figure, unless he's the only one that lived out of a dozen or so I put in there ten or twelve years ago. Sort of an old bachelor, you might say."

"So far so good. Now tell me, has Billy any chance of catching him, do you reckon?"

"That's a horse of another color," the miller answered, half sorrowfully. "He might and again he mightn't, as the saying goes. Matter of fact, I hope he does. I've been tryin' to stock the pond with perch, but that old hellion gobbles 'em down faster than I can put 'em in. He keeps the place clean as a hound's tooth. I've been campin' on his trail, off and on, for a long time, but he's still rampagin' around. Anyway, the boy's entitled to a little hope, ain't he? And besides, it will keep him satisfied."

"That relieves the situation somewhat," I told him. "I didn't want Billy to get his enthusiasm up for nothing."

"Humph!" he regarded me suspiciously. "Thought I smelled a rat. You're just calculatin' on payin' the pond a sociable little visit yourself, ain't you? But let me put a bee in your bonnet: fishin' for the Big Boss and all appurtenances thereunto, as the lawyers charge you for saying,' is the private privilege of Billy, and if I catch you snoopin' around down there with a rod and reel in your hands, well," he looked around and chuckled, "do you see that horsewhip over there, hangin' on the gate-post?"

That night the miller and I sat on the back porch, listened to the whippoorwills, marked the dismal baying of a hound in some darksome cove below, and told tall tales of "the days when." Billy and the miller's wife were busy in the kitchen, the boy absorbed in his tackle box, the miller's wife hovering solicitously over a fresh batch of teacakes. These nut-brown delicacies were destined, during the next two weeks, to cement the *entente cordiale* existing between Billy and the maker, and to subject the kitchen to periodic but discreet visitations on my part.

When I awoke the next morning, Billy was missing.

"Where's the boy?" I called downstairs to the miller.

"Shucks, that lad ain't a ten-o'clock scholar like his daddy. He's got get-up-and-get about him. Got his breakfast and left for the pond an hour ago, I guess. Maybe he's had his first run-in with the Big Boss by this time."

After breakfast I sauntered down to the pond, lingering reflectively about the weather-beaten old mill, the ancient overshot water-wheel, and the limpid pool beneath it. Then I walked up the path bordering the small reservoir. The pond was narrow and overgrown with willows but still deep. It extended perhaps three hundred yards up the ravine. At the upper end I found what I was looking for.

"What luck, brother?" I greeted.

With his breeches rolled up and his shirt tail flying at half mast, Billy was standing on a half-drowned sand-bar, smacking his blue-headed plug into a pocket in the lily-pads.

"Oh, it's you," he said. "Can't do much casting from the bank this way, but the boat is so full of holes I can't use it. Think I'll fix it up today."

"A good idea, son. We'll drag it out and see what can be done with it," I agreed.

"Much obliged, Dad; but if you don't mind, I'd rather not bother you. I heard you say you expected to be awfully busy getting your lectures in shape, and I can't expect to take up your time."

So that was the lay of the land! The young scalawag was intent on playing a lone hand. I was an uninvited guest, a fly in the ointment. I decided to leave him to his own devices.

The next time I saw the boat it was dry and seaworthy. Billy had pegged the knot-holes in the gunwales and talked the miller out of some roofing paint for the bottom. A workmanlike job, too.

At the end of the first day Billy returned to the house empty-handed but undiscouraged. He had been mostly getting things ready, he said. Of the Big Boss he had seen no signs. His hands were blistered and he was dog-tired, but he was happy with the quiet happiness of a man who has dedicated himself to high emprise.

"What part of the pond does the Boss stay in mostly, Uncle Will?" he asked.

"Well, being the Lord Mayor of the whole place, he naturally ranges all over, but I've noticed that early in the morning and late in the evening he hangs out in them tall weeds at the upper tip where the creek comes in," the miller informed him.

After tinkering with his reel for a while, Billy borrowed a battered alarm-clock from the miller's wife and went to bed. "I've got to get up early in the morning," he explained.

Along toward bedtime, the miller knocked his corn-cob pipe out and remarked: "I'm sort of figurin' on goin' to see a man about a dog. Right nice animal, that dog. Think you'd like to sashay along?"

"How far is it?" I asked, unsuspecting.

"I promise to get you back by midnight, if you don't try to overdo yourself. Come on."

He led the way to the smoke-house in the back yard. Fumbling around in the dark interior, he produced something and handed it to me. It felt like a long, slender stick.

"What's this?" I asked.

"Haven't you city slickers ever seen a reed quill? Here, stick it in the bunghole and sample 'er once."

A match flared up, revealing the outlines of a big black barrel. I thrust the quill into the hole and sucked, long and hard. Apple cider!

After a little I straightened up and handed the quill to the miller. "That," I told him, " is about the best-looking dog I've seen in many a day."

So, like two worshipers of some forgotten pagan god, we squatted by the black barrel and "calmly drinked and jawed." Thereafter our nocturnal visit to the smoke-house was a rite seldom neglected.

The second and third days brought no developments in Billy's campaign against his enemy. The Big Boss disdained everything he had to offer.

The miller called me aside: "You know, I'm sort of ashamed of myself for sickin' the boy on that bass. It's doin' the young fellow good, though. Did you see how he went for that buttermilk and those roastin' ears for dinner? But what bothers me is, I can't figure he's got a Chinaman's chance of catchin' the fish, and I'd hate like poison to see the boy disappointed after so much hard work."

"Maybe we can get him interested in something else and kind of wean him off," I suggested.

"That's an idea at least. I'll see what can be done."

The next day the miller tried his hand: "Billy, what's the chance of gettin' you to lend me a little help with some bee trees? I've got some prime ones I've been layin' off to cut for some time. We ought to get a nice parcel of honey."

"I'm sorry, Uncle Will, but I guess I won't have time this summer. Probably I can come back and help you next summer," Billy evaded.

"Well, what about goin' with me up the creek tonight to gig suckers. There are some rattling big ones up there, and we might run into eels, too."

"If you don't mind, Uncle Will, I broke a section of my rod today, and I have to fix that up tonight. I've got to go to bed early too, you know."

He was not to be weaned from his tournament with his bigmouthed adversary, nor to be seduced by the miller's blandishments.

"You say you cracked your rod today? Why not use your Dad's?"

"No, I'd rather not. You see, I bought this outfit myself, from money I made selling goldfish. It's my own, and it wouldn't be the same if I caught the Big Boss with somebody else's stuff. I've got another section I can put in."

So the first week passed, with nothing more eventful than our well-timed excursions to the smoke-house and periodic raids on the tea-cake stronghold in the kitchen. Billy was out early every morning. The tinny old clock he got from the miller's wife proved an insufferable nuisance, going off at five o'clock every morning with racket enough to raise the dead. I suggested to the miller the propriety of his issuing an injunction against the clock, but he snortingly protested that all decent and self-respecting people were out of bed by five o'clock anyway.

When Billy reported for supper Saturday night, however, we sensed something unusual in his demeanor. He carried with him an air of suppressed excitement and secretiveness. I called the miller aside for a confab.

"Something's up. Maybe. . . . "

"Hmm! I read the signs too. Suppose he's been flattered by a little attention from the Big Boss?"

But nothing whatever was forthcoming from Billy to indicate that anything of the sort had happened. He insisted he had had no encouragement whatever.

During the night, however, Billy seemed to have a spell of restlessness. Tossing about in his bed, he mumbled inarticulately at intervals. I went over and sat down in the chair by his bed. His fingers were twitching. His brown arm jerked spasmodically. Fishing in his sleep! Like a tired dog, stretched before the fireplace, re-enacting in his sleep the stirring episodes of the day's chase.

"You missed that time, did you?" he muttered presently.

"What missed, Son?" I asked softly.

"The Big Boss. Missed clean as a whistle. Strike when I'm having a backlash, would you? But I'll get you yet, damn you!"

So that was the way he talked to the Big Boss, was it? I turned him over on his side, and he soon lapsed back into the untroubled sleep that is the precious legacy of boyhood.

What an electric moment it must have been for the boy when the big fellow struck, and what a break that he should reserve his coquettishness for a dead plug! About the unwitting confession Billy had made in his sleep I observed a discreet reticence. This was certainly information to which I was not fairly entitled.

The next day was Sunday, and Billy was like a worm in hot ashes. It meant an enforced suspension of his campaign, and that, as I alone knew, at a most trying and unhappy juncture.

"Dad, why are Sundays always so much longer than other days?" he demanded.

"That boy is wearin' himself plumb out waitin' for Monday to come," was the miller's terse comment.

When Monday did come, Billy returned to the feud with renewed vengeance. After breakfast, I decided to take a casual stroll by the pond before starting the day. I didn't run into the boy, who was presumably gabbing with his bosom crony, the miller, at the lower end, but I did find his rod and reel, with the old plug dangling from the tip. I would sit down and wait for him to show up. But as I pushed the dew covered willow branches aside, a half-grown bullfrog scampered out. Picking up the frog, I tossed it into the water — at the very tip where the creek entered the pond.

Before you could have said Jack Robinson, it was over. The frog must have landed, by sheer luck, within a few feet of the giant bass. There was a heavy swirl, and my unbelieving eyes saw a pair of cavernous jaws flash up and gulp down the squirming frog.

"Now!" I said to myself. "If I drop this plug right where the frog fell, while the old boy is in a taking notion — "

I snatched up Billy's rod and measured the distance with a practiced eye. I brought the rod up and back for the flip. Then I brought it down again. I would have given my eyeballs for one cast, one timely little flip of the wrist, and I would have given a month's pay for the battle royal sure to follow, but a moment's reflection saved me from such folly.

If I had hooked and landed the Big Boss, Billy would not have forgiven me to his dying day, and I could hardly have blamed him. I would have forfeited his confidence, which I valued above all the big bass in the world. So I leaned the rod against a log as I had found it and sneaked off home.

I still think that my putting Billy's rod back without a single cast was perhaps the most heroic thing I ever did. Of course, I said nothing of my experience to the boy, because I had no business being down there at the pond, in the first place, and because. . . .

About five o'clock that evening I was surprised to run into Billy sitting out behind the woodpile.

"Why aren't you on the job?" I asked.

There was no answer. Billy reclined limply against the pile of wood, his head bowed dejectedly in his hands, his brown legs trailing inertly in the chips. His face was the picture of grief, utter and inconsolable. He had been weeping, the telltale signs ineffectually erased by a hastily requisitioned shirt tail.

"What on earth is the matter, Son?" I demanded anxiously.

The boy's mouth quivered. A single tear, over-riding restraint, coursed shamelessly down to the tremulous mouth and lingered there, glistening. Forlornly he pointed to the tip of the rod lying between his knees. Then I noticed that the plug was missing.

"Where is your plug?"

"I — I lost it," he faltered.

"My goodness! Isn't that something to take on so about! You can get another one exactly like it, or use mine," I encouraged.

"I know, but — but the Big Boss has it," he blurted.

Well, that was something else. I sat on the woodpile beside him. "Tell me about it. Did you really hang up with the old son-of-a-gun?"

"Dad, I never saw anything like it! It happened so suddenly it almost — scared me. You know, I had been casting for over a week, and nothing much happened, only a strike last Saturday, but he hit when I had a backlash and missed. Then this evening, at the upper end of the pond, in that little gut where the creek comes down, it happened. He hit like five hundred and almost pulled me overboard.

"I came to my senses and tried to reel him in, but he jerked the handle of the reel out of my hand. When I grabbed the handle again, I thought he was off. Then, right at the boat, he jumped clean out of the water. Dad, you never saw such a — and I jerked hard, and, and — " He stopped, his eyes dimming again.

"And what happened? Go on," I prompted.

"Then the line broke, right at his mouth, and he went off with the plug."

"That was a good line, Son. What made it break, do you reckon?"

"Well," he said shamefacedly, "you told me to cut off the end, where it was frayed from casting, and I forgot to do it. But I'll never forget it again as long as I live, and you can bet on that."

"Don't take it too hard, Billy," I comforted. "It's the element of chance that makes it a great sport. As for your beloved plug, you will get that back if you look over the pond tomorrow. The fish will get rid of that plug as sure as shooting. You can get it back, and probably try it out on the Big Boss again next summer. School starts next week anyway, you know, and we'll have to be getting home."

The big bass had outgamed the boy. He had lost his chance, and I decided the best thing to do was to reconcile him to going home empty-handed. I wondered how he would respond to the feeler I had offered. For a moment he sat like a piece of statuary; then his jaw set, and he grimly announced: "I'm going to stay up here in the mountains with the miller till I catch him."

"But school starts next week, Son."

"I know, but it's between him and me now; and school or no school, I'm not going back till I catch the Big Boss. I'm not!" Tears of rebellion welled up in his eyes.

I stalked off to find the miller.

"Look here, Will. I'll be jiggered if you haven't got me into a pretty mess! Billy broke his line on the bass today, and he swears he is not going back home, school or no school, until he catches him. This thing has gone too far."

"Don't I know all about it? Watched the whole business from the mill. Swallowed my heart three times to keep it down, and I don't blame the boy one bit. Fact is, I admire his spunk. Why, when I was growin' up, I got off one day to run down a rattlin' big turkey gobbler whose range I had spotted. Camped on that blamed gobbler's trail a whole week. Led me a dog's life. When I got back, I had lost my job, but I had my turkey, and I ain't regrettin' no regrets about it then or now. So, old-timer, you don't get much sympathy from me."

The next morning I fully realized I was in a predicament. What was I to do? Billy had delivered his ultimatum, and his resolution, secretly bolstered up by the miller I suspected, was unshakable. Yet I had to get back at the end of the week, and so did Billy, or run into a good scolding from his mother.

"Will, what is the chance of that behemoth's striking again?" I asked, half desperate.

"That depends. The Boss seems to have taken a likin' to the lad. Knows a dead game sport when he runs into one. That old bass is a pretty rambunctious fellow when he gets started. He may strike again; give him a few days to get his mouth back in shape. By the way, Billy found his plug this mornin' — floatin' in a clump of weeds where the old polecat spitted it out. He's up there ploppin' away now."

Three days passed without incident. The Big Boss had evidently had enough. The boy had fished his heart out without any further overtures from his arch enemy. I tried to convince him of what I felt to be true — that the bass would not strike again for some time — but Billy's only comment was. "I know, but he might." I also suggested that he try a live frog for a change, which met with prompt rejection: "I'm going to make him strike the plug if it takes till the cows come home. He started it, and he's got to finish it."

Came Friday. On the following day my time was up, and I simply had to get back and take Billy with me, whether or no. I was in a nice quandary, with a rebellious boy on my hands. Saturday morning came, and I awoke still perplexed. Billy, as usual, had crammed his pockets full of tea-cakes and betaken himself to the pond.

After breakfast I too walked down to the mill, hoping against hope that some kindly providence would intervene — that the big bass would take a notion to strike again. Approaching from the rear, I sat unobserved in the willows lining the bank and watched the boy. He was throwing with an accuracy that surprised me, dropping the plug by a submerged log or a clump of pads with a deftness that an older hand might well have envied. He had started at the other end of the pond and was working his way up toward me.

"Now he's in position," I told myself presently. "If he will just drop one lightly in that pocket, right at the mouth of the creek — "

And by jimminy he does, as light as a feather, in the exact spot. He begins to retrieve in the erratic way I had taught him, and then, as Billy said, "it happened."

*Smack!*

I jump up and stick my head through the willow branches. But my heart drops down into my stomach when I see the plug riding high and free, in the center of a big swirl. Missed! But the boy is as cool as a cucumber. He keeps playing the minnow, injecting into the big floating plug every seductive and tantalizing maneuver his wits can conjure up. Will he hit again?

*Slam!*

He hits again, with a malicious lunge that makes the water boil. I don't see the plug. For an interminable second I'm in an anguish of suspense. Is he hooked? He is!

The silk line zips through the water. Billy's rod bends almost double. He is playing his quarry like an old hand. But he must keep that bass from getting a straightaway on him. The line suddenly slacks. Bad business. The bass is going to rush the boat and break water.

"Hold him, Son, hold him! Watch that slack!" somebody yelled hoarsely from the bank. It was his dad. I could not have helped it to save me.

A powerful hand suddenly gripped my shoulder from behind, and another was clapped over my mouth.

"Shut up! If you don't, I'll brain you!" ordered the miller. "Hasn't the boy the right to lose his own bass in his own way?"

How the miller got there without my knowing it I haven't yet figured out.

But Billy has that baby well hooked. Up and out he leaps again, clearing the water with his mighty bulk. He stands on his tail and heaves prodigiously. The loose hooks jangle against the wooden plug, but he is still on. He breaks away for a long run again, but I begin to believe the boy has his number. Billy checks the spinning reel, only to have the flying handle snatched from his fingers.

Then, to my dismay, the reel drops into the boat. What's up? That danged gadget has slipped from the reel seat. Billy has the line and is horsing the fish in, hand over hand. He bends over the gunwale of the boat. Will he remember not to lift him in by the line alone? He does. He straightens up, one hand fastened in the big fish's gills.

I sit down, suddenly gone weak and limp in the knees, now that there is no occasion for doing so. The miller lets out a resounding whoop that must have echoed all the way back from Sandy Ridge.

Billy pulled ashore and stepped out with his pot-bellied and gasping adversary. The boy's mouth twitched and his eyes glistened a bit suspiciously, but he managed to grin and say: "I guess I'm about ready to — to go back to school now, Dad."

## Bob Is No Gentleman

THINGS happen to me that should not happen to a good bird hunter. Truth to tell, I am a beginner with twenty years' experience. In matching wits with Bob White, I still hang my head in discomfiture. Either he has gone forward, or I have gone backward. Either the thoroughness with which he is hunted nowadays has made him smarter, or my coordination isn't what it used to be. The odds are that it's Bob.

Not only has a more frugal agricultural regime, with the break-up of a lazy plantational system and the reclamation of marginal areas, circumscribed his feeding grounds, but ten men are gunning for Bob White today to every one a few years ago. Over-shooting has taught him the cunning of the cornered. He has had to be smart to live. Result: Bob is not the saucy gallant he used to be, but an ungentlemanly trickster.

When latter-day Bob pops off the ground, his first move is to put something between the shooter and the shootee. With the sole purpose of intercepting the shooter's line of vision, he makes a lightning inventory of the immediate landscape and adapts himself thereto. He reacts in mid-air to take advantage of what-ever the changing map offers. Upon such instant adjustment his life often hangs.

"Stand by that persimmon bush while I kick up this single," I told my gunless companion.

I walked forward and kicked, calculating that the single would make for the woods forty yards ahead. A cock popped out, flew directly toward me, and as straight as a martin to its gourd made for that lone persimmon. I wheeled about and lowered my gun in chagrin. If that bird had been logical, he would have flown toward the woods. But if he had been logical, he would have been dead. He had unerringly picked the one direction in which I could not shoot, although he had to fly straight at me to do so.

A harried bird will sometimes fly toward the gun when the gunner chances to be between him and his predetermined line of flight. And sometimes, I verily believe, he cunningly elects to fly toward the gunner. It is a bold stratagem which he uses when no other expedient offers itself. A disconcerting maneuver it is, whether done by accident or with malice aforethought.

Every bird hunter has seen a side-slipping single make for another member of the party. Ever had a quartering bird pick you out while a companion was frantically trying to get a bead on it? If so, you've been in a choice position to contemplate the fine old Latin motto about how *dulce et decorum* it is to die for one's country. Last season a friend of mine postponed immortality by collapsing to the ground in the infinitesimal nick of time.

I have had birds bounce out of an open field with a totally unobstructed shooting range — and hit a bee-line for a hitherto unobserved horse or cow. And who hasn't seen a brazen fellow loaf away just above the head of a bolting dog?

The last week of the season I caught an elusive swamp covey in the middle of a straw field. Thrilled at the prospect, I hastily inventoried the surroundings. Not a persimmon, sumac bush, or pine sapling in sight.

"Old Lady, we've caught 'em off base at last!" I chuckled, and confidently ordered Belle in.

A big covey sallied out, executed a careening half circle, and headed straight away. Now I'd lay tariff on those skulking swampers! I bided my time until I saw a converging trio down my gun barrel — and a few feet beyond, my wife composedly crocheting in the car I had parked. She had been working on that afghan for months, too; so I confessed myself outwitted and left those swampers to their own devious devices. That covey had reacted in mid-air to an unpredictable part of the landscape.

A segment of a covey once took refuge in a thick-topped live-oak alongside a highway. I tried to dislodge them, repeatedly stamping about the base of the tree and shooing with great vigor. They resisted my efforts, however, until a stream of cars came down the highway; then they impudently sailed over the tops of the cars. One bird, taking off belatedly, followed the end car two hundred feet down the highway, wheeling off only when out of range.

"That thar bird was a-lookin' out for No. 1," my ebony game-toter grinned appreciatively.

Does a covey of partridges decide what it's going to do before taking off or afterward? Does it caucus over the matter, or await the inspiration of the moment? On its habitual range, a covey is presumably familiar enough with the landscape and its natural modifications to determine its flight in advance. A sort of tacit agreement, as it were.

When a covey is caught off base, however, or the immediate environs offer no sanctuary, any such prearrangement would seem pointless. Whenever a decamping bevy takes advantage of such providential barriers as another hunter, a passing automobile or an ambling cow, its home-work is apparently done in mid-air.

But Bob needs little help from providence in making the average hunter look silly. Whatever there is he makes the most of. His alertness in catching the gunner at a disadvantage marks him as not only an opportunist but something of a wit.

Some years ago I chanced upon a birdy section in the flats of the upper James River. The ragweed stubble-fields were full of birds, but a rising covey unfailingly flew across the river and plummeted down on the other side. When I crossed over for them, they would methodically sail back to the bank I had just left, so that I spent most of the afternoon with my posterior extremity in the stern of a boat. It was exasperating business. Those birds appeared to take my innumerable crossings as a matter of course and seemed to enjoy my sporadic pursuit, as a cottontail enjoys a frolic with the neighborhood hounds now and then.

One of my favorite hunts used to be around the edges of a game preserve, catching the birds that overflowed into the adjoining fields. This preserve was privately owned by an eccentric millionaire who did little hunting himself but who visited retribution upon any luckless trespasser his outriders caught.

Although the preserve was overrun with quail, hunting in the neighboring fields soon petered out, because those errant coveys learned to stay on their side of the fence, or to skidoo to their side at any intimation of danger. Cagy veterans would evacuate at the approach of a hunter. As the dogs pointed and I walked up to shoot, it was not uncommon to see a chuckling covey pouring itself through the fence. I have known them to scamper ahead of the pointing dogs for a hundred yards; or if they did risk a take-off, they would brazenly light just beyond the line and begin whistling, as if reassured by the "No Hunting" signs with which the fence bristled.

Hunting at another time on land adjacent to a game sanctuary, I was amused and piqued by the way a surprised bird would head for the precincts of the refuge. One impertinent cock even lit on a sanctuary notice, stood like a peg-legged sergeant, and whistled a saucy challenge. It was a safety zone, and he evidently knew it.

Quail have what metaphysicians used to call a "natural affinity" for sunny fields near railroad tracks. Several times each season I tramp such a stretch, but my railroad coveys have a tricky habit that does my ego little good. The track runs through a deep cut for some distance. Down that cut these birds fly. A hundred yards down they lift easily out and deploy in the field. When I scramble across and flush them, they repeat the identical ruse.

It looks like easy shooting to a man on the rim of the cut. Actually, it is deceptive enough. It is shooting at a dropping target, because the birds drop sharply as they hit the opening. Such shooting is contrary to habit, and I over-shoot in spite of myself.

There is a certain hedgerow that I can't stay away from. Following an abandoned terrace for a full mile, it is studded with a low interlocking growth of crab-apple, prickly hawthorn and wild plum. The hedgerow bisects a wide field where partridge-peas and fat birds abound. And does every raised bird streak for that hedgerow! When I hunt one side they rattle out the other, sail down the row and back into it. When I disgustedly cross over, they pop out the side I have just left.

Sooner or later they're going to get befuddled and fly out the wrong side, I promise myself. But they seldom do. I can bag a few, however, by sending the dogs down the opposite side of the hedgerow. An occasional bird will see the dogs, make his own deductions, and rattle out my side. Or sometimes I send my 16-year-old son down the opposite side, but he always protests that the birds pick the worse shot to fly toward!

Most bird hunters know of coveys favored by habit and habitat to attain a ripe old age. Such are the "one-shot" swamp birds of the South Carolina low-country, where nearly every factor is against the hunter. In the deep South the quail's staunchest allies are the great ragged swamps and numberless "bays," which are smaller brakes and branch-heads too thick to navigate. Here they find a fast retreat. Some of these swamp coveys become legendary for their size.

Hunting the fringes of these swamps and bays is a snare and a delusion. "Swampers" are seldom caught napping. Some of them, in fact, never emerge from their darksome coverts, assuming a distinctively darker coloration. When they do venture into the adjacent fields, they keep a weather-eye open, and it's touch-and-go at the first sign of danger. When they are caught afield, they are sometimes loath to risk a take-off, scurrying ahead of the trailing dogs until they reach a bay. Then, when the hunter's nerves are away up in high C and it's too late to do anything about it, the air is suddenly filled with scudding bodies. These birds have learned a fundamental lesson: that safety lies in fear. Any bird or anybody who knows that is apt to hang up a record for longevity.

How well the sink-hole coveys have learned this lesson! Of all the birds on my calling list, hunting these is at once the least satisfactory and the most fascinating. Every trip to the sink-holes is my last one. I actually believe that, but when birds get scarce everywhere else. . . .

Stretching for miles down the Santee is a string of jagged, cup-like depressions formed by the leaching of soluble limestone in ages past. Some of these depressions are a hundred feet across and from thirty to fifty feet deep. A clump of sweetgums rim them about, while the crater-like holes themselves are over-grown with wild plum and entanglements of smilax, honeysuckle and jasmine.

The stretch of "sinks" which I hunt are, paradoxically, in one of the birdiest and most heavily shot sections of the state. The paradox explains itself when one learns the habits of these birds. There is prime feeding in the lazy fields surrounding these coverts, which are from a hundred to two hundred yards apart, and each of which has its own covey of fifteen or eighteen birds.

Whenever a feeding covey is raised, it makes for its particular stronghold and goes down into the hole. Hardly an errant bird splits off. I fuss around the rim, hoping to catch an unwary single, but vain is the hope. Then I sweat and swear and go tobogganing to the bottom of the crater, my dogs somersaulting behind in an avalanche of debris.

Down in the semi-gloom birds pop out like an epidemic, go slithering through the interlocking gums above my head, and buzz to the next sink-hole. Possibly I get one; probably I don't. Then I scramble out, trudge to the next hole, and repeat the performance. Maybe they went down at the edge of the next one, I tell myself, but it is a flattering unction. In a season of heavy shooting, I have known these birds to hole up in their headquarters for days.

Hunting sink-hole birds is a profitless business. I know it, but I can't stay away from them. Whenever I head toward them my son, in unspoken disgust, betakes himself to the swamp to shoot squirrels until my folly spends itself. And when I return from a sink-hole spree, I am short-tempered and dyspeptic — unless I have a few fat sink-holers in my coat.

But a bird's greatest defense is not his trickery, artful dodger though he be. It is the whir of his twin propellers on the take-off. That is Bob's ace in the hole. I seriously wonder whether it has not played a part in the survival of the species. To step into a skulking covey or to have an unannounced single explode under one's feet may well disconcert even a seasoned hunter.

"I'd about as lief step on a rattlesnake — jus' a little liefer!" a rabbit-hunting old darky ruefully complained to me. "Mout as well be kilt as skeered to death."

To walk unprepared into a bevy of birds unmans me. I am for the moment disarmed, all my resolutions gone a-glimmering. In fact, a rise of any kind seldom fails to thrill me. Not a very creditable admission, perhaps, but the unashamed truth. In spite of years of hunting, I have never gotten used to it. I hope I never shall. There would be little point in hunting if a covey rise left me unmoved.

My young son and I sometimes try to rationalize about it, but with dubious success. One afternoon last year, when the boy was in a missing streak, I said: "Son, don't let 'em rattle you. They don't fly so fast, really. It's just the noise they make. The thing to do is to reason about it."

The next instant a single exploded from the dry brush under my feet. Curveting about smartly, I leveled down on a perfect straightaway for a demonstration shot. For a full hundred feet I held unwaveringly on the bird, and then disgustedly lowered my gun without shooting. I had been too flustered to release the safety catch. Stood there squeezing the trigger like the veriest tyro.

The boy gave me a crooked grin, and some of my own medicine.

"Don't let 'em rattle you, Dad. It's just the noise they make. The thing to do is to reason about it. About the smartest thing a bird can do is to fly straight in front of you and me."

Now I ask you, is that the way for a son to talk?

I have seen crack shots at other game miss laughably at quail, mainly because of the disconcerting clamor of their wings. A friend of mine, whose experience had been rather confined to skeet, walked into his first covey of birds last season and missed with everything he had.

"What's the trouble?" I asked.

He smiled dismally. "There was too much applause from the gallery. And those scutters didn't wait for me to holler 'Pull!'"

I have know a number of good skeeters to have the same difficulty with quail, because they were accustomed to groove shooting. If the object of skeet is to improve proficiency in field shoot-ing, the flight of the targets should be patterned after the flight of the quarry itself. It should prepare the gunner for the un-expected and the unpredictable. But if an erratic machine throws a target a little out of its groove, hear the indignant squawks of the shooter! Quail don't fly in grooves.

After all, the thrill of quail hunting lies in its unexpectedness. You never know what a bird is going to do. Whatever you do, Bob will probably outguess you. By studying the ruses and flight habits that individualize him and by inventorying the land-scape before a rise, you might learn to anticipate him somewhat and reduce the element of the unexpected. But if you could outfigure Bob every time, there would be little point in hunting him. It would be time to quit.

# The Education Of The Wrecker

"I'LL SHOW you what I mean," I said, turning the three dogs loose.

The two aging hunters went faithfully to work around me, while a big rawboned setter raced through the flatwoods ahead. The flatwoods of our low-country South Carolina have low ground cover, are untimbered save for a soaring longleaf here and there, and you can see a dog a long way.

"A rambling wreck from Georgia Tech, ain't he?" admired Will. "Can he really cover a landscape!"

"Never saw a dog cover ground faster or more thoroughly," I said. "The other dogs seldom find anything behind him, and those doting old gals use a fine-toothed comb."

"Does he know what he's hunting for? I mean — "

"The son-of-a-gun has a single-track mind, all right. It's birds and nothing else with him. Spurns rabbits, larks, sparrows and everything of the sort," I truthfully reported.

"Nose?"

"Never owned a dog with a more remarkable nose. Pins his birds down instantly. No shilly-shallying with him. And his posture is peerless, like one of those calendar-cover dogs."

"Then why are you so down-in-the-mouth about him?" asked Will.

"Because he ain't worth a damn."

"But I don't understand," Will protested.

"Watch him and you will. Over there. Two hundred yards to the right. Near that brush pile. See him? Now watch what happens."

The big dog right-angled sharply and raced 40 yards to a full point, with head uplifted and white flag aloft. He was a black-and-white statue there in the somber pinelands.

"Lord, what a dog!" breathed Will.

Suddenly the black-and-white statue vaulted through the air. Even from a distance we could see fragments from the exploding covey.

"I see," said Will. "But he does put 'em into the air and give you plenty of singles-shooting. Let's go."

"Wait."

The big dog lifted his head, intently scanned the absconding bevy, and streaked away.

"What's he barking for?" asked Will a moment later.

"He's counting the singles as he bounces them. Watches them down and finds them before they hit the ground good. Then he barks every time he bounces one."

"Is this what you'd call a typical day afield with him?" Will asked.

"Yes. Finds more birds than any dog I've had for years, holds them like a rock for a moment, then goes berserk like that."

"What about his background?" pursued Will.

"He's got plenty of family behind him. You know how those Virginians are. But he was two years old when I got him, and there's the rub. Owner entered the service and the tyke was allowed to run wild over the countryside and hunt for himself. Now he's a casehardened self-hunter. Reckon you might call him a war casualty, in a way."

"Country is full of dogs that are war casualties like that. Owners couldn't train them at the right age, now they've become unbiddable or confirmed self-hunters. Sort of a lost generation with bird dogs. Most of them have missed too many trains, I guess. Great pity, too. By the way, what's his name?"

"He's down in the books as Light Horse Harry, but I just call him the Wrecker," I said, not very cheerfully.

"Well, the thing to do is to break the Wrecker down. Hunt him down to a nub and he'll be more tractable. A few days of hard hunting — "

"I hunted him four days straight, from can-see to can't-see as the Negroes say. And in rough country. Then I went to bed and hired another fellow to hunt him two days more. The next morning the Wrecker was r'aring to go again. Raised Cain because I was late starting. I got disgusted."

"That much stamina?"

"Tough as whit leather. Grew up following a wood truck in the mountains of Virginia."

"Tried weighting him down with dragline?" Will asked.

"Wore out $3 worth of good rope and half dozen chokes. Got a 25-foot drag on him now, but he doesn't know it. If I could just get my hands on him when he's pointing, and break his precious neck a few times — "

"But he's always too far away when it happens, eh?"

"Exactly. I've been fooling with spirited pups all my life, but I could get my hands on them now and then."

"Tried your vocal chords on him, of course? And a whistle?"

"Why do you suppose I had laryngitis the whole week?" I asked with some feeling. "And I've got a pocketful of whistles. But he's either too preoccupied or too self-willed to hear me in the field. Yet he's biddable enough around the house."

"How does he react to what the old schoolmasters used to call corporal punishment?" asked Will.

"The Wrecker has had brushings aplenty, but so much time elapses between the offense and the punishment that he probably doesn't know why I'm whipping him. He never whimpers during a licking, however vigorously I lay it on. When I'm through, he just climbs up and tries to kiss me, the blamed idiot. I can't help loving him, to save me, but how in the hell can you train a dog you can't get your hands on? That's what I'm asking."

"Have you considered a professional trainer?"

"Dave Bonnet kept him three weeks and sent my check back. Even prepaid the express when he sent him back. Dave wrote that his mother-in-law was ailing, but I got my suspicions."

"Maybe he'll quit chasing them when he finds he can't catch them," Will consoled.

"That's the sad part. The Wrecker caught two birds last week."

"You don't mean it!"

"Birds got up slow in heavy straw and he pounced on them."

"What did he do with them?"

"Cracked their heads and brought them to me, as proud as you please. See why I love the old scoundrel?"

"Our clinic ain't making much progress, I'm afraid," admitted Will. "The question before the house is: how in heck can you train a dog that you can't catch? Right? Of course, there's always a way of communicatin' your ideas in such a case. As a last resort."

"You mean a dose of bird shot applied to the rump at the proper distance and at the psychological moment. But I can't do that. I've considered and rejected the idea a dozen times."

"Why not? Better cure a wild dog than kill him outright. Sometimes it's the only method possible, and you know as well as I do that a good proportion of Southern bird dogs — "

"I know all that," I interrupted, "but I can't do it. I suggested such long-distance therapeutics in a magazine article once, and got a letter from a preacher in West Virginia telling me I was going to hell in five pages. Besides, I've promised my wife not to. And besides again, I love the old scamp too much."

"What are you going to do then, give him away? Reckon a man can always give a dog away."

"No. Not going to give him away, either. I'm going to break the Wrecker, that's what I'm going to do. Break him if it breaks me. Break him if it's the last — "

"How are you going to do it, may I ask?"

"Haven't figured it out yet," I admitted, "but I will. I've got more sense than he has. Reckon I have, anyway. It's going to be me versus the Wrecker from now on. He's going to hunt birds for me and do it right. You wait and see."

"Maybe he's just climbing fool's hill," Will encouraged. "Most dogs and most men have to do it, you know. And it's a harder climb for some than for others. In fact, some — ." He laughed. "But there is this to say for a hard-to-train dog: it seems to stick by him better. A lot of these easy-to-train dogs, these so-called naturals, are flashes in the pan. They backslide later."

I had called Will into the case as a consultant, but our clinic had accomplished nothing, except to confirm my determination to tame the Wrecker. A dog with his stamina, spirit, nose and ability to find birds was worth whatever effort it might take. Besides, my other dogs were in the twilight of their hunting days. Another season and it would be the Wrecker or nothing.

A week later I was still wracking my brain. Although I had hunted him almost daily, there had been no visible improvement. I tried everything anybody recommended, including a species of yoke suggested by a practical farmer. "Good for a roguish cow," he said. "Ought to be good for a roguish dog."

In spite of the scurvy tricks I played on him, the Wrecker was still wild about hunting, and he still thought I was a grand guy. He tolerated the devilish contrivances I afflicted him with as one friend tolerates the foibles of another. He loved me in spite of myself.

One afternoon I was leaning dejectedly against a pine, watching the Wrecker successively point and explode a covey 200 yards away. A moment later he began counting the singles for me. "How much longer," I said, "am I going to put up with him? What fools these mortals be, especially me."

As I trudged homeward, I passed a bony old cow. Her bell tinkled in the mellow twilight. "Drowsy tinklings lull the distant fold," I mused.

"Damn!" I jumped suddenly. "That's it. That will put the quietus on the Wrecker as sure as you are born. I've outsmarted him at last. Just wait until tomorrow, you old scapegrace!"

The next morning I went the rounds of the hardware stores. "I want a cowbell," I said, "one that will fit this dog collar."

"A dog collar around a cow's neck? If you'll excuse me for suggesting it, sir, most folks use a chain. Like this."

"What I want," I persisted, "is a full-sized cowbell that will fit this dog collar."

"Very well. That will be $1.25."

On arriving in the field, I buckled the bell around the Wrecker's neck. He acquiesced good naturedly. What new-fangled toy was the boss trying this time? Away he streaked. A raucous jangling tore the serenity of the pinelands to shreds.

The Wrecker slammed on his four-wheel brakes, a look of temporary befuddlement on his face. Again he bolted forward. Again he slammed on his brakes, an awful deduction on his face. That noise was coming from him! He turned around and looked at himself. He looked at me. Rashly he tried it again.

He brought up short. It was no go. This ungodly contrivance thumped him in the chest. It confused his senses and hurt his ears. It — . He suddenly decided there was something new under the sun, and he definitely did not relish it. A frolic was a frolic, but this thing was going too far. Much too far. He minced his way back to me.

"Whatever you've done to me, boss, undo it," he said. "Take this blasted thing off so I can get to work."

I ignored his overtures, pretending to be greatly interested in the other dogs. He decided to bark for a hearing, but the resultant jangle cut him off short. Then he squatted ruefully on his haunches and refused to budge, an indignant and outraged dog.

He got down and groveled in the dirt, a hangman's air on his face. He walled his eyes at me reproachfully. He whined futilely. Then he stretched out his neck like a turtle and glared venomously. But I hardened my heart and ignored the puzzled penitent.

Finally the Wrecker got up and followed dolefully at my heels. For half an hour he stayed behind, experimenting with that bell. He was figuring out some way to outwit that insolent thing about his neck. After a while he discovered he could walk without vexing his nemesis if he watched his P's and Q's. I watched him over my shoulder, practicing his steps like an adagio dancer. By mid-afternoon he had developed a mincing stiff-necked pace which did not set the accursed bell a-clamor, and he began to voyage out a little. Not too far.

When faithful old Tess pointed, I slipped a choke about the Wrecker's neck. When the covey flushed, the Wrecker bounded forward. This was what I had been waiting two months for. This was the very apex, the culmination of endless days, the *summum bonum* of my dreams. And I went to work with what you might call considerable dexterity.

The jangling of the bell and the taut choke hit the Wrecker simultaneously, and he somersaulted backward in an ignominious and chastened heap. It no doubt scared the birds into the next county. There the Wrecker lay, and refused to get up. And there I let him lie.

Getting no attention from any quarter, he ultimately got up and resumed his mincing pace by my side. Again Tess went down on a single, and again the Wrecker vaulted forward. Again he wound up in a raucous melee, gingerly stretching his neck to see if it was still there. I wasn't sure myself. I had put a lot of personality in my end of the rope. The third time Tess pointed, the Wrecker gave me a black look and said:

"Get somebody else to chase your damned birds for you!"

He wasn't anybody's dumbbell after all. I figured the idea would soak through his pericranium sooner or later, and it did. Two weeks later, he had become a pretty good citizen. He had perfected a sound-proof trot that enabled him to voyage out enough to find birds, but not too far for me to grab the checkline whenever necessary.

In time I removed the bell and checkline. Now we would see whether the Wrecker had learned his lesson. Finding a covey near me, he staunchly planted himself. So far, so good. But when the birds thundered up, I saw his haunches heave for the spring, and I had a pretty anxious moment. But the Wrecker suddenly bethought himself and glanced at me. I showed him the bell, sort of casually, and prayed. He walled his eyes venomously at me and resumed his point.

Thereafter, whenever the Wrecker got to feeling his oats too much, I would hold the bell up for his inspection. Just as a grisly reminder. And he would settle down to business again. "Pardon me, boss," he would say. "You don't have to knock me down with a hint."

Toward the end of the season, I took a visiting hunter out with me. Quite a judge of dogs he was, too. When the hunt was over, he slapped me on the back and said:

"Some folks have all the luck. A dog like that Light Horse Harry, for instance. Took to it naturally too, didn't he? Just a born hunter. Knew that as soon as I laid eyes on him. Some dogs train easily that way. Others are hard as the devil to train."

"Yes. I had one like that once. Called him the Wrecker," I said. "Think it'll rain tomorrow?"

# The Other Fellow

"YES, SIR! Many a fellow has gone a-gallivantin' all over the country when he could a-done better right at home," opined Sandy, methodically stuffing his pipe. "Now you take me, for instance. I spent five years a-courtin' down in North Car'lina, and then up and married the gal next door. If I'd a-saved all that time and money — "

Without being aware of it, Sandy had supplied me with a text, because the same thing applies to hunting and fishing. It took me years to find it out, I confess. Maybe I'm slow to catch on, as my wife has suggested from time to time. But I'm thankful for having learned it at all. As a rule, we learn the important things in life too late to do us any good.

I live among the "fishin'est folks" in the country. The population of my town is 62,391. On a fair day, 62,390 of these go fishing. Don't waste your sympathy on the one that is left behind. He'll be along as soon as he locks the city hall. The barometer doesn't bother us. If it's favorable, we say: "Let's go. There may be something to it." If it's unfavorable, we say: "Let's go. Darned thing's probably a fake anyway."

Yes, we have more fishers than we have fish down here, and places where a fellow might profitably wet a line are at a premium. If we mean to do a workmanlike job of line-wetting, we scurry far and wide, poking our noses into all sorts of remote and unreachable places.

About a mile from town, under a highway bridge, is what the poets call a limpid pool. A likely-looking hole it is, shadowy and foam-flecked. A hundred times I have crossed that bridge, glanced speculatively down, and said to myself: "There's an inviting spot, but of course it's been fished to death, being so convenient and close to town."

One afternoon in May, when there wasn't time to go anywhere else, I sneaked under that bridge with a pocketful of catalpa worms. Sheer folly, I kept telling myself. A seven-year-old would know better. But an hour later, I had an uncommonly fine string of bream. Nor was there any evidence of previous fishing. The claim had apparently not been worked by any predecessor.

As an endless stream of cars rumbled overhead I sat there slyly chuckling, as pleased as a boy and a girl in a railway tunnel. "You old buzzard!" I gloated. "Why in the heck didn't you try this sooner? Don't take anything for granted hereafter."

Have you ever noticed that nobody fishes near the boat-landing? Everybody takes it for granted that the other fellow has, and pushes off to more distant spots. The result is that —

Well, I've become a boat-landing fisherman, in a manner of speaking. For twenty-five years I have been a bass fisherman. It has been something of a specialty with me. Although I have never bagged a record-breaker, have never taken the "biggest" of anything in fact, any board of appraisers would rate me a better-than-middling bass man.

I have gone a-courtin' of *Huro salmoides* — fancy name for a tramp — in several states, driving the-Lord-knows-how-many thousand miles in my efforts to "frame him in formaldehyde." Old bigmouth, you know, is a Democrat. He belongs to the Solid South and votes a straight ticket. He doesn't grow to real manhood in your chilly Republican waters up North.

Sometimes I made worth-while catches. Sometimes I didn't. You know how it is. And I often observed that the size of my catch was not in proportion to the distance I had traveled. I didn't do any serious fishing near by, because there wasn't anything to fish for. Everybody said so. All the near-by ponds had been fished out by the other fellow. Everybody said so. You had to get back where the other fellow didn't go.

But one night, while I was frogging in a tiny pond near home, a big something jumped into the boat. My flashlight went overboard. When that varmint began cavorting around my legs in the dark, I thought it was a hitch-hiking 'gator, and was personally in favor of giving him a quit claim to the boat and all appurtenances thereunto.

"Well," I said, "this is a small pond. An unprotected pond, and within plain view of the highway. Theoretically, it is all fished out, but actually — "

I hefted the interloper dubiously and laid him on the scales. An eight-pound bass can upset a lot of theory. Incidentally, while frogging or alligator hunting at night, I have occasionally had a bass jump into my boat, but never such a war-horse as this.

A week later, in a corner of my own county, I chanced upon an overgrown mill-pond. The miller was hospitable but discouraging.

"You're welcome, mister, but this here pond was fished plumb out years ago. Ain't nothin' in it a-tall, they say."

For a week I flirted with the place, inventorying its possibilities. Then one memorable afternoon I reeled in a ninepounder from a lily-pocket. The miller's eyes popped. So did mine.

Many of these supposedly barren ponds have half a dozen abdominous old roustabouts in them, crafty customers who gobble up everything else. Restocking is useless. Whatever you put in goes into their cavernous maws. They are a bad rubbish and a good riddance, if you can catch them.

So I'm getting a bad case of "localitis." A man may do a **deal** of exploring in his own back yard, and find it to his liking. There is no pleasure like discovering things for ourselves. Familiarity may not breed contempt, but it does breed incuriosity. I have found far more fish hereabouts than I ever suspected, although orthodox methods may not get them. I figure it this way: you can fish extensively or intensively. You can go a long way from home, or fish differently.

In the tumbling waters under rotting dams, in half-forgotten and supposedly fishless ponds, in the black creeks that creep sinuously through our swamps and the little lost lagoons adjacent thereto — I have found something to fish for. I am getting my share of bream and redbreast, the most savory morsel over which the son of man ever licked his chops; and bigmouth bass and bounding pickerel, locally know as pond-jack and growing up to six pounds.

I am getting more fish per mile than ever before. And since I have renounced my roving proclivities I have found that my wife is, after all, a rather charming person. Not that I am henpecked. I've never been at home long enough for that. But a man's wife does come under the head of practical considerations, and I see no reason for not admitting a fact that speaks for itself.

Then there is the incident of the Forty Dollar Duck, which my wife ate — and never forgot.

Duck hunters are a people unto themselves. They have a far-away look in their eyes. They talk of tides and time-tables, and make reservations. They lie in their comfortable beds and dream of distant flyways and smoky horizons, of lonely marshes and marrow-chilling winds, of a pallet on the floor and the humble corn pone.

I used to be something of a long-distance ducker, getting up at unheard-of hours, driving twelve or fifteen hours at a stretch, and heading for bankruptcy by leisurely stages. Sometimes I brought back ducks; sometimes I brought back lumbago and memories. Sometimes I ran into a revamped edition of the world's oldest lie: "Man, if you had just been here last week! In that very blind!"

From one three-day trip I brought back exactly one duck. Heck, it was all I saw. Anyway, it inspired my wife to do a little arithmeticking, with the result that it was thereafter known as the Forty Dollar Duck, and thereafter my long-distance ducking was over.

"Can't you find ducks nearer by to shoot at?" she asked.

"No."

"Why not?" she pursued.

"There aren't any nearer. You have to go away for ducks. Everybody knows that."

"What about some of those ponds and things you discovered last summer?"

Under the head of "things," I bethought myself of some places I had found while fishing, all in my own bailiwick. By snooping circumspectly here and there — and thinking like a duck thinks — I managed to bag a pretty respectable quota of ducks during the season. The expense was negligible, and not a single night away from home.

So I'm getting philosophical, something I never expected to be. Which is better, I asked myself, four hundred miles and ten ducks, or twenty miles and four ducks?

Nobody expects to find much quail hunting near a city as large as mine. It is one of those taken-for-granteds. When we want serious bird shooting, we head for the Low-Country, by which we mean not Holland, which surrendered to the Germans, but Charleston, which never yet surrendered to anything or anybody.

But the Low-Country is a hundred miles away. To drive a hundred miles, hunt all day, and drive another hundred back — well, you've got to get good hunting to justify it. I've had some superb hunts and some unaccountably birdless hunts. Again, there seemed to be no figurable ratio between the distance I went and what I brought back.

An experience I had three years ago was a revelation to me. On the opening day of the quail season, I got up before daybreak, put my four setters into the car, and headed for a coastal county 150 miles away. It rained the livelong day. For hours I sat and watched it drenching the fields and sluicing down the windows of my car. In bitter disappointment, I finally turned homeward.

About ten miles from town the rain eased up and the sun broke through a rift in the clouds.

"Let's take a sashay in that pea-field," my companion suggested.

"Too close to town and too near a highway," I demurred. "No birds in a place like that. Why, everybody and — "

"We've got only an hour left, and the day's ruined anyway," he persisted.

Just to be agreeable, I stopped and let the setters out. An hour later, we had raised three whopping coveys and I had fifteen birds in my bag. It's the hunt I am fondest of telling about. It redeemed a day that needed redeeming badly, and opened up for me a new vista.

Now a deal of my quailing is done in my own precincts. I am finding birds in the most unlooked-for places — in close-lying areas spurned by my predecessors, in fields so convenient that they were taken for granted by the other fellow. Since I began hunting locally, I have made a bird map of fifty distinct coveys within thirty miles of town in one direction only.

Indeed, I have found four coveys within the city limits. Bob is a sociable fellow, if you'll let him be. Privileged characters, these suburbanites are, but the very thing for training puppies in scraps of time.

There is a real advantage, too, in hunting the same coveys year after year. The birds are more predictable. They become more or less known quantities. You learn their range, their dinner hours and their flight habits. They become old friends.

Long trips are time-consuming, expensive and often disappointing. The element of fatigue, the hazards of the highway, the prolonged absence from home — all make against them. The "hang-over" hangs over so much longer too. It is harder to sweet-talk your conscience the next time you want to go. The way to hunt and fish is oftener, not longer.

It may be your misfortune to live in a relatively gameless section of the country. Nature just short-changed some of us in this respect. But wherever you live, if you will cultivate your own neighborhood closely enough, you will probably find game resources you never suspected. If you still can't find anything to fish for or shoot at, give it back to the Indians and come on down here. You are a sap for staying there, and you have nobody to blame but yourself.

"But all the hunting land near by is posted," someone hollers from the audience. Certainly some of it is. I sometimes wish more of it were posted down here. If one farm in every five throughout the South were protected, we'd all have better shooting. A protected area not only provides a hatchery from which game can overflow into the surrounding territory, but also supplies a refuge for over-harried game. I have a thousand acres myself, and it's all posted, but that doesn't mean a fellow can't hunt it, if he will ask permission and handle himself like a gentleman and sportsman.

When a state sells a man a hunting license, it is selling something it doesn't own. The state can't sell me the right to hunt on your land. When the government charges a man for the right to hunt, it ought to provide a place for him to hunt on. Unless it does, it is profiteering at the expense of either the hunter or the landowner. And it encourages trespassing. But we can't try that case right now.

Most farmers who post their land have ample reason for doing so. They may enjoy hunting themselves, or they may expect, and rightfully, some compensation for the privilege. Conscienceless game hogs might have abused their hospitality, shown them some discourtesy, or damaged their property. Whenever you discover the spirit behind a no-hunting sign, you are pretty apt to be sympathetic.

In the section where I used to hunt, there was a large plantation that I would have given my eyeballs to get on. Closely protected for years, it was teeming with over-ripe coveys. But the place bristled with no-hunting signs, threatening trespassers with fearful penalties. A dozen fellows who had ventured too close had been summarily haled into court and fined.

A rather pleasant fellow, the owner seemed to be, and I wondered what lay behind his feud with hunters. Surely there must be some semblance of reason. One day I drove through the pecan grove to his house.

"See you don't allow any hunting," I overtured.

"Anybody can see that," he returned.

"Well," I conceded, "I don't blame a man for saving his game for himself."

"It's not that. Never hunt myself."

Then, while we cracked pecans together, he told me the story. A few years before, in his absence, a gang of cutthroats had invaded the place with automatics, had hounded his game to death and, by their indiscriminate shooting, had so frightened a fine horse that the animal became entangled in a fence and was horribly lacerated. For a month that farmer had tenderly doctored the suffering horse, cursing the hunters daily in his heart, until it died.

"I never could catch them," he added grimly. "Reckon it was a good thing I didn't. I don't mean to be ungenerous to you fellows, but that's what happened."

"Nobody could blame you, I guess."

"As a matter of fact," he remarked, "right now I'd like to have a few birds for a sick neighbor. If you'd just brought your gun along — "

"Well," I suggested, "I *do* have a little 20-gauge in the car."

"I'm in favor of light guns. Gives the game a chance and doesn't scare the stock so badly. If you'd just brought along a dog — "

"Come to think of it," I said with a sheepish grin, "I happen to have a little setter in the car too."

The farmer walked with me over the place, showing me where the coveys were, and a most companionable fellow he proved to be. By nightfall he had birds for his neighbor and himself too.

"Feel sorta bad about taking your birds," he apologized. "But I'll tell you what. You and the frisky miss and that little gun come back whenever you like. Those signs are for blacklegs. Maybe all hunters aren't alike."

Behind many a posted sign is a just grievance, or such a rankling sore as this. Behind many another is a lonely farmer saying: "If you are the right sort, you'll come and ask me. If a thing ain't worth asking for, it ain't worth having."

What I started out to say was this: it took me twenty-five years to learn that the grass on the other side of the fence only *looks* greener. What used to be the most gamy and inaccessible places are now the most heavily hunted and fished. Whenever I've taken particular pains to get back where the other fellow didn't go, I've found him there in big numbers.

If you want to hunt and fish where the other fellow doesn't, go right back of his house. The other fellow isn't at home. He's a sap too!

🍁    🍁    🍁

# Indian Summer

JUDGE RANDY lived in that part of the country where tracing kinship is one of the fine arts, where you can still get up an argument about Calhoun and states' rights, and where the magical phrase "before the war" still refers to the War between the States. The old Judge had invited me down for a day's hunting, receiving me with a warmth that made me wonder whether visitors weren't few at the once historic but now half-forgotten homestead.

"Bless my soul, young fellow! So glad to see you. You've driven a good piece to get here and I know you're anxious to get into the field. Everything is ready and we'll start right away. A fine chance of partridges on the plan'ation this year, sir, a fine chance."

Call him Bob White, quail, bird or whatever you will in the rest of the country, but to elder sportsmen of the South this saucy little patrician is still partridge. It is *lese majesty* to call him anything else. And a dog doesn't point, he *stands*. Nor does a dog 'honor' another, he *backs*. Staunch is always *stanch*. And such a phrase as "a bevy of quail" instantly identifies the user as a rank outsider with probable leanings toward Republicanism.

A few minutes after greeting me, the Judge emerged from the rambling house with an ancient double-barrel under his arm. A heavy-bodied pointer stalked sedately behind him. When I looked at the corpulent and graying old hunter, my hopes slumped. Obviously, old Falstaff had seen his best days. A two-hundred mile drive, a fine prospect for birds, a mellow Indian summer day ahead, and a superannuated relic to hunt with. Why hadn't I disregarded the footnote in my host's letter and brought my own dogs! But Judge Randy seemed to sense my chopfallen appraisal of the aging pointer.

"Major is not so young as he once was, I know. Matter of fact, he and I are about the same age, considering. He was twelve last spring, and I'm sixty-nine. But the old reprobate grows fatter and fatter, while I grow leaner and leaner. But still a middlin' good dog, sir, a middlin' good dog."

From a cabin in the yard shuffled an old darky with the remnants of a once-costly hunting jacket, — the castoff largess of some long forgotten guest I surmised, — bulging about his middle. A dilapidated single barrel was slung across his shoulder.

"Is you gennermans ready for de journey?" He tipped his hat and gravely bowed.

"This is Simon, my factotum," explained the Judge. "Always take him along to tote the snack and the game."

The snack-toting role was agreeable enough, but I had to repress a smile at the Judge's optimism about the rest of Simon's duties.

Entering the field, old Major moved along as leisurely as if time were of no consequence. He had evidently learned to conserve himself, a habit doubly valuable to him now in the infirmity of age. I soon guessed that he had that uncanny gift, rare enough in the best of dogs, of covering a field with the least expenditure of energy. Watching him, I smiled and pondered the wisdom of the ancient saw: "Who drives fat oxen should himself be fat."

In the second field Major sniffed interestedly. Right-angling a path down which we were walking, he trailed a hundred feet and planted himself statuesquely near an overgrown terrace. Beckoning to me, the Judge leisurely walked up.

"We are ready, Major. You may advance," he said quietly.

A populous covey erupted from the hedgerow. Whirring wings filled the air. I shot quickly, dropping one bird and missing another. Unemotionally the Judge raised his double-barrel hammer and waited, waited until it seemed he had forfeited every chance. Then he affectionately fingered the right trigger, shifted imperceptibly, and repeated with the left. The birds fell in the broomstraw a hundred feet away. He calmly reloaded, utterly disregarding Major and the location of the fallen birds.

Major ambled over and picked up the far bird. Instead of returning to his master, he crisscrossed and picked up another. Then he clambered heavily up on the Judge and extended his big muzzle.

"I'm surprised at your manners, Major," the Judge gently reprimanded. "That gentleman is our guest. Take them to him."

With great dignity Major made me the beneficiary, and such a tender-mouthed job did he make of the double retrieve that hardly a feather was ruffled. From that moment, I conceived a new respect for the ponderous old pointer.

Facing about, Major headed straight for the spot where the nearest single had lit in a briar patch. The Judge confidently followed, although he had paid scant attention to the absconding covey. But the straight line that was the nearest distance between two points intersected a rail fence, which Major didn't feel like negotiating. Squatting on his fat haunches, he looked expectantly at Simon.

"Pick him up, Simon, and tote him across the fence."

"What dat, Jedge? Me tote dat lazy good-fer-nothin' dawg over de fence? He done sp'iled now twill he rotten, I specks."

"Don't be so garrulous, Simon, and do as I tell you. First thing you know, I'm going to get rid of you and get me a nigger that's some account."

"Garrylous! Dat a masterpiece, Jedge!" He smacked his lips over the word. "Garrylous! I gwinter try hit out on Cinthy. 'Shet up, Cinthy, yo' low-down garrylous varmint!' Dat what I gwinter tell 'er."

He picked up the dog and lifted him over the fence, scolding and fussing all the while. Once over, Major led us unerringly to the spot where the single had grounded. Thus another bird fell to the Judge's old hammer gun, and still another to my light twenty.

As Major lowered his head to pick up the second bird, a rabbit popped up from behind a stump and went scurrying through the underbrush. Caught off guard for a second, the old pointer reverted to a folly he had put away with puppy-hood — made a single ragged break for the rabbit. Realizing his miserable blunder, he walked forlornly back and delivered the bird. With head averted and tail drooping, he turned ashamed from his master and crept away, a picture of self-abasement and reproach. Sitting down on a log, the Judge took Major's head in his lap and toyed consolingly with the graying muzzle.

"There's no fool like an old fool, is there? They say it's once a man and twice a child, and I reckon that goes for both of us, old fellow. That sinister Simon must have been taking you on his rabbit-hunting debauches, and you just forgot which pulpit you were preaching in. Now quit pulling that long face, you pious fraud, and get back to work."

In the meanwhile Simon was in hot and clamorous pursuit of the cottontail, lugging his cumbersome Long Tom through the bushes and making the hills echo with his hue and cry. The harassed rabbit crossed and recrossed open patches within shooting distance of the darky, but true to the traditions of his race, he declined to risk a shot at a fleeing quarry.

The immemorial technique of the Southern Negro consists in whistling a rabbit to a standstill and then shooting it. So Simon jumped on a stump and whistled mightily. Presently his antique blunderbuss thundered and Simon, who had only a precarious footing on the stump, fell sprawling into a briar patch.

Major sat on his haunches and cocked his head at the disreputable figure. I collapsed on a convenient log, while the Judge laughed so immoderately he had to lean against a sapling. When the paroxysm had passed, he demanded, in a voice made to sound as indignant as possible:

"Simon, what in the name of the great Beelzebub is wrong with you?"

"Musta been dat super-sumpin' shell dat fine gennerman gin me," he explained, pointing toward me. "Iffen hit shoots front-wards lak hit shoots back'ards, I sho' Lawd done got me a rabbit."

"Simon," reprimanded the Judge severely, "how many times have I told you that it is poor sportsmanship to shoot anything sitting still? I have been trying for fifty years to make a gentleman and a sportsman of you. This sad exhibition shows what a failure I've made. You have not the slightest conception of sport."

"You kin hab de spote, sah, iffen I gits de rabbit. Ole nigger cyan't eat spote. Shootin' at birds and things runnin' is white man's foolishment. What de sense in shootin' at a rabbit runnin' when I kin whistle 'im down? 'Sides, I mout miss him runnin'."

When a second cottontail popped up a little later, old Simon thought to redeem himself in his master's eyes. He gave noisy chase until he was out of earshot, then commenced a subdued whistling. But the Judge, chancing to look down a path some distance ahead, saw the rabbit come to an abrupt halt and prick up its ears. The next second a gun boomed away and the animal toppled over in the path. In a few minutes Simon gleefully returned.

"Was that rabbit running when you shot it, Simon?" the Judge asked with disarming casualness.

"Was he runnin'! Lawd, Jedge Randy, he was a-goin' lak a streak o' greased lightnin', dat he was. Runnin' lak de berry Debil. I done kick 'im outen de bed and make 'im run for spote, sah."

The Judge sorrowfully propped his gun against a tree and addressed himself to the business at hand.

"Simon, you low-down lying blackguard, you contemptible disciple of Ananias, you mendacious double-jointed son of Ham. I saw that rabbit sitting in the path when you shot it."

The English language developed uncommon resources whenever the Judge lit in on Simon, and both of them enjoyed it.

"Lawdy, Jedge, say dat agin! You sho' sound lak a 'ristocrat dat time. Po' buckra cyan't talk dataway. I feels lak I done bin washed in lye water. What I means to say, dat rabbit was runnin' lak de berry Debil jes' *afore* I shot, sah. Dat what I mean. De blame fool done took and stop jes' as I pull de trigger, but how I know what he gwineter do, sah?"

With two rabbits dangling from his waist and a quarter in his pocket, — a tribute he had levied on me, — Simon felt pretty saucy. Swinging along behind his master, his piping voice intoned an old plantation melody about Brer Rabbit:

"Ole Molly Hyar,
What yer doin' dar?
Settin' in de cornder,
Smokin' yo' ci-gar.

"Ole Molly Hyar,
Yo' tail mighty white,
Yes, by Gawd, gwinter
Take hit outer sight."

In the next field Major's systematic quest proved fruitless, but at the edge of an adjoining woods he appeared to discover something of interest. The Judge and I followed leisurely behind. The trail he was following led under a big log, over which the pointer laboriously dragged himself, Simon not being present to perform that service for him.

The moment he was atop the log, Major's senses seemed to call a peremptory halt. Unable to maintain his balance, however, he let his forefeet slide forward, so that when we arrived on the scene he was pointing in almost a perpendicular position. It was an awkward and trying posture, especially for an old dog, but he continued to hold the picturesque pose for several minutes while I looked admiringly on. In spite of our distracting presence and comments, he held inflexibly, with the immobility of marble itself.

It was that way with Major. There were no half-way measures or compromises with him. A prematurely flushed covey was not in his scheme of things, and his judgment told him that any effort to extricate himself from the awkward position might spill the beans.

The covey was ensconced in a thicket of pines and cedars, where it was almost impossible to shoot. As I was eloquently bemoaning this fact, I heard the Judge chuckling contentedly to himself. It was not his way to complain because the natural

breaks were against him. Indeed, he liked nothing better than
being taken at a disadvantage. Another man's forlorn hope was
his meat.

"We are ready, Major. You may advance."

In such close quarters the covey scattered like chaff before
the wind. I got one bird as the bevy rocketed upward, and was
duly thankful therefor. Calmly the old Judge caught one "lad-
dering" over a tall cedar, then pivoting nimbly about, he caught
two distant absconders above a low pine. Major dutifully
retrieved the Judge's triple. Then Major congratulated the
Judge, and the Judge congratulated Major, after which dog
and man went into an affectionate huddle.

"That was something of an eye-opener, wasn't it?" He stroked
the dog's heavy muzzle, caressed his ears and soliloquized softly,
as if both were unaware of an alien presence. "We may have a
little age on us, you and I, but we are not quite ready for the
cider press yet, are we? Sounds like a doddering old fool maybe,
but if you and I have as much fun hereafter as we've had here,
there'll be two satisfied customers wherever we go."

Major gravely lifted a big paw into his master's hand, and
I felt that somehow there had been a meeting of minds.

When lunch time came, we stretched out in a sheltered spot
against a cliff, from which issued a hidden spring that glinted
and sparkled in the sun. From his antique hunting jacket, Simon
produced three pones of crackling bread, half a dozen cakes of
fragrant pork sausage, and a bottle of artichoke pickle. We ate
slowly, basking in the lazy sun. The Judge divided his snack
with Major, who thereupon stalked over to Simon and reminded
that worthy not to make a hog of himself.

"Tain't no use to come a-sniffin' around me, yo' good-fer-
nothin' scallawag," Simon protested. "You make old nigger tote
yo' wuthless hide over de fences an' ditches, and den laugh
at 'im when he fall in de briar patch. I ain't gwinter gin you
nary a scrap, sah, nary a scrap." But even as he jawed at the
interloper, Simon broke his last sausage cake and meticulously
divided it with him.

Lunch over, we drank deeply from the cooling spring and
sauntered on. As we entered an adjacent field Major found
a single, which the Judge neatly downed. Major ambled over

to retrieve, but there was nothing to retrieve. The bird had fallen in a spot clear of vegetation and the dog was mystified. Perhaps it was only wounded and had scampered away. But no, the trail started and ended here, and there was nothing whatever here — nothing but the whitened skull of a dead cow.

Major was above all else a dignified animal, with an almost human fear of appearing ridiculous, yet his nose told him that beyond a doubt the winged bird had taken refuge under the crumbling skull. The old fellow was in a quandary. In all his life he had never encountered such a crazy situation. Well, something had to be done about it. He couldn't go on bluffing all day. Gingerly nosing the skull over, he found the bird stone-dead. The comical relief registered on Major's face made the incident one of those foolish memories every bird-hunter treasures.

We spent the afternoon hunting the brown fields together, choosing the sunniest slopes and the easiest grades. Never once did the Judge instruct or rebuke the dog. Never once did he presume to tell Major how or where to hunt. That was Major's business. He knew the wide-spreading fields of the old homestead and the habits of each individual covey, as a good dog knows the territory over which he hunts year after year. They seemed to hunt together with a tacit gentleman's agreement.

As the afternoon waned and a nip of autumn began to steal into the air, the Judge started slowly homeward.

"We still have an hour of shooting ahead, sir," I hopefully suggested.

"Yes, and the choicest hour of the day at that," he answered. "But we lack only two birds of having our bag, and that's the best time to quit. The true sportsman imposes his own limit upon himself. For me, that is always one or two under the lawful bag. Always quit before you get enough, young fellow!"

Now that the hunt was over, the Judge and I walked some distance ahead, leaving Simon and Major together. The old darky was gabbing as usual, trying out on the unperturbed Major the mouth-filling phrases his master had used on him. Surmounting the brow of the red hill, we came to a set of drawbars, over which the Judge climbed and passed on, while I hung back to bring up the rear with Major and Simon.

With a general aversion to any sort of labor, Simon preferred crawling under the fence to pulling down the draw-bars. Then he looked back to see Major sitting soberly on his hams on the other side. Simon called but got no response. Then he tried to coax Major through, offering as enticement a morsel of crackling bread he had found in his pocket. That maneuver failing, Simon resorted to threats, winding up by wearing out his newly acquired vocabulary on the obdurate Major. In extremity, Simon climbed back under the fence and faced the dog.

"Lissen, yo' lazy white trash! T'ink I'm gwinter take down de bars for let you pass? T'ink I'm gwinter humor you dataway? Well, you mighty mistaken. Done sp'iled to death anyway. Wusser'n a free-issue nigger, you is. Yassah, I kin wait here jes' as long as you kin. I'm gwinter stay right here twill de cows come home, 'fore I pulls dem bars down for you. I'm gwinter set right here twill de bats fly and de owls hoot. You low-lifed, garrylous, prognosticatin' ole son-of-a-gun!"

Major yawned to show his lack of interest in the proceedings, and Simon started in afresh. The duel was finally broken up by Judge Randy, who had started back to see what the trouble was. Down the slope tumbled a blistering, volcanic rush of words. Old Simon jumped and answered meekly.

"Yassah, we's a-comin'."

Still arguing in a discreet voice, he proceeded to take down the draw-bars one by one, hoping for a compromise with his adversary, but not until the last bar had been removed did Major condescend to move. Then with great dignity he strode through, looking neither to the right nor the left, and followed his master up the winding lane to the big house, behind which a mellow Indian summer sun was setting.

# Not Always The Smartest

"MAN, I'VE got the finest puppy you ever laid eyes on!" the Doctor warmly assured me. "Only five months old and pointing birds to beat the band. Give him a little seasoning and, Mister, I'll show you a dog!" His eyes shone with a light that never was on sea or land.

Two years later I ran into the Doctor on a week-end hunting trip.

"By the way, Doc, what became of that precocious pup?" I asked.

"Precocious pup?" he repeated. "Oh, you mean that young buckaroo I had down in Georgia. Well, I'm afraid he didn't live up to expectations. Learned his a-b-c's fast, but busted out before he got to college. Turned out to be the most hard-headed, incorrigible cuss you ever saw. Can't tell about dogs, you know."

"Too bad," I sympathized.

"Yes. But I've got a youngster now that really has the makings. Some of Judge Goode's stock from Virginia, you know, and he's the most promising pup I ever had. Why, just the other day . . . "

And the old love-light crept again into the Doctor's eyes, convincing me afresh that the poet had doting dog trainers in mind when he wrote:

> "Hope springs eternal in the human breast;
> Man never is, but always to be, blest."

A number of my friends have had similar experiences with precocious pups. Some time ago one of them hailed me jubilantly: "Got a story for you to write!"

"What about?"

"What about? Why, that new dog of mine, of course. Man, I've really got a natural this time!" he beamed pridefully.

"A natural?"

"Sure. Remember that pup I bought two months ago? Well, sir, would you believe that little scutter is pointing and retrieving already? Didn't have to tell him a thing. Do I know how to pick puppies! And if he's that good now, what will he be in a year or so? Yes, sir, a natural if ever there was one."

What will he be in a year or so? I wondered about that myself. When I met the same fellow in the field later, I noted with interest that the dog whose promise he had so rosily depicted was not in his menage.

"Where is that natural you were theme-songing about last year?" I asked.

"How's that? Oh, you mean that Cap'n Kidd dog. I hate to admit it, but he was a thoroughgoing bust. Better at six months than he ever was afterwards. Wound up the most self-willed and intractable hellion in seven states. Flash in the pan, I guess. Dogs are funny that way. Thought I had a natural, and he turned out to be a natural damned fool."

His willingness to switch to another topic led me to suspect that here was another chastened citizen. I say "another" because I am a member of the chastened class myself. A charter member, in fact.

I once had a pointer pup whom in an over-fond and unguarded moment I christened "Miss Demure." A lovely little miss she was, patrician in every line. But she stole my heart and sold me out.

She had been following the other dogs on easy hunts, more for the exercise than anything else, and I had been paying her scant attention. I really intended for her to have her "coming-out" party the next season. But one red-letter day I found her stretched out on the loveliest point you ever saw, as staunch as patience on a monument. She had her birds tacked to the map too, and instantly retrieved the single I shot for her. I marveled that one so young could have a head so old.

Hugely pleased, I sat down in the broomstraw and gave my heart to her then and there. I hugged her to my palpitant bosom, told her she was the apple of my eye and the darling of my dreams, and that I would never love another woman. The rest of the season she was a prodigy and nothing less, pinning down coveys and singles alike, and performing her chores with a sweet dependableness that left nothing to be asked in a youngster.

"Well, at least here's one dog that won't have to be worried about," I clucked complacently.

I took pictures of her on point to damn the eyes of my skeptical friends, and had her written up in the society columns of the local paper. I wish, gentle reader, I most ardently wish that I could tell you that that pup, like the doughty hero in the stories of Horatio Alger, went on from there to marry the banker's daughter, to become chairman of the board, and ultimately to win the thanks of a grateful republic. In short, that she took Grand Junction and all the lesser junctions by storm.

I said I wish I could tell you that. But the mortifying truth is that she wasn't worth a horse trader's damn. My pride and joy became an acute pain in the neck, a recalcitrant little spitfire and an undisciplined wench. The older she got the worse she got. As Jeff, my ebony factotum, feelingly remarked: "Cap'n, dat dawg sho' done backslide clean into hell!"

Verily, I said, man that is born of woman is few of days and full of trouble. I fell out of love with Miss Demure, and straightway began to set my cap for a winsome little setter in my neighbor's kennel. It was the same old story of a precocious pup that didn't pan out. In one respect a bird dog is like a politician: too often there is a whale of a gap between pre-election promises and post-election performance.

The trouble with a prematurely bright puppy is that his owner is liable to take him for granted, allowing him to go his undisciplined way during the impressible age, so that the dog naturally becomes confirmed in error and incorrigible later. Assuming that he knows enough, we leave the youngster to his own devices. Little faults, correctible if caught in time, are allowed to crystal-

lize until the dog becomes intractable. It is like letting a bright
student "skip too many grades," which we often rue later.
Precocity of any kind is not always a happy augury for the fu-
ture.

A dog that "takes to it natural" will naturally contract the
habit of hunting for himself and not for you. The paramount
point in training any kind of hunting dog is, of course, to train
him to hunt for you and not for himself. And the time to teach
a dog is when he is at the teachable age. If you allow him to
miss too many trains. . . .

"The first year I didn't have to tell him anything. The second
year he was so hard-headed I couldn't tell him anything," a dis-
enchanted friend of mine remarked.

You may be able to teach an old dog a new trick now and
then, in spite of the proverb, but it is generally cheaper to buy
a new dog. You can break some undesirable traits, such as rab-
bit-running, but did you ever try to teach an old dog to retrieve?
I spent the better part of a season trying to teach an old setter
to bring me a bird, and never got to first base with her. The old
lady was too set in her ways.

Puppies that are reasonably hard to train often make the best
hunters. A dog that learns easily may forget easily. Easy come,
easy go. Many an agile-witted "grade-skipper" has to be sent to
coaching school now and then, or requires a brushing-up, and
sometimes a brushing down, at the beginning of each season.

But a dog that learns the hard way, by dint of constant repe-
tition, is apt to have the lesson indelibly etched on his memory.
There is less danger of such a dog's reverting during periods of
enforced inactivity, or when he falls into the hands of some other
person than his trainer, or when conditions are not conducive to
what the psychologist calls the maintenance-of-skills.

I once had a strain of setters that were all C students. Not
one Phi Beta Kappa in the lot. They were plodding, slow-witted
fellows that had to be told the same thing over and over again.
What they learned they got at the University of Hard Knocks,
by perspiration rather than by inspiration, and they seldom paid
any dividends until after the second season. Yet as a whole they
made uncommonly fine hunters. They got better as they got
older.

"I don't especially mind a slow pup," I heard a master trainer say. "Reckon I was pretty dumb in school myself, and I know how 'tis. Many a smart man was a dumb-bell in school, you know, and many of the bright boys have wound up keeping books for him."

There is, of course, no such thing as a "natural" in the sense of a perfectly functioning dog that never required any training. It is true enough, however, that puppies vary tremendously in their trainableness, their responsiveness to instruction. They run the whole gamut from brilliance to idiocy, as do the men who hunt them!

Occasionally a lucky fellow does get a brainy pup whose responsive instincts and birdy birthright provide him with able preceptors enabling him to pick up much that he needs to know. If you are one of those lucky owners, pay your preacher regularly and buy your wife a present — and don't stretch your luck too far! Don't assume that your pup's precocity relieves you of the necessity of training him. Don't take him out of school merely because he is ahead of the class. And don't, whatever you do, hurry him along too fast. A first-class gentleman's shooting dog was never yet trained by an impatient man or a game-hog.

A really well-trained dog represents months, often years, of painstaking work on somebody's part — and a very special kind of patience, intelligence and temperament. It is a specialty in itself, and why everybody with money enough to buy a dog thinks he has sense enough to train it passes comprehension.

Not more than one bird hunter in five is so situated and so constituted that he can undertake the training of a puppy with a reasonable prospect of success. Indeed, a large number of the trained dogs that are sold are ultimately ruined by the men who buy them. Remissness and over-indulgence on the part of the hunter, conniving at occasional slips until they become habitual, may eventually undo years of proper training.

The ability to train a dog, then, presupposes certain traits. And any man who hasn't these traits had better hire a man who has them to do his training for him. Better a little money than a lot of grief.

There once lived in London a famous diagnostician, Dr. Abernathy, whose name lives partly because of a smart answer he gave a patient who tried to wangle free medical advice from him.

"Oh, Dr. Abernathy," a tight-fisted dowager sidled up to him at a social function and asked, "if a patient came to you with such and such a symptom, what would you recommend?"

"Why, I would recommend Dr. Abernathy," he replied.

I've got sense enough to know I haven't got sense enough to train some dogs, and on a tight case I never hesitate to "hire Dr. Abernathy." With an idea of getting a little free advice from a trainer, I once asked, "If you had a dog that wouldn't honor another's point, what would you do?"

"I'd hire me to train her," he shot back.

Which I did.

About the hardest nut I ever tried to crack was a dog named High Pocket, a big-headed setter, wiry and long-muscled, and in all respects save one a magnificent hunter. High Pocket ate his birds. He didn't merely mouth them or rough them up. No, sir-ee! He bodaciously gulped them down. And not merely as a periodic spree, but as standard diet. How or when he acquired the nice habit I can't say, since he was two years old and thoroughly confirmed in his table manners when I got him.

Now I realize there are a number of ways of curing a bird-eating dog. I tried everything I could think up, and everything you could think up too, Mister! I cajoled and wheedled him. I gorged him with raw meat before taking him out. Whenever he ate a bird, I called him in and manhandled him in a way that might have disabled a lesser dog. That was one thing I loved about the rugged brute: he always came in and took the worst licking I could give him without a whimper. Also without mending his ways in the least.

I devised a highly ingenious muzzle for the improvement of his morals. I even disembowled birds and loaded their carcasses with such *hors d'oeuvres* as castor-oil and quinine, and on one inspired occasion with tabasco sauce. All of which High Pocket devoured with impartial gusto and touching gratitude, showing not the least ill effects from his gastronomical indiscretions. That dog had the alimentary immunities of a billy goat in a hard winter.

This is only a partial catalogue of the dastardly tricks I tried on him. As my wife tartly remarked, if I had studied my job as hard as I had the dog, I might have been made president of the company. And after all my fancy thinking and devising, the thing that finally cured High Pocket was an accidental discovery.

One afternoon I shot two birds on a covey rise, whereupon High Pocket blithely gulped them down, wiped the feathers from his mouth, and trotted toward me with a satisfied look on his face. "Nice going, boss. That double helped a lot."

Following the singles, he soon pointed again and expectantly waited for me, licking his chops in anticipation. As I raised my gun a wave of revulsion swept over me. This was too much, much too much. Utterly disgusted, I lowered my gun without shooting and stalked away toward the car. No longer would I be a caterer for a dog, a graceless glutton of a dog. I'd been played for a sucker long enough.

A hundred yards away, I chanced to look back. There was High Pocket still on point, casting bothered glances in my direction. I walked wearily on. In a moment he overtook me, trotted ahead, barked ingratiatingly, and then started back toward the broomstraw field.

"Boss, there's a whole field full of birds down yonder you've left," he said.

"No. I'll just be damned if I'm going to spend my time shooting birds for you to eat. After all, you're not paying taxes on *me*, you old renegade!"

Again he trotted in front of me and barked anxiously.

Finally I relented. "All right, I'll try you just once more, you unregenerate son of Belial, and if you eat this bird, so help me. . . . "

I walked back, he resumed the point, and I dropped a single. He recovered the bird, and just as he started to eat it I turned abruptly away — more out of disgust, I confess, than with the idea of enforcing a moral. Over my shoulder I saw him drop the bird and eye me in great perplexity. Then, to my utter amazement, he overtook me, pranced coquettishly in front, and handed me the bird as a peace-offering.

"You — you precious old scallawag!"

Half fearfully, I went back, found and shot another single, and pretended to walk away. Again he overtook me with the bird and tried to wheedle me into going back. After a great show of indifference, I capitulated and followed him, with the same incredible result.

For the next few weeks, whenever he picked up a bird I invariably stalked away, and he just as invariably ran me down with his offering. After a few weeks of this psychological dosage, High Pocket renounced his bird-eating habits altogether and added trustworthy retrieving to his other fine qualities.

When he finally came through, I felt like a doting father who finally attends the graduating exercises of a beloved and thick-headed son. But it did my ego no good to reflect on all the cleverness I had wasted before chancing upon so simple a remedy. It was like a fellow's going to the hospital and having his appendix removed, and then discovering that all he had really needed was a dose of bicarbonate of soda.

## Quail Guns And Loads

THE MOST-MISSED game bird in America. That, I think, is the dubious distinction of the Bob White quail. An incredibly easy target at times, yet the speed and disconcerting clamor of his take-off, his genius for ensconcing himself in unshootable places, his erratic flight and his unpredictable habits combine to make him the most-shot-at and the most-missed bird in the country. And ways and means of encompassing his downfall are likely to prove lively issues in any company.

This is not a technical article. I don't know enough about the subject to be technical. All it aspires to be is a practical statement regarding the gun-and-ammunition issue as it relates to quail-shooting under actual field conditions. And I should like to underscore *actual field conditions.*

Nor is this article written for the perusal of good shots. If you are already a crack partridge man, don't read this or any other disquisition on how to shoot. Go dry the dishes for your wife, or play dominoes with your grandchildren. If you are already an expert performer in any field, never listen to the other fellow's theories.

As it relates to quail-shooting, this gun-and-ammunition business depends as much *on the man as on the bird.* Of this I am perfectly sure. One man is effective with one type, another with another type. Nothing is more absurd than putting the same gun into the hands of everybody and saying: "This is what you need for quail." You can make guns uniform, but you can't make the men who use them uniform, nor the quail they shoot at. One man's meat —

There is a prevalent notion that the gun to give a tyro at quail-shooting is a small guage. "As soon as you get proficient with this little one, you'll be ready for a big one," the good-intentioned mentor advises. But the unreasonableness of this procedure is patent. It is adding a handicap to a handicap, — that of inexperience to that of an inadequate tool.

Believe me, the man who is inadept at quail-shooting needs every advantage he can get, especially if he is hunting under average field conditions and not on some millionaire's over-stocked preserve. Let him provide himself with a 12-guage gun, with bore and barrel-length to insure a quick wide coverage, and small shot.

And let him pray more or less fervently whenever he points at a brown target hurtling through the thicket or rocketing through the tree-tops, for that is where the majority of his shots will be. Unless, of course, he is shooting a plutocrat's pampered preservelings. Now don't misunderstand me. I'm in favor of plutocrats and preserves and pampering too, but as a catch-as-catch-can bird-hunter, I don't get much of either.

I do not mean to belittle small-gauged guns. Surely, they have their niches of usefulness. They are lighter to carry, and appreciably easier to handle. Under some conditions, these advantages more than compensate for a corresponding lack of load. There are times when *wieldiness* is more important than sheer power.

Nor do I mean to underrate the effectiveness of small gauges' in the hands of proficient users. Last season I saw a gentleman walk into the field with a little .410 and drop ten birds out of eleven shots. You will observe that I called him a gentleman! That man could *afford* to handicap himself, but I can't, and I'm not sure you can.

But I do reject the theory that a small-gauged gun is the proper weapon for an inexperienced gunner or an indifferent

performer who addresses himself to quail. And I vigorously reject the notion, so frequently encountered nowadays, that it is
"sportier" to use a small gauge on quail. A long, improbable or
ten-to-one chance is conventionally referred to as a sporting shot.
Sporting to whom? may I ask. Certainly not to the bird that
flies off, or scurries beneath the honeysuckle, and ultimately dies
of its wounds or is devoured by a lurking cat or other marauder.

Even under the best conditions, a sickening percentage of
wounded quail go unrecovered by the gunner and ultimately
perish. A larger percentage, I think, than of any other game
bird. The sporty shot is that which kills quickest and cleanest.
No thinking sportsman uses a bird to test the pattern of his gun
on. He does his experimenting on things inanimate.

Throughout the South, the orthodox load for quail is number
8 shot. Go into any store, however remote, and ask for bird-shot
and that is what you will unfailingly get. I had used 8's all my
life until two seasons back, when the ammunition "freeze" caught
my shell stock woefully depleted. Finally I found an isolated
country store with a case of number 10's.

"Why in the devil they sent me a whole case of sparrow-shot,
I don't know," the owner spat disgustedly.

In desperation, I bought the case of "sparrow-shot" and
opened the quail season with them. The result was a revelation
to me. With number 10's, I could drop them with considerable
consistency in the woods, "bays," and thickets where latter-day
Bob is rather-more-than-likely to be. True enough, they were
not all dead when downed, but a superb retriever looked after
that. Old black Joe, a shaggy and aging Gordon, was one of
the most patient and thorough workmen in the retrieving department I ever saw.

The majority of my shots were admittedly of the close variety,
but so will the majority of yours admittedly be, unless Lady
Luck smiles on your undeserving carcass. More often than otherwise, you will either shoot close or not at all. So I have become
a convert to number 10's, particularly for close quailing and
when I am aided and abetted by a good retriever.

But last season old Joe was gathered to his fathers, his succes-
sors were undistinguished retrievers, and I found it necessary to
use somewhat larger pellets that would drop my birds dead or

disabled. For the rest of my hunting days though, whenever I have a good retriever, or whenever my shooting slumps or my confidence wanes, I'll use number 10's and thank you too.

If I were a consistently good shot, I would not need the extra advantage that number 10's give. I could take almost any gun and any load and thumb my proboscis at *C. virginianus.* But if-ing is bootless business, and there is no escaping the fact that in quail-shooting the load depends as much upon the shooter as upon the shootee.

Every season I spend an enchanted week hunting quail on a 4,000 acre plantation in the famed low-country of South Carolina, as the guest of an old-fashioned gentleman whom I should like to introduce. Col. Longstreet Pettigru calls his sprawling estate his "plan'ation." That's the surest way you can tell whether a Southerner's great-grandfather was born in the South. If he says "plantation," he is an *emigre* and outlander, regardless of whatever amiable qualities he might have.

"But if he omits the "t" from plantation and pronounces John C. Calhoun "Caloon," you can be sure that he is still a States' Rightist and roundly distrusted Roosevelt although he voted for him, that his great-grandfather figured in a famous duel, and that there is a prized mint-julep recipe in the family.

Well, Col. Pettigru says "plan'ation," and in character and appearance he is a stalwart symbol of an *ancien regime.* Despite his seventy years, he is hardy and keen-visioned, and the best quail shot within twenty miles. An original thinker and a forthright man is the Colonel, and an astute judge of quail dogs and guns. All of his guests bring him their shooting troubles, and his diagnosis always commands respect.

"Come in, Charlie. Been sort of expectin' you," said the Colonel, as a distinguished-looking gentleman with a somewhat harried air came in and plopped down. "What's the trouble?"

"Same old ailment, sir. I'm just one of those too-soon shooters. Too nervous and excitable, I guess, and birds kind of scare me. Even on an open-field rise I shoot too quickly for my pattern to open up. Just impossible for me to hold my fire. I've read everything and tried everything, but can't help it to save my life. Guess I took up bird-hunting too late in life," he said dejectedly.

"Let's see your gun," invited the Colonel.

"Here it is, sir. Made in England and set me back a cool thousand. Everybody who sees it admires it, but maybe it hasn't got the right choke or something."

"Any choke is too much choke for you," commented the Colonel, fingering the gun. "Twenty-gauge, isn't it? Handsome gun. Yes, sir, a handsome weapon. Give it away as soon as you can."

"But, sir, my gunsmith said that a twenty — "

"Yes, a twenty is a fine gun for some people and some things, but the man who sold it to *you* for quail should be bashed in the head. Give it away."

"Well, I brought along a sixteen, with one barrel improved-cylinder and the other a modified choke, with a comb-drop of one-and-a-half, with a pitch and heel-drop — "

"You know too much about guns to be a good shot," the Colonel laughed. *"That gun fits you best of which you are least aware.* Take that old twelve gauge by the fireplace — the Battle of Manassas the boys call her — and that box of number 10's settin' by it, and tell Jed to give you a good retriever. Now you can go out and be as nervous as you please."

That night, when the harried gentleman came in, he was no longer harried. Instead, he was beaming like a schoolboy upon whom the demure little girl at the next desk had finally smiled.

"Colonel, that old gun is the medicine for me. The shootingest thing I ever handled. Got eight birds out of twelve shots this afternoon. Eight out of twelve. Imagine *me* doing that! Took me ten years to discover the right gun."

"And the right shot — for you," amended the Colonel. "You and the Battle of Manassas were sort of made for each other, I reckon. She's nervous too."

The next day the Colonel's clinic had another visitor, a surgeon from Memphis.

"What's ailin' you, Doc?" inquired the Colonel. "Thought you were right smart of a partridge man."

"I dunno," the doctor rubbed his chin ruefully, "a right debatable point, I'd say. Birds haven't been in the fields for days. All holed up in woods and thickets. Peculiar weather we've been having, I guess. Anyway, it's mighty close shooting and

I've been missing them for days. Reckon I ought to have brought some thicket loads or something."

"And you've promised to send some birds to those grandsons in Memphis to show 'em *rigor mortis* hasn't got the old gray mare yet, haven't you? Let me see your gun."

"If I ever get your carcass on an operating table — " the doctor laughed.

"Handsome gun," the Colonel admired. "Mighty handsome gun. Give it away."

"But Colonel — "

"But me no buts. Take old Manassas over there and that box of number 10's and bring some partridges home for your grands — if you don't want 'em to think you're a has-been. And tell Jed to let you have old Prince to do your retrievin' for you."

Another satisfied customer came in that night, his pockets a-bulge with swamp quail.

"This old rélic," he patted it affectionately, "is a humdinger. With a gun like that, you sure can invade their privacies. When I get back to Memphis, I'm going to do some tall gun-swapping."

Still other guests came in from time to time with their shooting troubles. One attributed his ineffectiveness to an attack of indigestion and a sleepless night. Another complained of a temporarily impaired vision. Another still was baffled by a protracted slump. And in every case the old Colonel admired their guns, took them away, and prescribed the Battle of Manassas, or the Slumper, as some of the boys called it, and number 10 shot.

Did the Colonel prescribe the same medicine for all his patients? Was old Manassas a panacea for all their shooting ailments? Well, hardly. One day a wiry young fellow came in looking "powerfully unhappy," as the Colonel phrased it.

"I'm training my puppies. They are a little high-strung and nervous yet, and my birds are getting up out of reach. But I've got to kill some birds over those buckaroos to settle them down. What do you suggest, Colonel? Now don't start pointing at that precious old relic by the fireplace this time!"

"Go upstairs, son, and fetch my old turkey gun by the bed. No, don't *fetch* it, bring it. You damyankees have plumb ruined my low-country English. You can reach 'em with old Kingdom

Come. But it takes right smart of a man to handle 'er. Better chew some of Doc's precious vitamins before you start out. And don't get the old girl into the habit of missin'," he chuckled.

Around the spacious fireplace with its smouldering hickory logs, the Colonel and his guests often held gun-and-dog clinics, during which they sipped hot toddies and "discussed the pros and cons of this and that." In all such discussions, the Colonel was by common consent referee and court of last resort, an honor properly accorded him as the "best partridge man in the county."

For the Colonel disdained the word *quail* as an upstart, however much his guests bandied the term about. Bob White was a Southerner. *Partridge* was his traditional Southern name, and partridge it would be. Just as he disdained the new-fangled word *honor* and clung to *back-stand* instead. And never a dog the Colonel trained would respond to the Yankeyism, *fetch!*

"Old Manassas there, however popular she is with you boys when you're slumpin', ain't the proper gun for a lot of people," the Colonel began. "Remember young Tuck Whitaker of New Orleans who was here last season? Well, I took away his 12 and gave him a 16. Then I took away his 16 and gave him a 20. And that ain't all. Henry, you and I saw him go to a skeet field in Savannah and crack 24 out of 25 *with a .410.* After that, I took his 20 and had him shootin' birds with a .410, and he liked it.

"An open-barreled 12 wouldn't have been any fun for Tuck, — and I wouldn't have had any birds left! Sometimes you got to handicap the man, sometimes the bird. By the way, Tuck ain't shootin' partridges now. Read the other day about a medal he got for pickin' off Jap machine-gunners.

"The point I'm makin' is this: the proper gun depends upon the man as well as the game, and on *how the game's behavin'.* And often on a man's dogs. Now partridge-huntin' ain't what it used to be, not by a jugfull. The partridge used to be an up-standin' field bird, a-willin' to take his chances fair and square. Now he's a *politician.* And a son-of-a-gun. And it takes a bush-whacker to get him. Maybe Bob has lost his nerve. Maybe he has degenerated, but *he's still alive,* and that's something.

"And to find 'em you got to hunt 'em where they are, not where they ought to be. To demonstrate what I mean, let's take a census right here. During the last two days, what percentage of your shots have been in the open? Now you boys figure a minute and speak up."

"About thirty percent of mine," answered Henry.

"Forty percent of mine, I'd say," contributed the Judge.

"Possibly forty percent, maybe less," added the Doctor.

"Thirty for me, and glad to get 'em," supplied another.

"Not over fifteen percent for me," still another mournfully announced.

"My stars and garters!" exploded an old timer. "You boys must have been hunting the pea patches to get that many open shots. I've been after those big coveys across the bay, and so help me, I've had only two open shots all day."

"That speaks for itself," resumed the Colonel. "This is fair-to-middlin' partridge country, yet on the whole, fewer than a third of your shots have been in the open. The others were fundamentally brush-shots, and with that kind of shootin' it's either now or never. *If you don't get 'em quick, you don't get 'em at all.* Gentlemen, we've got to accommodate our guns and loads to the habits of the quarry, and there's no dodgin' that fact.

"And another thing," continued the Colonel. "You boys have pretty good dogs, but how many of the birds you shot at today were actually pointed? Let's take another census. Henry, suppose you lead off."

"Only five out of twelve, for me."

"Only seven out of thirteen."

"Seven out of twelve."

"Five out of eleven."

"Eight points and seventeen shots."

"Nine points and twenty shots."

"Now that's what I'm a-leadin' to," continued the Colonel. "In spite of good dogs, fully half of your shots were unpointed. Birds stay in such heavy cover, and their behavior is so erratic that a dog is at an awful disadvantage. They scurry around under a network of brush, briars and honeysuckle, and your dogs are naturally baffled. They point here-and-there-and-everywhere and finally the culprit pops up over yonder or behind you. Am I right?

"That picture on the cover of that magazine there looks powerful pretty. Three dogs on a stylish point, in the middle of a beautiful field. Not even a persimmon or sassafras bush in sight. You can even count the birds on the ground. Now that gent was a fine artist and a nice fellow, no doubt, but you boys know you get powerful few magazine-cover rises these days.

"The other day I read an article about footwork. The first principle in shootin', the writer said, was a good stance so you could swing free and easy in any direction. Now he was a smart fellow, and no doubt he was right, but what kind of stance do you get in bird-shootin' nowadays? Like as not one foot is in a stump-hole, or under a log, or tangled up in honeysuckle, or in mid-air when the bird pops up. Like as not too, you're duckin' your head, wardin' off the briars, or pullin' a thorn out of your nose.

"Now under the conditions I've been talkin' about, and I'm sorry to say they are what you might call prevalent, a hunter's liable to need all the help he can get. I'm not a-fussin' with Bob, of course. What he does is his own business, and it's up to me to make it mine. I'm just sayin' that *unless a fellow's a crack partridge man,* he needs plenty of shot and a pattern that'll sort of make allowances. For most people, that means a good old-fashioned 12, with cylinder or improved barrels, and small-shot. Unless, of course, he's using some compensatin' attachment on his gun.

"I've got a crow to pick with the gun people too. To illustrate my point, will you go out and pattern your gun for us, Judge?"

The Judge tacked up a circular card-board, backed off, counting his steps as he went, and raised his gun.

"Now wait a minute," interrupted the Colonel. "How far are you from the target?"

"The standard distance. Forty yards."

"That's the very crow I want to pick. Forty yards. The standard distance. All the books say so, don't they? Yet how many birds do you shoot at that distance? How many do you even shoot *at* at that distance? Answer me that."

"Almost none, come to think about it. Too far. If you wait for a bird to get that far away, he's apt to be out of sight."

"Do you see what I'm drivin' at, boys? Forty yards is an absurd distance to pattern a bird gun. A gun should be patterned *accordin' to what's expected of it,* — accordin' to the game, and the man who uses it. Both the distance and the thirty-inch circle are impractical for birds.

"Everybody's inclined to over-estimate the distance at which he kills his game. Just human nature to exaggerate, I reckon. Now a partridge is pretty apt to be shot going away from you. It already has enough momentum to carry it a few feet even if shot dead in mid-air. The impact of the shot will carry it still farther, so you normally pick up your bird several feet farther away than you actually shot it.

"Make allowance for such driftage, and I'll bet the Battle of Manassas against a gun-shy dog that the average bird-hunter, under average conditions nowadays, will shoot most of his birds within *twenty* yards instead of forty. And a precious lot of his shootin' will be closer than that.

"And another thing," the Colonel continued, "have you noticed how Jed, the boy who works for me, can shoot? He knows nothing about gun-smithin'. Doesn't know whether he shoots with one eye open or both, and doesn't give a darn. Yet Jed can pick up any gun and any shell, and out-shoot any of you two-to-one. And most of these other local bird-hunters can do it too. The good Lord did it to sort of balance things, I reckon.

"Why can Jed shoot so well? Partly because it's not too *important* to him. He's not trying to bag enough birds to show his prowess or send somebody back home. But mainly because Jed is a product of the *outside,* as you boys are products of the *inside.* He has *country* eyes, and *country* nerves. You all have *city* eyes, *city* nerves, and *city* digestive systems. You think too much. A man can't shoot well when half of him is worryin' about things at home. He's got to be all there.

"No," he shook his head with mock solemnity, "rich and distinguished citizens ain't apt to be good bird-shots, and you might as well reconcile yourselves to that. But you can *improve,* and that's what counts. Courtin' is a lot more fun than celebratin' anniversaries anyway," he twinkled.

My own observation and experience lead me to side with the Colonel. Three-fourths of the bird-hunters, on three-fourths of the shots they get on an average day, need all the help they can get. The other fourth? Well, who in the hell's worrying about them?

# My Health Is Better In November

Does your health show a marked improvement during the hunting season, and do your honest ailments get scant sympathy from a suspicious household the rest of the year? If so, you are ripe for membership in the order of Misunderstood Husbands, Unincorporated, and entitled to all the rights and privileges thereunto appertaining.

I know a man who feels like the Wreck of the Hesperus for nine months of the year. He chews expensive vitamins. He sits for hours in the doctor's office, reading out-of-date magazines. His medicine cabinet is filled with strange nostrums in ill-assorted bottles. He is subject to neuritis and lumbago, and is plagued by nondescript aches and pains.

His digestion is so bad that he pays dearly for the slightest dietary indiscretion. And night brings him little respite; for sleep, sweet sleep that so poetically "knits up the ravel'd sleave of care," leaves him fagged and haggard. Nightmares use him to practice up on. His family regards him, and perhaps not without provocation, as moody and irritable. This fellow is really in an unenviable fix, but somehow he manages to drag his creaking chassis along . . . until November comes.

He is not a malingerer. Nor a neurotic. Nor one of those who *enjoy* bad health and revel in imaginary symptoms. He is honestly ailing. Once he went to a famous diagnostician who examined him for three days, charged him $100, and said: "You will live forever and feel like hell." The second part of the diagnosis he can verify, the first part he is not so keen about verifying. Forever is too definite.

But when the first frost comes, there is a noticeable improvement in his health. And when quail season arrives, he is a new man. Tonics and elixirs and tinctures of this-and-that are consigned to the attic. The medical profession has to eke out its existence without his munificent patronage.

He is no longer susceptible to colds, neuritis, and lumbago, although he tramps the countryside in the unfriendliest of weather and is often in wet clothing the livelong day. He sleeps the sleep of the innocent, unharried by nightmares. His outlook is buoyant, his disposition amiable, and the household hears nothing of his woes — not a solitary complaint — for the next three months. For the master of the household is paying ardent court to Bob-White and his bashful bevy.

This man sounds like a suspicious character, but let's not convict him on circumstantial evidence. A moderately honest and hard-working man he is, and I have a deal of sympathy for him. I know him well. In fact, I might be pardoned for saying that I hold him in peculiar esteem, for with all my faults I love *me* still. He is the gent who has been living with my wife for twenty-five years.

The fact that the improvement in my health coincides with the advent of the quail season doesn't mean that my ills during the rest of the year are imaginary. For outdoor pursuits have a recognized therapeutic value. Especially quail hunting.

After a day-long tramp behind a brace of ambitious dogs, a man doesn't need an appetizer when he sits down to dinner. Nor does he require a lullaby to put him to sleep. And it's a hardy neurosis indeed that will outlast a few busy and sparkling days afield in the autumn of the year.

For who could ask a better bracer than a covey of birds deployed in a sedge field at twilight? A rarer cordial than a *tableau* of hunters tensed about that bombshell poised in the ragweed? Or a more potent elixir than a bevy that pirouettes about your head and goes zigzagging through the treetops?

Farmers seldom have nervous break-downs. They haven't time. People who lead a brisk outdoor existence don't go in for neuroses, psychoses, and other expensive and fashionable complaints. For a stirring day in the field purges the mind. There is such a thing as mental constipation too, you know. What this country needs right now is a *mental* laxative.

The quail hunter leaves a hierarchy of troubles and worries behind him. He is not wondering whether the bank is going to foreclose, or when that next note will be due. He is not wondering whether he has coal enough in his basement, whether that insurance policy has elapsed, or whether he has enough cash on hand for his next income-tax installment. He is for the time being one of those men who are born free and equal.

His biggest concern now is whether there's a covey in the edge of that pea patch, whether the singles went in here or deeper, whether he will get a double or an inglorious miss, or whether that overanxious little debutant pointing in the stubble field will hold until he gets there.

And these are all transient worries that will soon resolve themselves, to be followed by others equally absorbing and equally transient. After all, a man is entitled to enough trouble to keep his mind occupied. As David Harum so feelingly remarked, "A reasonable amount o' fleas is good fer a dog — keeps him from broodin' over *bein'* a dog."

I am one of those who through some whim of fortune or skullduggery of chance became a white-collar man. I am a country boy who wound up in the city, and it goes hard with me. For twenty-five years my wife has been trying to make a gentleman out of me.

I dream of a springy sod beneath my feet, a nip of autumn in the air, and of a lemon-eared pointer loping across the golden broomstraw, while I pound the pavements or sit behind a desk and tell hundreds of people I'm glad to see them.

But don't waste your sympathies on me. That pavement-and-desk routine is just for nine months of the year. During the hunting season I am a rebel and a renegade, away from the job so much that I stand in imminent danger of being fired. I always leave full instructions for my successor, just in case. Yes, I get quail hunting aplenty for three whole months, and that's the only time I don't feel bad when I get up and worse as the day progresses.

Some of you who fish and hunt are probably like that too. We spend nine months of the year waiting for the other three. We are children of the earth. When they try to civilize and regiment us, we fret and fume. Our colons become spastic, our pancreatic juice becomes unhappy, and our old chronic ailments go to work on us. We are not unlike the Titans, the earthborn giants of mythology, who were invincible in battle only as long as their feet were planted on the good earth.

I'm no Jeremiah lamenting his fortunes. I'm not complaining. I'm just explaining. And all I am asking is a little consideration for the state of my health *between* hunting seasons. I'm tired of having my every complaint met with the same wifely reception, namely:

"Oh, you'll get over it when the hunting season opens."

"Now don't tell me that drying the dishes and mowing the lawn affects your neuritis, when you can tote a shotgun all day."

"Yes, I know. Sitting up in church gives you lumbago. Moving a trunk to the attic gives you lumbago. Pulling morning glories out of the garden gives you lumbago. Waxing the floor gives you lumbago. Yet day after day you can hunt your dogs to death, and I never hear lumbago once."

See what I mean? I repeatedly tell my wife that hunting is different. That it is also self-sustaining, since in quail season I save enough on doctor and medical bills to pay all field expenses, which is the gospel truth. But as a college freshman wrote: "It's like water on a duck's back — in one ear and out the other."

Is your health seasonal too? And do you feel qualified for membership in the Order of Misunderstood Husbands? If so, you can send in your dues and call me brother, for I am secretary and treasurer, president, and chairman of the board.

❧   ❧   ❧

# Havilah Babcock: Virginia Carolinian
## (1898–1964)
### By Claude Henry Neuffer

IN 1926 Havilah Babcock, Virginian, Master of Arts from Mr. Jefferson's University and professor of English at William and Mary College, came to the University of South Carolina on a year's leave of absence. He found the hunting and fishing so good and the people so hospitable and so much like his native Virginians that he remained to become a distinguished professor and head of the University's English Department for twenty-seven years. Here, where he taught for thirty-eight years, he was an institution and the kind of man about whom truths and legends were freely circulated. As a teacher he was incomparable and unpredictable and happily incapable of pedantry or dullness. He might begin a class by saying, "I'll give twenty-five cents to anyone who can spell Houyhnhnm." On the day after a rare Southern snowfall, he greeted his arriving students with a fusillade of snowballs. His classes resembled Robert Frost's poems: they began in delight and ended in wisdom. The cordial rapport between student and teacher made his courses the most sought after at the University, causing students to sign up a year in advance for English 129. In this vocabulary and semantics course students learned of the charm and power of words as they listened to a master of word craft deal with their nuances and constantly shifting connotations.

Even though Havilah Babcock was an excellent teacher and referred to school-teaching as his trade, his particular genius was writing, and from his first school composition to his final prose tale he worked hard to attain perfection in his craft. His writing career began in Appomattox, his birthplace, in the sixth grade when his teacher agreed to promote him to the eighth grade if he would write a short novel during the summer. Young Havilah bought himself a fat ten-cent tablet and began writing. In three weeks, he had filled the tablet and finished his novel, which the teacher examined and pronounced fine prose for a boy of twelve and promoted him to his desired first year of high school.

In his undergraduate days at Elon College and the University of Virginia he absorbed Poe and determined to be a writer. However, it was some years later that he perfected his unique prose genre, the informal, whimsical, essay-like tale of hunting and fishing in the Carolina Low Country. These are the prose pieces that will ultimately take a quiet place in American Literature comparable to Izaak Walton's *The Compleat Angler* in English Literature. The tales and essays were first published in *Field and Stream* and other magazines, and later the best were brought out in four collected volumes: *My Health Is Better in November* (1947); *Tales of Quails 'n Such* (1951); *I Don't Want to Shoot an Elephant* (1958); and *Jaybirds Go to Hell on Friday* (1964).

Havilah Babcock found his "briar patch" and ideal authorial habitat in South Carolina, where bird hunting and bream fishing are passions as well as pastimes. Like William Faulkner he drew his strength as writer and man from the soil, preferring also the company of hunters, farmers, and fishermen to writers, critics, or professors.

As a man Havilah Babcock's loyalties were divided between South Carolina and Virginia. Reminders of his Old Dominion background often appear in his writing. In dealing with a fine dog's ancestry, he will usually trace him back to some noble Virginia canine F.F.V. During his years of teaching in South Carolina he never failed to return in the summer to his native Appomattox—sometimes for three months, sometimes for three days. Regardless of other matters, he was always a Virginian.

However, as a writer his subject was essentially Low Country South Carolina, which he lovingly described as a bird hunter's elysium:

> Of all the things I have enjoyed on this terraqueous globe—that I am willing to set down on paper—the one I have enjoyed most has been bird hunting in the fabled Low Country of South Carolina. The Low Country is conservative and sparsely populated, with life centering around its great plantations and tempered by a leisureliness and gentility savoring of an ancient, half-forgotten regime.
>
> You somehow have the feeling that this country looks very much as it did a hundred years ago, that the on-rushing stream of progress has thankfully passed it by, and that you are part of a brooding and twilight civilization that is perhaps tinged with a mild melancholy.

This land of spacious fields and few fences has a long tradition of hunting and hospitality, and another man of the woods and fields, John James Audubon, after visiting here in 1831, wrote to his Charleston collaborator, Dr. John Bachman, of "the noble and generous spirit of the hospitable Carolinians," adding, "I certainly have met with more kindness in this place than anywhere else in the United States." Havilah Babcock also expressed a similar sentiment for his adopted home: "South Carolina is a fine place for a Virginian to live."

A notable nineteenth century forerunner of Havilah Babcock was William Elliott of Beaufort, South Carolina, an honor graduate of Harvard in 1809, and a man of literary tastes and talents. He found time from the managing of his plantations to write hunting and fishing sketches signed in the Waltonian manner Venator and Piscator. These writings were later collected and published in book form under the title *Carolina Sports by Land and Water* (1846). Mr. Elliott's sketches possess both the quiet, contemplative spirit of Izaak Walton and the familiar, personal tone of Havilah Babcock.

Of the South Carolina partridge, Babcock's patrician of birds, Elliott remarks:

> The partridge is the same bird which is miscalled in the Middle States the quail. It is a veritable partridge—though smaller than the English partridge or the red-legged partridge of Spain.

Mr. Elliott continues to commend the partridge highly both to the hunter and the epicure, quoting an encomium on the red-legged Spanish species "it should be eaten with none but champagne sauce, and in no posture but on one's knees—through thankfulness."

But it was without champagne sauce that Havilah Babcock found in the fields of his adopted state the ideal subject for his gun and pen— *Colinus Virginianus*, the Southern partridge, the *nonpareil* of game birds—described by him as "an unreconstructed Rebel if ever there was one. In the South, where gunning for him is both a pastime and a passion, he is still called partridge. You Yankees, who can name things better than you can hit them, insist on *bobwhite quail*. Well, that sets him apart. But he doesn't depend on the English Language to get that done. He sets himself apart."

"Call him Bob White, quail, bird or whatever you will in the rest of the country, but to elder sportsmen of the South, this saucy little patrician is still partridge. It is *lèse-majesté* to call him anything else."

Havilah Babcock has offered other rhetorical accolades to this patrician of gamebirds:

"Although I hunt Bob hard I hunt him fair. I would be loth to take an ungentlemanly advantage of so gallant a gentlemen."

"Most old-fashioned bird hunters feel this way. An acquaintance of mine who owns a fine Low Country plantation once said rather pointedly:

'Come back and hunt whenever you wish. And bring an occasional friend with you. But be sure the fellow compares favorably with a partridge.'

"I have often said that the bobwhite is America's most superb game bird, and that the pursuit of this gallant little fellow is the pastime of a scholar and a gentleman. I may not fit either of these categories but few men have pursued *Colinus Virginianus* longer or more ardently than I."

In his last published volume, *Jaybirds Go to Hell on Friday,* recalling his recovery from a serious operation, he speaks with reverence and rapture of his old friend Bob White:

"For a while it was touch and go with me in the hospital and at times my spirits sagged. But during an especially black mood when I was at the bottom of the doldrums a sound floated through the open hospital window that brought instant delight and set my heart to singing. It was the clear, bold, lilting call of Bob White! Bob White! coming out of the misty daybreak. I held my breath and with pure joy drank in the musical cadences of the call which has always thrilled me beyond others. And from then on I began to think about hunting and decided I had a chance of pulling through."

And he did pull through for two more years of hunting, teaching, and writing; and in his valedictory story, "When a Man's Thoughts Are Pure," he wrote a muted elegiac on the hunter at daybreak:

"Whenever I go for a day's hunting I like to get up an hour or so *besun,* to use a grandfatherly phrase. The breaking of day is for me a quiet miracle, bringing balm to hurt spirits and a moment of privacy in which to contemplate the day ahead. Forever old and forever new, a sunrise is always and never the same."

Although Doctor Babcock was capable of such a contemplative, meditative tone, his works more often possessed a genial humor and an acutely skeptical view of the passing men and events.

On some of the shortcomings of scientific agriculture he speaks with conviction:

"The vanishing of the rail fence from the Southern scene was due in part to the widespread use of barbed wire, that invention of the devil. A bygone regime could look indulgently upon a sprawling rail fence but modern agriculture, with its emphasis on maximum land utilization, must have fences that are straight, efficient, and characterless.

"The rail-fence and the honeysuckle thickets in Virginia have often been the partridges' salvation. Throughout the quail-hunting South, the honeysuckle and the brier patch is perhaps his most used harbor of refuge.

"Social historians and agronomists have long poked fun at the old fashioned farming of what it pleases them to call the benighted South. Old fashioned it was. Unscientific it was and sometimes inefficient and wasteful. But it was the precise type of agriculture most congenial to the incidental production of game. Let's not forget that."

On idyllic notions concerning boyhood, nightingales, and un-requited love he humorously observes:

"I sometimes wonder whether boyhood is all that it is cracked up to be. For time out of memory poets have depicted it as an idyllic existence, a sweet Elysium of unruffled waters and cloudless skies. But boyhood apparently improves with age, poets waiting until it is safely behind them before writing panegyrics about it. And the more remote it is the nicer boyhood seems to become. I have been struck by the shortage of what might be called contemporary poetry about the subject.

"There has probably been more literary lying about boyhood than any other subject, with the possible exception of nightingales and unrequited love. As for nightingales, only people who have never heard a mockingbird on a telephone pole at daybreak could go into ecstasies about them. And as for unrequited love, it is seldom fatal, Shakespeare having observed with great sapience: 'Men have died from time to time, and worms have eaten them, but not for love.' "

Of South Carolina *pilaus* and *bogs* he writes with reservation:

"A Virginian by birth I like everything about South Carolinians except their weakness for *bogs* and *pilaus* of one kind or another. These concoctions are too Democratic for me, their prepetrators having no qualms about tossing into the *omniumgatherum* whatever is not otherwise disposable. I once saw a scorpion fall into a pot of pilau, and the clerk of the works didn't bat an eye."

On the finer distinctions between horses, mules, and *tacky* ponies, he speaks with authority:

"Take a horse for dignity, a mule for safety. Take a horse to have your picture made on, a mule to get you back home. Not that a mule gives a darn about you; he just doesn't want to get hurt himself. What I'm trying to say is that a horse has more education, a mule more sense.

"The finest hunting mounts I have ever ridden were the *tacky* ponies Bernard Baruch used to get from Hilton Head and other islands off the Carolina coast. Easy-riding, intelligent, and sure footed, these ponies are said to be descendants of horses brought over by the Spaniards in the 16th century."

But there are some subjects, such as grandsons and bird dog puppies, that always held a special place in the heart and memory of Doctor Babcock, and of these he wrote with a fervent but reverent spirit. The matter of the proper things to leave a grandson is recorded in one of his finest stories "Miss Priss." Here the authorial Babcock, a retired school teacher and grandfather, is a man "who had always figured that the best legacy a man could leave his grandson was a good gun and a good bird dog, a hunter of proud lineage whose feet would disdain the faltering pace of groundlings." He found a young dog just right for the boy because the grandfather believed: "A boy and dog should grow up together, making their own mistakes and discoveries, each molding himself to the other. One man's hat seldom fits another."

In another story, "I Went to See a Man About a Dog," a schoolmaster grandfather expresses a like ambition:

"I want Princess here to be a faultless retriever. It's retrieving that makes partridge hunting a gentlemen's diversion. I'm training Princess for my grandson, and she must be as proficient in all departments as possible. That dog,—and this watch—are about the only legacies I can leave him. And it would hurt me powerfully, sir, to think that I had left my grandson a dog that might embarrass him."

Both these grandfathers, although teachers and men of letters, would have agreed with General Archibald's grandfather in Ellen Glasgow's *The Sheltered Life,* who insisted "that hunting had given greater pleasure to a greater number of human beings than all the poetry since Homer."

Next to describing the proper bringing up of grandsons, Doctor Babcock wrote most lovingly of the proper training of young bird dogs and the inexplicable joy of viewing the first point your puppy makes:

"There are certain events which enshrine themselves in a man's memory. As Virgil said two thousand years ago, and as you and I declaimed when the world was young: 'Perhaps it will delight you to remember these things in days to come?' "

In a fine story, "The Deacon's Grandpa," the young incorrigible puppy Deacon is at last taught to properly back the older dog Preacher:

"Nervously lolling his tongue, he glanced at Preacher with profound respect. Then he gingerly backed two steps until his head was even with Preacher's rump, the proper place for a grandson, after all. There he planted himself for the whole world to see. As I watched the tableau with swelling heart, the menace in Preacher's throat subsided into a soft murmur of approbation.

"For five minutes I let them stand. I am no longer a young man, I reminded myself. In the span that may be vouchsafed me by the Bountiful Giver I may not walk this path again. I will hang this picture in the gallery of my mind to enliven my fancy in days to come. And if I felt the taste of salt in my mouth, it was nobody's damned business but mine."

There are two other matters on which the dog-loving Babcock could speak from the heart—the classic beauty of a perfect point and the priceless boon of a good retriever:

"A gracefully pointing dog is to me a perennial delight—a scene which, however often beheld, has always a newness about it, one which never fails to bring me a quickening of the senses and a long moment's rapture.

"A beautiful retriever is like a virtuous woman. Her price is far above rubies. For retrieving is what makes the difference between a good dog and a great one. It is the icing on the cake, the cherry atop the sundae, the lace on the bride's pajamas. It is the *summum bonum* of an autumn's day in the field. It is of fortune's cap the very button, and that which makes bird hunting peculiarly a gentleman's pastime.

"It is something that makes you say twenty years later: 'I once owned a dog'—or 'There is where it happened in a patch of beggar's lice just back of the old orchard.' This is the very stuff that reminiscence is made of."

Almost as much as he loved his dogs Doctor Babcock was attached to his hunting and fishing companions. And they were a varied lot of all sorts and conditions: his son Huck Babcock; Bernard Baruch, South Carolinian and man of large affairs; Dr. J. E. Copenhaver, professor and research chemist, with whom he hunted every Thanksgiving Day for twenty-five years; Rhett Shuler and Doc Rhodes, farmer-planters of Low Country South Carolina; Dr. Yeaton Wagener, his long-time English Department colleague and incomparable raconteur; Dr. Ben Miller, Columbia physician and devoted friend; Honey Chile, a six-feet-four *overlooker* of game on Doc Rhodes' 3,000-acre plantation, who knew the whereabouts of most of the circulating coveys on the place and could always see where a bird fell or where the singles went down; and the writer of this profile, a professor of American Literature, described by Doctor Babcock as "an unfailing colleague and the world's greatest walker," who hunted with him for fifteen years and never carried a gun.

Of Doctor Copenhaver, his hunting companion of longest standing, Doctor Babcock has spoken from the warmth and certitude of an old friendship:

"For twenty-five years I have hunted with the same companion, which must establish some sort of record for mutual tolerance. Now, there are both advantages and disadvantages in having the same sidekick so long. We know the idiosyncrasies of our dogs, which enhances the pleasure of the hunt. We also know the idiosyncrasies of each other, which *sometimes* enhances the pleasure of the hunt.

"During the twenty-five years of companionship any two men will accumulate a fund of experience to talk about, but long association tends to reduce the necessity of conversation. We know each other so well that we don't have to talk. A monosyllable may effect a meeting of minds, a meaningful glance may recall some experience memorable to both."

For Havilah Babcock hunting was a social pastime which he enjoyed with men and dogs as his beloved companions. He often said that the best way to gauge a man's character was to take him bird hunting, for there his virtues and vices were sure to crop out since "people are inclined to behave naturally outdoors."

He was also sometimes partial to dogs as companions saying that "a trait which makes a dog good company is his imperfectness. They partake of our own frailties. After all, it is not strength but weakness that endears. You don't make friends by being right all the time."

In one of the last pieces he wrote, "When a Man's Heart Is Pure," Doctor Babcock speaks somewhat in the manner of Izaak Walton concerning good company and good discourse making the way seem short:

"No dissertation on the pleasure of hunting and fishing should leave out the titillating effects of good conversation. A great beguiler of time and abridger of distances is conversation, for what so shortens a trip as good talk? The charm of good conversation lies in its spontaneity and disrespectfulness, the way it rambles without apology from one topic to another. Lay down rules for the conduct of a conversation and you wind up with a conference, which is a swapping of ignorance and an exercise in mutual boredom. The first requirement of good conversation is that nobody should know what is coming next.

"Good conversation, of course, demands good companionship. A man may work alone, but it is improbable that he will get much playing done without the companionship of others. Bird hunting is one such social pastime. Companionship is, in fact, half the hunt and may go far toward redeeming a bad day. Certainly it should be listed among the pleasures of hunting, but tastes in companionship may vary.

"I want a companion to be friendly, but not too friendly; to be talkative, but not too talkative; to have a good dog, but not quite as good as mine; to have a sense of humor without being a humorist. I also want a companion who is a good shot, but not too damned good. The first rule of companionship in hunting is not to embarrass the other fellow.

"Surely not the least of my pleasure in hunting and fishing is getting back home. And having somebody there who is glad I'm back, and is interested in the kind of day I've had, someone to call out, 'Any luck?' "

And Alice was always there.

Next to his ardent lover's battle with bobwhite, Doctor Babcock pursued another incomparable beauty close to the hearts of all South Carolina anglers—the Edisto River redbreasted and the copperhead bream. To these *nonpareils* of Carolina's rivers he has paid splendid tribute in his first collection of tales, *My Health Is Better in November*.

"The copperhead bream is almost legendary with South Carolinians. In a manner of speaking, he is our state fish, the piscatorial laureate of the commonwealth. Bound up with memories of the ante-bellum, with States Rights and pistols-for-two and coffee-for-one, the bream is held in unique esteem. From time out of memory, anglers have acclaimed his mettle, epicures his meat.

"Did not Yates Snowden [one of Doctor Babcock's colleagues at the University] more than half a century ago, write:

> And here was mooted many a day
> The question on which each gourmet
> Throughout the parish had his say:
> > "Which is the best:
> Santee or Cooper River bream?"

Doctor Babcock wisely does not attempt to answer this question but he does proceed to excoriate lexicographers for their inadequate and colorless descriptions of the bream and their pronunciation: *breem*, when "any Southern boy big enough to button *britches* knows it is *brim*." Instead of a scientific discourse on the nature and characteristics of the species, he speaks with a more authentic voice:

"The finest tribute to him I ever heard came from an old bream fisherman with a week's beard on his face and poetry in his heart. 'The bream,' he fervently announced, 'is one fish God a'mighty made for a fly rod and a gentleman.' "

In his long sojourn in South Carolina Havilah Babcock learned to dearly love this proud domain of hunters, planters, and fishermen and became one of them.

"During the full moon in May, we South Carolinians have a seasonal sickness. It is the bream fever. We go around with rapt expressions on our faces. We talk a language of our own. We are subject to strange going-and-comings, to sudden exits and unpredictable absences."

In this land of what he called the huntingest and fishingest folks in the world even certain family names are synonymous with perfection in the use of the flyrod or the bird gun. If a man's name is Boykin or Hampton, he is expected to always get two birds on the covey rise. Here people don't pick a day to lay aside business and go fishing, but now and then they choose a day to stay at home and tend to their affairs. It is also a peculiar province where as Doctor Babcock says: "Every loyal citizen has three ambitions. He wants to refight the Battle of Gettysburg, run for governor on a States'-Rights platform, and inherit a grove of catalpa trees [source of the famed caterpillar bream bait]." And he knows that if Stonewall Jackson had been at Gettysburg, the outcome would have been different.

Although Doctor Babcock as a converted Carolinian never ran for governor or succeeded in restaging the Gettysburg engagement, he did possess one luxuriant catalpa tree in his backyard, shading the pen where Whitey and Fleet, his pair of English setters, resided. And in one of his finest accounts of the mystic rites of bream fishing he speaks eloquently of catalpa trees:

"When I am ready to retire from schoolmastering, I shall ask no better annuity than a well-ravaged grove of catalpa trees in the bream-fishing country of the Deep South.

"But I shall know better than to call them catalpa worms, for *catalpa* is almost an alien word in the lower South, having long ago abdicated in favor of the homely *catawba*. Southerners have a genius for nicknaming things. The crappie has resigned itself to the ungracious appellation of *goggle-eye*. The warmouth bass has degenerated into *Molly*. The lithesome chained pickerel is always stigmatized as a *jack*, while the unmentionable bowfish is invariably a *Mud*. The bigmouth bass, on the other hand, is commonly promoted to *trout*, and my fellow Carolinians imperturbably bag eight-and-ten-pound *trout* in Lake Murray and Santee-Cooper reservoirs!"

There are times when Doctor Babcock's fishing tales take on a quieter tone and resemble the reflective, leisurely observations of the grand old classic of the fishing art, Izaak Walton's *The Compleat Angler*, which offers this contemplation on the virtues of angling:

"Angling was, after tedious study a rest to his mind, a cheerer of his spirits, a diverter of sadness, a calmer of unquiet thoughts, a moderator of passions, a procurer of contentedness; and it begot habits of peace and patience in those that professed and practiced it."

Doctor Babcock speaks in a similar voice on the worth of fly casting:

"It is beyond peradventure the most leisurely and tranquilizing form of fishing. What will so banish the cares that infest the day as the rhythmic swish of a fly rod over a lily-crowded cove tip at eventide.

"Whenever I need a psychiatrist, I go fly fishing, holding a boat to be superior to a couch any day of the week. A fly rod is good for whatever ails a man. Any curable infirmity to which the flesh is heir is sure to respond to its persuasive therapy."

In a quieter mood also is this little vignette of the black water creeks of lower South Carolina:

"Our low-country creeks and spillways are famed for their fishing. A serpentine black-water creek that steals its way through a brooding cypress swamp is to me a thing of dark enchantment, a mystic and primeval region where the strangest things happen naturally. And nowhere else on the habitable globe, I think, will one find such an amazing variety of game fish in comparable water."

And Doctor Babcock would surely agree with Izaak Walton's little Epistle to the Reader:

"I shall stay him [the reader] no longer than to wish him a rainy evening to read this following discourse; and that, if he be an honest angler, the east wind may never blow when he goes a-fishing."

Havilah Babcock could rightly say with Montaigne, "It is myself I portray." And since this self is a perceptive, unique professor country-gentleman, distinguished by a delightful difference, and one who sees much in many things, he will eternally charm his reader with the way he sees the world:

"There comes a time in every man's life when he is either going to go fishing or do something worse."

"She [the aging bird dog] knew why she had been brought along, and she knew her own limitations, which is about the finest thing either dog or man can learn."

"Every country boy is entitled to a creek. If no creek's handy, maybe a meandering branch will do for awhile. But it must have a few holes that he can't see the bottom of. That is an absolute requisite, and there is no getting around it."

"After all a dog is a dog, and I wouldn't want him to be much smarter than he is. It might prove embarrassing."

"A boy wakes up new every morning."

It is such writing as this that moved Henry Cavendish, reviewer of Doctor Babcock's *The Education of Pretty Boy* for the *New York Times*, to write a letter directed to Havilah Babcock, Professor of English,

Somewhere in South Carolina:

"I have just finished the other day your *Jaybirds Go to Hell on Friday,* sampling it along from time to time for I'd reckon something more than a year. Sort of like sampling along a rare old Bourbon you want to make last as long as possible while living along in between times on the regular old piney woods moonshine."

And this from the brief Valedictory in the April (1965) issue of *Field and Stream:*

"We shall miss our friend and his inimitable cronies, but our loss is tempered by the fact that his stories bear reading and rereading. Like a good wine, they grow better with age."

Doctor Babcock's professorial self gets into his writings by way of the numerous quotations from English and American Literature and a rhetorical style instinctively following the pattern of the masters he has taught. On one page in his story "Puppies Incorporated," he weaves quotations from Bacon, Shakespeare, Bunyan, and Wordsworth into the pattern of his prose:

"Whoever lavishes affection on a puppy, gives hostages to fortune."

"Few businesses are so subject to the arrows of outrageous fortune as that of raising and training puppies."

"When your soul is in the slough of despond, a wayward tyke gallops up and drops dead on his maiden point. Then your heart with rapture thrills, and hardships are forgotten."

Also occasionally even in describing a bird dog, he uses a line which still carries the imprint of the exquisite Petrarchan Renaissance poets: "Her right foot did delicately scorn the ground."

Another characteristic of Doctor Babcock's writings is that he drew his strength from the land, the soil: hunters, farmers, and fishermen were more often his associates than professors and critics. He described his kind of person thus:

"We are children of the earth. We are not unlike the Titans, the earthborn giants of mythology, who were invincible in battle only as long as their feet were planted on the good earth."

He wrote best when his story was firmly set in the Virginia or South Carolina that he knew and loved best, such as the reminiscence of his return to the little branch of his boyhood in Appomattox:

"At my feet was a straight ditch, in which a beaten stream flowed dully. Gone were the well-remembered pools, the foam flecked eddies and the noisy little cascades that had made up my branch. In their place was an efficient ditch, in which there were no signs of fish. It was a nice job of engineering, no doubt, but it wasn't my branch. I was suddenly a stranger among strangers, standing embarrassed, in the presence of my own boyhood."

This kind of writing possesses a deceptive simplicity, but beneath the seeming effortlessly written prose there is the hand of the devoted craftsman of words who worked diligently at the lonely and arduous task of writing well. His was the hand of the lapidary; his sentences were carved carefully by an artist seeking to get the inevitable word in the right place, and his best prose happily fulfilled Thoreau's dictum:

"A sentence should read as if its author had he held a plough instead of a pen could have drawn a furrow deep and straight to the end."

Havilah Babcock was the master of the hunting and fishing tale which transcended the limits of such stories to be enjoyed and relished by people who never shot a covey of partridges or cast a flyrod for a red-breasted brim or a rainbow trout. The style, the humor, the disarming simplicity, and the essential humanity of these writings will insure their permanence in our literature among our minor classics.

The author of these tales was a man who loved both simplicity and perfection. In the only foreword he ever wrote, he speaks from the heart of these things:

"As I grow older I am inclined to thank God for simple things: for a staunch dog silhouetted against the setting sun; a night's untroubled sleep; the soft swish of a paddle at sunrise on the Ashepoo or Cumbahee; a cooling drink from a sequestered spring at noontide."

There were also other grandly simple things which he revered: Kenneth Graham's *Wind in the Willows*, Homer's *Odyssey*, a good bird dog or a good friend, a gracefully written sentence or a fine crop of beans.

Doctor Babcock's health was always better in November when the bird season opened and he could leave his academic duties to spend whole days from *besun* to *nightcome* hunting his favorite game bird,

*Colinius Virginianus* the Southern partridge. On such days he was always young in heart and spirit and physically able to walk fifteen miles over any good bird country.

As a writer Havilah Babcock labored at the lonely task of turning out good prose, and in this endeavor he had the true artist's regard for perfection. In his story, "I Went to See a Man About a Dog" after listening reverently to an old bird hunter telling of his meticulous training of a faultless retriever he utters what might well be a summation of himself as a writer:

"The lesson lives in the passionate heart of one who loves but has never quite achieved perfection."